A CENTENNIAL EDITION

LEWIS CARROLL'S
The Hunting of the Snark

ILLUSTRATED BY HENRY HOLIDAY

The Annotated Snark by Martin Gardner

The Designs for the Snark by Charles Mitchell

The Listing of the Snark by Selwyn H. Goodacre

EDITED BY JAMES TANIS AND JOHN DOOLEY

LOS ALTOS · CALIFORNIA

William Kaufmann, Inc.

IN COOPERATION WITH BRYN MAWR COLLEGE LIBRARY

Library of Congress Cataloging in Publication Data

Carroll, Lewis, 1832-1898.
    Lewis Carroll's The hunting of the snark.

    Bibliography: p.
    Contents: The annotated snark / by Martin
Gardner — The designs for the snark / by Charles
Mitchell — The listing of the snark / by Selwyn H.
Goodacre.
    I. Holiday, Henry, 1839-1927. II. Tanis,
James, 1928-   . III. Dooley, John.
IV. Gardner, Martin, 1914-   .   V. Mitchell,
Charles, 1912-   .   VI. Goodacre, Selwyn Hugh.
The listing of the snark, 1981.   VII. Title.
PR4611.H8 1981b   821'.8   81-17212
ISBN 0-913232-36-X   AACR2

ISBN 0-913232-98-X (collector's ed.)
ISBN 0-913232-51-3 (subscriber's ed.)
ISBN 0-86576-023-3 (pbk.)

First printed in November 1981.
Reprinted with emendations in February 1982.
Printed in the United States of America

DEDICATED TO

TWO HUNTERS OF THE SNARK

Erwin O. Freund

&

George Howe

A PREFATORY NOTE

✥ ✥

"IT's A SNARK!" . . . for whatever else can it be? Yet in a suburban guest room, it's not what one is prepared to see. In that guest room, on first opening the weathered remnants of the binding which Henry Holiday had designed to hold his original drawings, I was awed by the silvery beauty of his pencil and the deep black of his ink, fresh and vibrant in spite of a hundred years.

The volume was then owned by Mrs. Walter (Helen Howe) West, Jr., daughter of the Philadelphia bibliophile George Howe. The drawings, having left Holiday's hands early in the century, had lain quietly in the Howes' possession since last displayed in New York at the Carroll Centenary Exhibition in 1932. Mrs. West generously gave these drawings to the Bryn Mawr College Library in honor of her father.

Spurred on by the excitement of these treasures, we set out on a new hunt—not a hunt for the Snark itself but for its graphic remains. First to be located were the sheets of study sketches, also displayed in the New York show and later acquired by the Princeton University Library. Then, slowly yielding to clues and dark traces, the intermediate drawings and the proofs of the wood engravings were discovered in two private collections. These had been in the London Centenary Exhibition of 1932. Following that show, these materials became a part of the remarkable Carroll Collection acquired by Erwin O. Freund, a passionate devotee of the *Snark*. His assemblage included the long-lost picture of "The Boojum," which Carroll had rejected, and an unpublished roundel of "Hope," which Holiday had drawn for a binding design. The present owners of these important works graciously deposited them at Bryn Mawr, so that they could be studied together with the Howe-West drawings. Last to be located were the original woodblocks, cut by Joseph Swain from Holiday's designs. These had been purchased a decade ago for the Osborne Collection of Early Children's Books at Toronto Public Library.

Soon after the Howe-West volume came to Bryn Mawr, we learned that an edition of the *Snark* was being prepared to mark the centennial of its publication in 1876. Its author, Martin Gardner, and its publisher, William Kaufmann, kindly invited Bryn Mawr to share in the venture. To our delight, the English Carroll enthusiast Selwyn H. Goodacre then agreed to join the Hunt with an updated text of his *The Listing of the Snark*. Hence we have this opportunity to join the tale of Henry Holiday's most creative moment with the enduring allure of Lewis Carroll's fanciful text. We launch it now, trusting that lovers of the *Snark* everywhere will pursue it "with forks and hope."

James Tanis
Bryn Mawr College Library

CONTENTS

THE HUNTING OF THE SNARK

But, should the play
Prove piercing earnest,
Should the glee glaze
In Death's stiff stare,

Would not the fun
Look too expensive!
Would not the jest
Have crawled too far!

EMILY DICKINSON

INTRODUCTION

❖❖

Martin Gardner

ALTHOUGH Lewis Carroll thought of *The Hunting of the Snark* as a nonsense ballad for children, it is hard to imagine—in fact one shudders to imagine—a child of today reading and enjoying it. Victorian children may have found it amusing (there is a grim record of one little girl having recited the entire poem to Carroll during a long carriage ride), but even they, one suspects, were few in number.

"It is not children who ought to read the words of Lewis Carroll," writes Gilbert Chesterton, "they are far better employed making mud-pies." Carroll's nonsense should be read by

sages and grey-haired philosophers . . . in order to study that darkest problem of metaphysics, the borderland between reason and unreason, and the nature of the most erratic of spiritual forces, humour, which eternally dances between the two. That we do find a pleasure in certain long and elaborate stories, in certain complicated and curious forms of diction, which have no intelligible meaning whatever, is not a subject for children to play with; it is a subject for psychologists to go mad over.[1]

The Hunting of the Snark is a poem over which an unstable, sensitive soul might very well go mad. There is even a touch of madness in the reverse, looking-glass procedure by which it was written. The time was 1874. The Reverend Charles Lutwidge Dodgson, that shy and fastidious bachelor who taught mathematics at Christ Church, Oxford, was then forty-two and something of a celeb-

rity. He had written two masterpieces that were to immortalize his child-friend, Alice Liddell, and he had published *Phantasmagoria*, a small book of (mostly dull) nonsense poems. On the afternoon of 18 July, in Guildford, the town in Surrey where his sisters lived, Carroll went out for a stroll. This is how he tells the story:

I was walking on a hillside, alone, one bright summer day, when suddenly there came into my head one line of verse—one solitary line—"For the Snark *was* a Boojum, you see." I knew not what it meant, then: I know not what it means, now; but I wrote it down: and, some time afterwards, the rest of the stanza occurred to me, that being its last line: and so by degrees, at odd moments during the next year or two, the rest of the poem pieced itself together, that being its last stanza.[2]

Carroll first mentioned the poem in his Diary on 23 November 1874 when he showed Ruskin some of the pictures that Henry Holiday had drawn to illustrate the book. He was much disheartened to hear that Ruskin saw no hopes of Holiday doing the work satisfactorily.

Holiday, whom Carroll had first met in Oxford in 1870 and already approached in January 1874 as a possible illustrator of another book, "if *only* he can draw grotesques," was a prominent London

---

1. "The Library of the Nursery," in *Lunacy and Letters*, 1958.

2. "*Alice* on the Stage," *The Theatre*, April 1887. Morton N. Cohen, in his article "Hark the Snark" (see bibliography), argues convincingly that the ballad's genesis was closely related to Carroll's state of mind during this long and sad vigil in Guildford. Carroll was there to minister to a cousin and godson who was dying of tuberculosis.

painter and sculptor, and later a celebrated designer of stained-glass windows. His autobiography, *Reminiscences of My Life*, reproduces a number of his murals: mostly historical scenes, painted in a classical manner and swarming with nudes and Grecian-robed figures. His stained-glass windows were shipped to churches all over the globe, including dozens in the United States, some in large cities, some in towns as small as Wappingers Falls, New York, and Thermopolis, Wyoming. His best works, he thought, were the windows—in particular the two huge scenes of the Crucifixion and the Ascension—that he designed and cast for the Church of the Holy Trinity at 316 East Eighty-eighth Street in Manhattan. (They are worth a visit. I sometimes wonder how many of the parishioners, worshipping on Sunday morning, are aware of the fact that these pious patterns of colored glass were designed by the illustrator of *The Hunting of the Snark*.)³ If anyone had suggested to Holiday that he might be remembered chiefly for his pictures in the *Snark*, or that his autobiography would be collected mainly because of its references to Carroll, he would have been incredulous; as incredulous as Dean Henry George Liddell's official biographer if someone had suggested that among the academic associates of Alice's father, the one destined for the greatest fame was a man nowhere mentioned in the biography!

How well the academician Holiday succeeded in producing grotesques for the *Snark* (it is the only work of Carroll's that he illustrated) is open to debate. Ruskin was certainly right in thinking him inferior to Tenniel. His published drawings are, of course, thoroughly realistic except for the oversize

heads and the slightly surrealist quality that derives less from the artist's imagination than from the fact that he was illustrating a surrealist poem.

In his article on "The Snark's Significance," Holiday tells how the poem came to be illustrated. He describes how Carroll, after he had completed three fits of it, asked for three pictures, and how before they were finished he wrote another fit and asked for another picture, going on, fit after fit, until there were nine pictures in all. One of Holiday's sketches was never used (see plate XII). This is how he explains it:

In our correspondence about the illustrations, the coherence and consistency of the nonsense on its own nonsensical understanding often became prominent. One of the first three I had to do was the disappearance of the Baker, and I not unnaturally invented a Boojum. Mr. Dodgson wrote that it was a delightful monster, but that it was inadmissible. All his descriptions of the Boojum were quite unimaginable, and he wanted the creature to remain so. I assented, of course, though reluctant to dismiss what I am still confident is an accurate representation. I hope that some future Darwin, in a new *Beagle*, will find the beast, or its remains; if he does, I know he will confirm my drawing.

Carroll records in his Diary on 24 October 1875 that he has the sudden notion of publishing the *Snark* as a Christmas poem. But five days later his plan collapses when he hears from Macmillan that it will take at least three months to complete the wood engravings. On 5 November he mentions sending Macmillan the text of three fits. The following day he writes four more stanzas, "completing the poem." On 7 November he sends his "finished" manuscript to Macmillan, but in January of the following year we find him still working on new fits and adding more stanzas to the old ones.

The book was finally published in late March 1876, shortly before Easter. This gave Carroll an excuse for inserting into the volume a small pamphlet (later sold separately) entitled *An Easter Greeting* (see plates XLIII–XLIV). He realized that the religious sentiments in this greeting were out of keeping with the ballad, but he may have had a vague, uncomfortable feeling that the gloom and

3. I do not have a complete listing of other churches in Manhattan that have stained-glass windows by Holiday, but I do know of two. The Grace Church, 802 Broadway, has windows depicting Joseph and Benjamin, the four Mary's, the raising of Lazarus, and the raising of the daughter of Jairus. The Church of the Incarnation, Madison Avenue and 35th Street, has windows showing the resurrection and ascension of Jesus, Jacob blessing his children, Jesus commissioning St. Peter, and the Virgin Mary and Dorcas. For a listing of churches in Philadelphia, Chicago, St. Louis, Washington, D.C., and other U.S. cities, for which Holiday designed windows, see the article by Baldry under references on Holiday.

pessimism of his poem needed to be balanced by a reference to the Easter message of hope.

On 29 March Carroll records that he spent six hours at Macmillan inscribing some eighty presentation copies of his book. Many of these inscriptions were acrostic verses on the names of little girls to whom the books were sent.[4] The following two have often been reprinted:

"ARE you deaf, Father William?" the young
    man said,
"Did you hear what I told you just now?
"Excuse me for shouting! Don't waggle
    your head
"Like a blundering, sleepy old cow!
"A little maid dwelling in Wallington Town,
"Is my friend, so I beg to remark:
"Do you think she'd be pleased if a book
    were sent down
"Entitled 'The Hunt of the Snark'? "

"Pack it up in brown paper!" the old man
    cried,
"And seal it with olive-and-dove.
"I command you to do it!" he added with
    pride,
"Nor forget, my good fellow, to send her
    beside
"Easter Greetings, and give her my love."

MAIDEN, though thy heart may quail
And thy quivering lip grow pale,
Read the Bellman's tragic tale!

Is it life of which it tells?
Of a pulse that sinks and swells
Never lacking chime of bells?

Bells of sorrow, bells of cheer,
Easter, Christmas, glad New Year,
Still they sound, afar, anear.

So may Life's sweet bells for thee,
In the summers yet to be,
Evermore make melody!

Is it life of which it tells? If so, what aspect of life is being told? We know that the *Snark* describes "with infinite humor the impossible voyage of an improbable crew to find an inconceivable creature," as Sidney Williams and Falconer Madan put it in their *Handbook of the Literature of the Rev. C. L. Dodgson.* But is that *all* it describes?

Every serious reader of the *Snark* has pondered this question, and many have tried to answer it. Carroll himself was, of course, asked it repeatedly. On the record, he answered it five times.

1. "Periodically I have received courteous letters from strangers," Carroll wrote in "*Alice* on the Stage," "begging to know whether *The Hunting of the Snark* is an allegory, or contains some hidden moral, or is a political satire: and for all such questions I have but one answer, '*I don't know!*' "

2. In 1876 he wrote to a child-friend: "When you have read the *Snark,* I hope you will write me a little note and tell me how you like it, and if you can *quite* understand it. Some children are puzzled with it. Of course you know what a Snark is? If you do, please tell *me*: for I haven't an idea what it is like. And tell me which of the pictures you like best."

3. This from a letter written in 1880 to a not-so-little girl of nineteen: "I have a letter from you . . . asking me 'Why don't you explain the *Snark*?,'

---

4. One charming acrostic, to Alice Crompton, did not come to light until 1974 when it was reprinted in *The Lewis Carroll Circular,* No. 2, edited by Trevor Winkfield:

Alice dear, will you join me in hunting the Snark?
    Let us go to the chase hand-in-hand:
If we only can catch one before it gets dark,
    Could anything happen more grand?

Ever ready to share in the Beaver's despair,
    Count your poor little fingers & thumbs:

Recollecting with tears all the smudges & smears
    On the page where you work at your sums!

May I help you to seek it with thimbles & care?
    Pursuing with forks & hope?
To threaten its life with a railway-share?
Or to charm it with smiles—but a maiden so fair
    Need not trouble herself about soap!

The Victorian cane-to-lips gesture. From *Punch*, 2 July 1870.

a question I ought to have answered long ago. Let me answer it now—'because I can't.' Are you able to explain things which you don't yourself understand?''

4. In 1896, twenty years after the ballad was published, he is still struggling with the question.

As to the meaning of the *Snark*? [he writes in a long letter to a group of children] I'm very much afraid I didn't mean anything but nonsense! Still, you know, words mean more than we mean to express when we use them: so a whole book ought to mean a great deal more than the writer meant. So, whatever good meanings are in the book, I'm very glad to accept as the meaning of the book. The best that I've seen is by a lady (she published it in a letter to a newspaper)— that the whole book is an allegory on the search after happiness. I think this fits beautifully in many ways— particularly about the bathing-machines: when the people get weary of life, and can't find happiness in

town or in books, then they rush off to the seaside to see what bathing-machines will do for them.

5. Carroll's last comment on the *Snark* was in a letter written in 1897, a year before his death:

In answer to your question, "What did you mean the Snark was?" will you tell your friend that I meant that the Snark was a *Boojum*. I trust that she and you will now feel quite satisfied and happy.

To the best of my recollection, I had no other meaning in my mind, when I wrote it: but people have since tried to find the meanings in it. The one I like best (which I think is partly my own) is that it may be taken as an allegory for the pursuit of happiness. The characteristic "ambition" works well into this theory —and also its fondness for bathing-machines, as indicating that the pursuer of happiness, when he has exhausted all other devices, betakes himself, as a last and desperate resource, to some such wretched watering-place as Eastbourne, and hopes to find, in the tedious and depressing society of the daughters of mistresses of boarding-schools, the happiness he has failed to find elsewhere. . . .

There is no reason to suppose that Carroll was in the slightest degree evasive in denying that he had intended his poem to mean anything at all. But, as he himself pointed out, words can mean much more than a writer intends. They can express meanings buried so deep in an author's mind that he himself is not aware of them, and they can acquire meanings entirely by accident. Nonsense writing is a peculiarly rich medium for both types of "unintended" meaning.

"I can remember a clever undergraduate at Oxford," writes Holiday in "The Snark's Significance," "who knew the *Snark* by heart, telling me that on all sorts of occasions, in all the daily incidents of life, some line from the poem was sure to occur to him that exactly fitted. Most people will have noticed this peculiarity of Lewis Carroll's writing." When a Carrollian nonsense line suggests one of these neat metaphorical applications, who can say, particularly in the case of the *Snark*, whether the fit is fortuitous or whether it derives from a level below the Fit—that dark, unconscious substratum of intent that underlies all great creative acts?

Many attempts have been made to force the whole of the *Snark* into one overall metaphorical pattern. A writer with the initials M.H.T., in a note appended to Holiday's article on the ballad's significance, argues that the Snark represents material wealth. "I am always lost in astonishment," he says, "at the people who think it can be anything else. Observe the things with which its capture was attempted. Why, the mere mention of railway shares and soap is sufficient of itself to establish my thesis." The Boojum, according to this writer, is that type of unexpected good fortune that lifts a man "into a sphere in which he is miserable, and makes his wife cut the greengrocer's lady."

A second note to Holiday's article, this one signed St. J.E.C.H., takes the position that the poem is a satire on the craving for social advancement, the tragedy of the person who tries to climb into society but never gets higher on the ladder than the local Browning club.

Two events that took place at the time Carroll's ballad was being written gave rise to two popular theories about the poem. One event was the famous trial of the Tichborne claimant, discussed in note 54. The other was an arctic expedition on two steamships, the *Alert* and *Discovery*, that set out from Portsmouth in 1875, returning in the fall of 1876. The expedition was much in the news before and after the publication of the *Snark*, and many readers apparently supposed that the ballad was a satire on an arctic voyage, the Snark a symbol of the North Pole. There is little to recommend this theory, although the polar expedition, like the Tichborne case, undoubtedly added to the topical interest of the poem.

A theory closely related to the material-wealth theory of M.H.T. was proposed in 1911 by Devereux Court in an article in the *Cornhill Magazine*. Court thought that the poem satirized an unsound business venture. The ship's company is the business company. The vessel has been "floated." The men on board are the men on the company's board of directors, all of them speculators fond of "quotations." The Bellman is the chairman of the board, the Boots the secretary. The Snark is a land shark who brings about the company's downfall.

The latest variant of this interpretation was advanced in the early thirties by Dean Wallace B. Donham of the Harvard Graduate School of Business Administration. His views are defended at length in an article, "Finding of the Snark," by Arthur Ruhl, in the *Saturday Review of Literature*, 18 March 1933. Dean Donham's opinion is that the *Snark* is a satire on business in general, the Boojum a symbol of a business slump, and the whole thing a tragedy about the business cycle. In 1933 the United States was of course in the midst of the great depression. The poem's allegorical level is worked out with considerable ingenuity: the Boots is unskilled labor, the Beaver is a textile worker, the Baker a small businessman in a luxury trade, the Billiard-marker a speculator, the hyenas are stockbrokers, the bear is a stock market bear, the Jubjub is Disraeli, and so on. The Bandersnatch, who keeps snatching at the Banker in Fit 7, is the Bank of England, repeatedly raising its interest rate in the wild optimism that preceded the panic of 1875. It was Dean Donham's belief that "no single quatrain in the *Snark* goes contra to the interpretation," but the reader will have to consult Ruhl's article for a fuller defense of that statement.

The most elaborate and witty of all Snark theories is the tongue-in-cheek concoction of the philosopher Ferdinand Canning Scott Schiller. Schiller is almost forgotten today, but at the turn of the century he was recognized, along with William James and John Dewey, as one of the three principal leaders of the pragmatic movement. Schiller had a zest for logical paradoxes, practical jokes, and outrageous puns. (He would have made a sterling member of the Snark hunting crew, under the name of the Bachelor; he managed to avoid marrying until he was seventy-one.) In 1901, when he was teaching philosophy at Oxford, he persuaded the editors of *Mind*, a philosophical journal, to bring out a parody issue. Schiller's "A Commentary on the *Snark*," for which he used the pseudonym of Snarkophilus Snobbs, is the highlight of this issue. It interprets Carroll's ballad as a satire on the Hegelian philosopher's search for the Absolute. The full text of this commentary will be found in the appendix of this section, so I shall say no more about it here.

Is there more to be said about the *Snark*? Yes, there is yet another way of looking at the poem, an existentialist way if you will, that for several reasons is singularly appropriate to our time.

The key to this interpretation is in the last five stanzas of Fit 3. The Baker's uncle, perhaps on his deathbed, has just informed the Baker that if the Snark he confronts turns out to be a Boojum, he will "softly and suddenly vanish away, and never be met with again!" In the next four stanzas the Baker describes his emotional reaction to this solemn warning. In keeping with the Bellman's rule-of-three, he says it three times to underscore the truth of what he is saying. He is in a state of acute existential nausea.

> "It is this, it is this that oppresses my soul,
>   When I think of my uncle's last words:
> And my heart is like nothing so much as a bowl
>   Brimming over with quivering curds!"

This state of existential anxiety, as the existential analysts like to call it (earlier ages called it simply the fear of death), is of course a thoroughly normal emotion. But, for one reason or another, both individuals and cultures vary widely in the degree to which they suppress this emotion. Until recently, at least in England and the United States, death as a natural process had become almost unmentionable. As Geoffrey Gorer puts it in his article on "The Pornography of Death,"[5] one of the peculiar features of our time is that while violent death, and the possibility of violent death, has greatly increased, and while it plays an "ever-

growing part in the fantasies offered to mass audiences—detective stories, thrillers, Westerns, war stories, spy stories, science fiction, and eventually horror comics," talk about natural death has become "more and more smothered in prudery." It is the great conversation stopper of parlor discourse.

Lewis Carroll lived in a different age, an age in which death was domesticated and sentimentalized, an age in which readers were able to weep real tears over the passing of Dickens's Little Nell. Carroll thought a great deal about death and, I am persuaded, about the possibility of his own nonexistence. Jokes about death abound in his writings, even in the *Alice* books. His rejection of the doctrine of eternal punishment was his one major departure from Protestant orthodoxy. In the introduction to his book *Pillow Problems* he speaks of the value of mental work at night in keeping one's mind free of unholy thoughts. "There are sceptical thoughts, which seem for the moment to uproot the firmest faith; there are blasphemous thoughts, which dart unbidden into the most reverent souls; there are unholy thoughts, which torture with their hateful presence, the fancy that would fain be pure."

I believe that Carroll is describing here a state of existential dread. I think it is what he had in mind, perhaps not consciously, when he has the Baker say:

> "I engage with the Snark – every night
>   after dark –
>   In a dreamy delirious fight:
> I serve it with greens in those shadowy scenes,
>   And I use it for striking a light."

Its use for striking a light—the light of faith—is the central theme of Miguel de Unamuno's great existential work, *The Tragic Sense of Life*. Scores of books have been written in the past few decades about the existentialist movement, but for some impenetrable reason most of them do not even mention Unamuno, the Spanish poet, novelist, and philosopher (he died in 1936) whose outlook is

5. *Encounter*, October 1955. Since this appeared "thanatology" has received increasing attention as a topic of both public and academic interest.

"And believes that they add to the beauty of scenes – A sentiment open to doubt." From *Punch*, 9 Sept. 1876.

certainly closer to Kierkegaard's than that of many philosophers who wear the existentialist label. The Baker's remarks about his uncle's last words are a metaphorical compression of scores of passages that can be found in Unamuno's writings. Here is a moving example from his commentary on *Don Quixote*:

. . . one of those moments when the soul is blown about by a sudden gust from the wings of the angel of mystery. A moment of anguish. For there are times when, unsuspecting, we are suddenly seized, we know not how nor whence, by a vivid sense of our mortality, which takes us without warning and quite unprepared. When most absorbed in the cares and duties of life, or engrossed and self-forgetful on some festal occasion or engaged in a pleasant chat, suddenly it seems that death is fluttering over me. Not death, something worse, a sensation of annihilation, a supreme anguish. And this anguish, tearing us violently from our perception of appearances, with a single stunning swoop, dashes us away—to recover into an awareness of the substance of things.

All creation is something we are some day to lose, and is some day to lose us. For what else is it to vanish from the world but the world vanishing from us? Can you conceive of yourself as not existing? Try it. Concentrate your imagination on it. Fancy yourself without vision, hearing, the sense of touch, the ability to perceive anything. Try it. Perhaps you will evoke and bring upon yourself that anguish which visits us when least expected; perhaps you will feel the hangman's knot choking off your soul's breath. Like the woodpecker in the oak tree, an agony is busily pecking at our hearts, to make its nest there.

It is this agony, the agony of anticipating one's

loss of being, that pecks at the heart of Carroll's poem. Did he realize that *B*, the dominant letter of his ballad, is a symbol of "be"? I sometimes think he did. At any rate, the letter sounds through the poem like a continuous drum beat, starting softly with the introduction of the Bellman, the Boots, and the others, then growing more and more insistent until, in a final thunderclap, it becomes the Boojum.

The *Snark* is a poem about being and nonbeing, an existential poem, a poem of existential agony. The Bellman's map is the map that charts the course of humanity; blank because we possess no information about where we are or whither we drift.[6] The ship's bowsprit gets mixed with its rudder and when we think we sail west we sail east. The Snark is, in Paul Tillich's fashionable phrase, every man's ultimate concern. This is the great search motif of the poem, the quest for an ultimate good. But this motif is submerged in a stronger motif, the dread, the agonizing dread, of ultimate failure. The Boojum is more than death. It is the end of all searching. It is final, absolute extinction, in Auden's phrase, " the dreadful Boojum of Nothingness." In a literal sense, Carroll's Boojum means nothing at all. It is the void, the great blank emptiness out of which we miraculously emerged; by which we will ultimately be devoured; through which the absurd galaxies spiral and drift endlessly on their nonsense voyages from nowhere to nowhere.[7]

Perhaps you are a naturalist and humanist, or a Sartrean existentialist. You believe passionately in working for a better world, and although you know that you will not be around to enjoy it, you take a kind of comfort—poor substitute that it is!—from the fact that future generations, perhaps even your own children, may reap the rewards of your labors. But what if they won't? Atomic energy is a Snark that comes in various shapes and sizes. A certain number of intercontinental guided missiles—the U.S. Air Force has one it calls the Snark—with thermonuclear warheads can glide gently down on the just and unjust, and the whole of humanity may never be met with again.

For the Snark was a. . . .

We are poised now on the brink of discovering the unsuspected meaning that Carroll's poem acquired in 1942 when Enrico Fermi and his associates (working, appropriately, in a former "squash" court) obtained the first sustained nuclear chain reaction.

Consider for a moment that remarkable four-letter word *bomb*. It begins and ends with *b*. The second *b* is silent; the final silence. *B* for birth, non-*b* for Nothing. Between the two *b*'s (to be or not to be) is *Om*, Hindu symbol for the nature of Brahman, the Absolute, the god behind the lesser gods whose tasks are to create, preserve, and destroy all that is.

"I believe it [the atom bomb] is the greatest of all American inventions," declared H. L. Mencken, "and one of the imperishable glories of Christianity. It surpasses the burning of heretics on all counts, but especially on the count that it has given the world an entirely new disease, to wit, galloping carcinoma."[8] This disease advanced to a new stage in August 1961, when Khrushchev announced that the Soviet Union would unilaterally resume nuclear testing, perhaps build a 100-megaton bomb. A political cartoon in the *Boston Traveler* showed Khrushchev sticking his head around a corner, a cloud mushrooming from his mouth and bearing

6. "If thought of as isolated in the midst of the ocean, a ship can stand for mankind and human society moving through time and struggling with its destiny. . . . *The Hunting of the Snark* is a pure example of [this] use. . . ." —W. H. Auden, *The Enchafèd Flood.*

7. There is no evidence that Carroll ever read *Moby Dick*, but more than one critic has found parallels between Melville's novel and Carroll's ballad. No one has discussed the parallels more fully or more profoundly than Harold Beaver (author of an annotated *Moby Dick*) in his essay "Whale or Boojum" (see bibliography). At the top of his essay he quotes the following passage from Melville's chapter on whiteness: "Is it that by its indefiniteness it shadows forth the heartless voids and immensities of the universe, and thus stabs us from behind with the thought of annihilation, when beholding the white depths of the milky way?"

8. As quoted in *Life*, 5 August 1946.

the single word "BOO." No Snarxist need be told "the word he was trying to say."

A bookish pastime, recommended for whiling away the hours left to us in these tropical climes of cancer, is that of searching odd corners of literature for passages unintentionally prophetic of the Bomb. Here, for example, is Vincent Starrett's poem "Portent."[9]

"Heavy, heavy—over thy head—"
    Hear them call in the room below!
Now they patter with gruesome tread,
    Now they riot with laugh and blow.
    Tchk! What a pity that they must grow!
"Heavy, heavy—over thy head—"

"Heavy, heavy—over thy head—"
    Winds are bleak as they coil and blow.
Once the sky was a golden red;
    Once *I* played in that room below.
    Sometimes I think that children know!
"Heavy, heavy—over thy head—"

Paul Goodman's novel *The Grand Piano* (1941) closes with its hero, Horatio Alger, wiring an explosive to the piano key of B flat (Carroll's B again!) just below the center of the keyboard. The idea is to play a composition in which the tones cluster

9. From *Flame and Dust,* 1924.

around the death note, never touching it, but always calling for it as a resolution.

This is, of course, precisely the wild, demonic music that the U.S. and the U.S.S.R. have been playing, and in which other, less skillful musicians are joining. It is this background music that gives to Lewis Carroll's poem, when it is read today, a new dimension of anxiety. The Baker is Man himself, on the Brink, erect, sublime, wagging his head like an idiot, cackling with laughter and glee.

Suddenly that startled, choked-off cry, " It's a Boo—"

Then silence. . . .

Perhaps otherwise. Perhaps the Bomb will prove to be not a Boojum but only a harmless variety of Snark. The human race will continue to creep onward and upward, stretching out its hands, as H. G. Wells liked to say, to the stars. Take comfort from such happy thoughts, you who can. The Boojum remains. Like T. S. Eliot's eternal Footman, it snickers at the coattails of every member of humanity's motley crew.

Twilight and evening bell,
And after that the Snark!

These lines could serve as a caption for the poem's final illustration. Beyond the craggy precipice, in the shadows of a terrible twilight, a man of flesh and bone is vanishing. Send not to know, dear reader, for whom the Bellman's bell tolls.

THE
ANNOTATED
SNARK

Martin Gardner

Inscribed to a dear Child:
in memory of golden summer hours
and whispers of a summer sea.[1]

GIRT with a boyish garb for boyish task,
   Eager she wields her spade: yet loves as well
Rest on a friendly knee, intent to ask
   The tale he loves to tell.[2]

Rude spirits of the seething outer strife,
   Unmeet to read her pure and simple spright,
Deem, if you list, such hours a waste of life,
   Empty of all delight!

Chat on, sweet Maid, and rescue from annoy
   Hearts that by wiser talk are unbeguiled.
Ah, happy he who owns that tenderest joy,
   The heart-love of a child!

Away, fond thoughts, and vex my soul no more!
   Work claims my wakeful nights, my busy days –
Albeit bright memories of that sunlit shore
   Yet haunt my dreaming gaze!

1. Of the many acrostics that Lewis Carroll wrote for his child-friends, this is perhaps the most ingenious. Not only do the initial letters of the lines spell Gertrude Chataway, but her name is also indicated by the first words of each stanza: *Girt, Rude, Chat, Away.*

Carroll made friends with hundreds of little girls, but there were several of whom he was particularly fond and who received more than his usual attention. The first and most intense of these special friendships was, of course, with Alice Liddell, the original of his fictional Alice. Gertrude was the second. He first met her in 1875 on the beach at Sandown, a small bathing resort. She was with her parents and three sisters. Gertrude was then almost eight. This is how she later recalled the occasion (from *The Life and Letters of Lewis Carroll*, by Stuart Collingwood):

"I first met Mr. Lewis Carroll on the sea-shore at Sandown in the Isle of Wight, in the summer of 1875, when I was quite a little child.

"We had all been taken there for change of air, and next door there was an old gentleman—to me at any rate he seemed old—who interested me immensely. He would come on to his balcony, which joined ours, sniffing the sea-air with his head thrown back, and would walk right down the steps on to the beach with his chin in air, drinking in the fresh breezes as if he could never have enough. I do not know why this excited such keen curiosity on my part, but I remember well that whenever I heard his footstep I flew out to see him coming, and when one day he spoke to me my joy was complete.

"Thus we made friends, and in a very little while I was as familiar with the interior of his lodgings as with our own.

"I had the usual child's love for fairy-tales and marvels, and his power of telling stories naturally fascinated me. We used to sit for hours on the wooden steps which led from our garden on to the beach, whilst he told the most lovely tales that could possibly be imagined, often illustrating the exciting situations with a pencil as he went along.

"One thing that made his stories particularly charming to a child was that he often took his cue from her remarks—a question would set him off on quite a new trail of ideas, so that one felt that one had somehow helped to make the story, and it seemed a personal possession. It was the most lovely nonsense conceivable, and I naturally revelled in it. His vivid imagination would fly from one subject to another, and was never tied down in any way by the probabilities of life.

"To *me* it was of course all perfect, but it is astonishing that *he* never seemed either tired or to want other society. I spoke to him once of this since I have been grown up, and he told me it was the greatest pleasure he could have to converse freely with a child, and feel the depths of her mind.

"He used to write to me and I to him after that summer, and the friendship, thus begun, lasted. His letters were one of the greatest joys of my childhood.

"I don't think that he ever really understood that we, whom he had known as children, could not always remain such. I stayed with him only a few years ago, at Eastbourne, and felt for the time that I was once more a child. He never appeared to realize that I had grown up, except when I reminded him of the fact and then he only said, 'Never mind: you will always be a child to me, even when your hair is grey.'"

A pencil sketch and a photograph that Carroll made of Gertrude, wearing her "boyish garb," are reproduced opposite page 476 in *The Letters of Lewis Carroll*, edited by Morton N. Cohen with the assistance of Roger Lancelyn Green (1979) and the sketch is also reproduced herein (see plate 1). Carroll's friendships with little girls usually cooled when they reached adolescence, but Gertrude was an exception. When she was twenty-five he wrote her an affectionate letter, recalling "like a dream of fifty years ago" the "little bare-legged girl in a sailor's jersey, who used to run up into my lodgings by

the sea." In his Diary Carroll notes on 19 September 1893 that Gertrude (then almost twenty-seven) arrived for a visit at his lodging in Eastbourne. The next entry, four days later, is: "Gertrude left. It has been a really delightful visit."

It was this visit, Roger Green discloses in his commentary on the Diary, that prompted a letter from Carroll's sister, raising the question of whether it was proper for him to permit young ladies, unescorted, to visit him at the seaside. Carroll's reply, quoted from *The Letters*, is characteristic:

"... I think all you say about my girl-guests is most kind and sisterly. . . . But I don't think it at all advisable to enter into any controversy about it. There is no reasonable probability that it would modify the views either of you or of me. I will say a few words to explain my views: but I have no wish whatever to have 'the last word': so please say anything you like afterwards.

"You and your husband have, I think, been very fortunate to know so little, by experience, in your own case or in that of your friends, of the wicked recklessness with which people repeat things to the disadvantage of others, without a thought as to whether they have grounds for asserting what they say. I have met with a good deal of utter misrepresentation of that kind. And another result of my experience is the conviction that the opinion of 'people' in general is absolutely worthless as a test of right and wrong. The only two tests I now apply to such a question as the having some particular girl-friend as a guest are, first, my own *conscience*, to settle whether I feel it to be entirely innocent and right, in the sight of God; secondly, the *parents* of my friend, to settle whether I have their *full* approval for what I do. You need not be shocked at my being spoken against. *Anybody*, who is spoken about at all, is *sure* to be spoken against by *somebody*: and any action, however innocent in itself, is liable, and not at all unlikely, to be blamed by *somebody*. If you limit your actions in life to things that *nobody* can possibly find fault with, you will not do much!"

When Carroll completed his acrostic poem to Gertrude, about a month after first meeting her, he mailed a copy to Mrs. Chataway with a request for permission to print it some day. Evidently she did not notice the concealed name because after hearing from her, Carroll wrote again to call her attention to the double acrostic and to ask if this made any difference in the permission she had given. "If I print them," he wrote, "I shan't tell anyone it is an acrostic—but someone will be sure to find it out before long."

Ten days later he wrote again to tell Gertrude's mother of his plans to use the poem as a dedication in his forthcoming book, *The Hunting of the Snark*. "The scene is laid," he writes, "in an island frequented by the Jubjub and Bandersnatch—no doubt the very island in which the Jabberwock was slain."

2. In Carroll's first version of this poem, as he sent it to Gertrude's mother for approval (see *A Selection from the Letters of Lewis Carroll to His Child-friends*, page 107), the last two lines of the first stanza read:

> Rest on a friendly knee, the tale to ask
> That he delights to tell.

A third version of the poem, with minor alterations, appears as the inscription of Carroll's book of poems, *Rhyme? and Reason?*

PREFACE BY LEWIS CARROLL

IF – and the thing is wildly possible – the charge of writing nonsense were ever brought against the author of this brief but instructive poem, it would be based, I feel convinced, on the line,

> "Then the bowsprit got mixed with the rudder sometimes."

In view of this painful possibility, I will not (as I might) appeal indignantly to my other writings as a proof that I am incapable of such a deed: I will not (as I might) point to the strong moral purpose of this poem itself, to the arithmetical principles so cautiously inculcated in it, or to its noble teachings in Natural History – I will take the more prosaic course of simply explaining how it happened.

The Bellman, who was almost morbidly sensitive about appearances, used to have the bowsprit unshipped once or twice a week to be revarnished, and it more than once happened, when the time came for replacing it, that no one on board could remember which end of the ship it belonged to. They knew it was not of the slightest use to appeal to the Bellman about it – he would only refer to his Naval Code, and read out in pathetic tones Admiralty Instructions which none of them had ever been able to understand – so it generally ended in its being fastened on, anyhow, across the rudder. The helmsman* used to stand by with tears in his eyes: *he* knew it was all wrong, but alas! Rule 42 of the Code, "*No one shall speak to the Man at the Helm,*" had been completed by the Bellman himself with the words "*and the Man at the Helm shall speak to no one.*" So remonstrance was impossible, and no steering could be done till the next varnishing day. During these bewildering intervals the ship usually sailed backwards.

As this poem is to some extent connected with the lay of the Jabberwock, let me take this opportunity of answering a question that has often been asked me, how to pronounce "slithy toves." The "i" in "slithy" is long, as in "writhe"; and "toves" is pronounced so as to rhyme with "groves." Again, the first "o" in "borogoves" is pronounced like the "o" in "borrow." I have heard people try to give it the sound of the "o" in "worry." Such is Human Perversity.

This also seems a fitting occasion to notice the other hard words in that poem. Humpty-Dumpty's theory, of two meanings packed into one word like a portmanteau, seems to me the right explanation for all.

For instance, take the two words "fuming" and "furious." Make up your mind that you will say both words, but leave it unsettled which you will say first. Now open your mouth and speak. If your thoughts incline ever so little towards "fuming," you will say "fuming-furious"; if they turn, by even a hair's breadth, towards "furious," you will say "furious-fuming"; but if you have that rarest of gifts, a perfectly balanced mind, you will say "frumious."

Supposing that, when Pistol uttered the well-known words –

> "Under which king, Bezonian? Speak or die!"

Justice Shallow had felt certain that it was either William or Richard, but had not been able to settle which, so that he could not possibly say either name before the other, can it be doubted that, rather than die, he would have gasped out "Rilchiam!"

---

* This office was usually undertaken by the Boots, who found in it a refuge from the Baker's constant complaints about the insufficient blacking of his three pair of boots.

THE HUNTING

OF THE SNARK

An Agony, in Eight Fits[3]

3. *Agony* is here used in the old sense of a struggle that involves great anguish, bodily pain, or death. Carroll also may have had in mind the "woeful agony" that periodically seizes Coleridge's Ancient Mariner, forcing him to tell to strangers his "ghastly tale."

Fit has the double meaning of a convulsion and a canto. *The Oxford English Dictionary* quotes Samuel Johnson: "A long ballad in many fits," and Lord Byron: "one fytte of Harold's pilgrimage." Phyllis Greenacre, in her psychoana-lytical study of Carroll (*Swift and Carroll*, 1955), thinks there is some connection between the fact that Carroll's poem has eight fits and Carroll had eight younger siblings.

Carroll had once before punned on the word *fit*. In the first *Alice* book, during the trial of the Knave of Hearts, the King quotes the poetic line, "before she had this fit." "You never had fits, my dear, I think?" he asks his wife. When she replies "Never!" the King says, "Then the words don't *fit* you." This produces dead silence in the courtroom.

FIT THE FIRST

THE LANDING

1   "Just the place for a Snark!"[4] the Bellman[5] cried,
        As he landed his crew with care;
        Supporting each man on the top of the tide
        By a finger entwined in his hair.[6]

2   "Just the place for a Snark! I have said it twice:
        That alone should encourage the crew.
        Just the place for a Snark! I have said it thrice:
        What I tell you three times is true."[7]

4. Beatrice Hatch, in her article "Lewis Carroll" (*Strand Magazine*, April 1898, pages 413–23), says that Carroll once told her that *Snark* was a portmanteau word for *snail* and *shark*; but "one suspects," writes Phyllis Greenacre, "that snake has crept into this portmanteau." Stephen Barr, a correspondent in Woodstock, N.Y., suggests *snarl* and *bark* as another pair of meanings that may be packed together here.

5. *Bellman* is another word for a town crier. The Bellman is, of course, the captain of the ship and the man who organized the Snark hunt. On early ships a bell would be struck every half hour to indicate the number of half hours that had elapsed in each four-hour watch, so perhaps this is one of the Bellman's chores. Perhaps, also, there is a connection between the agony's eight fits and the fact that eight bells marked the end of a watch.

Contemporary readers fancied a resemblance to Tennyson in Holiday's pictures of the Bellman. The Bellman appears, whole or in part, in every illustration except the one of the Butcher sharpening his hatchet.

In her biography, *Lewis Carroll* (Schocken, 1979), Ann Clark reports that the *Oxford University Statutes*, which Carroll swore to uphold during his matriculation ceremony at Christ Church, provided for an officer called Le Bellman, or the "ringer." Whenever an important university person died, the bellman's duty was to give notice of the burial by going about ringing a hand bell. Because the Snark hunt proved fatal to the Baker, Ms. Clark argues plausibly that Carroll may have had this officer in mind when he included a bellman among the ship's crew.

6. The crew member shown supported by his hair in Holiday's illustration for this stanza is the Banker. He is carrying a telescope (see Fit 5, note 44). The word *Swain* in the lower right corner is the surname of Joseph Swain, the man who made the wood engravings from Holiday's original drawings.

7. The Bellman's rule-of-three is invoked later (Fit 5) to establish the presence of the Jubjub, though the Beaver has considerable difficulty making sure that three statements have in fact occurred. Norbert Wiener, in his book *Cybernetics*, points out that answers given by a computer are often checked by asking the computer to solve the same problem several times, or by giving the problem to several different computers. Wiener speculates on whether the human brain contains a similar checking mechanism: "We can hardly expect that any important message is entrusted for transmission to a single neuron, nor that any important operation is entrusted to a single neuronal mechanism. Like the computing ma-

3   The crew was complete: it included a Boots —[8]
          A maker of Bonnets and Hoods —
      A Barrister, brought to arrange their disputes —
          And a Broker,[9] to value their goods.

4   A Billiard-marker,[10] whose skill was immense,
          Might perhaps have won more than his share —
      But a Banker, engaged at enormous expense,[11]
          Had the whole of their cash in his care.

chine, the brain probably works on a variant of the famous principle expounded by Lewis Carroll in *The Hunting of the Snark*: 'What I tell you three times is true.' "

Another mathematician says it this way in the preface to his *Introduction to Matrix Analysis* (1970). "The human mind being what it is, repetition and cross-sections from different angles are powerful pedagogical devices. In this connection, it is appropriate to quote Lewis Carroll in *The Hunting of the Snark*, Fit the First—'I have said it thrice: What I tell you three times is true'—The Bellman." And who is the author of this textbook? Richard Bellman!

In arithmetic, an ancient rule for calculating ratios was well known in Carroll's day as the rule-of-three. Carroll refers to it in the dedicatory poem of *A Tangled Tale*, and the Mad Gardener's song in *Sylvie and Bruno* also mentions it:

He thought he saw a Garden-Door
    That opened with a key:
He looked again, and found it was
    A Double Rule of Three:
"And all its mystery," he said,
    "Is clear as day to me!"

Carroll's quite different rule-of-three plays a central role in the plot of a bizarre science fiction story, "Chaos, Coordinated," by John MacDougal (pseudonym of Robert Lowndes and James Blish). The earth is at war with a distant galaxy, where the various races are coordinated by a gigantic computer. An earthman manages to disguise *The Hunting of the Snark* as an "observational report" and feed it to the giant brain. The brain accepts literally the order "What I tell you three times is true." All it had been told once or twice in the past is regarded as unverified, and new observational reports are not accepted because they are made only once. As a result the entire galaxy becomes, so to speak, snarked. The machine issues blank star maps, distributes bells to spaceship captains, stocks medical chests with muffins, ice, mustard-and-cress, jam, two volumes of proverbs, and a recording of riddles beginning with "Why is a raven like a writing desk?" (See Fit 3, stanza 1.) The story appeared in *Astounding Science Fiction*, October 1946.

The American writer Edith Wharton was fond of the *Snark* when she was a little girl. In her autobiography, *A Backward Glance* (1934), pages 311–12, she tells of a lunch with President Theodore Roosevelt, whom she had known since her childhood. "Well," he said, "I *am* glad to welcome to the White House someone to whom I can quote *The Hunting of the Snark* without being asked what I mean! . . . Would you believe it, no one in the administration has ever heard of Alice, much less of the Snark, and the other day, when I said to the Secretary of Navy: 'Mr. Secretary, *What I say three times is true*,' he did not recognize the allusion, and answered with an aggrieved air: 'Mr. President, it would never for a moment have occurred to me to impugn your veracity!' "

8. A "boots" is a servant at a hotel or inn, formerly assigned to such low tasks as cleaning boots and brushing clothes. No one knows what the Boots looks like; he is the one crew member who does not appear in any of Holiday's illustrations.

9. Not a pawnbroker, but one licensed to appraise and sell household goods. When a landlord took possession of the furniture of those unable to pay rent, the broker would be called in to "value their goods." Anti-Semitic caricatures of such brokers, with bowler hats and Disraeli sidelocks, were common in the cartoons of Victorian England, and in novels and plays. "People hate and scout 'em," wrote Dickens, "because they're the ministers of wretchedness, like, to poor people."

10. A "billiard-marker" is the employee of a billiard parlor who keeps a record of the game by marking the points made by each player.

I like to think that the crew's Billiard-marker is none other than the billiard-marker whom Sherlock Holmes and his brother Mycroft observed, many years later, strolling down Pall Mall with his friend the Boots. After leaving the Bellman's crew, the Boots had enlisted in the Royal Artillery. He was discharged after honorable service in India, but was so fond of his boots that he continued to wear them (as Mycroft noticed) after his retirement from service. (See the story of "The Greek Interpreter" in *Memoirs of Sherlock Holmes*. For the friendship between Holmes and Carroll, see William

5   There was also a Beaver, that paced on the deck,
          Or would sit making lace in the bow:
      And had often (the Bellman said) saved them from wreck,
          Though none of the sailors knew how.

6   There was one who was famed for the number of things
          He forgot when he entered the ship:
      His umbrella, his watch, all his jewels and rings,
          And the clothes he had bought for the trip.

7   He had forty-two boxes, all carefully packed,
          With his name painted clearly on each:[12]
      But, since he omitted to mention the fact,
          They were all left behind on the beach.

8   The loss of his clothes hardly mattered, because
          He had seven coats on when he came,
      With three pair of boots – but the worst of it was,
          He had wholly forgotten his name.[13]

S. Baring-Gould, *Sherlock Holmes of Baker Street,* Clarkson Potter, 1962, pages 26–27.)

11. I am indebted to Wilfred H. Shepherd for telling me that "engaged at enormous expense" was, and still is, a ritual phrase used by masters of ceremony in British music halls when they introduce the star of the show. The syllable "nor" in "enormous" is heavily accented, and the audience joins in reciting the entire phrase. "The effect," writes Shepherd, "is much like that of a breaking wave, and as inexplicably pleasant to the ear."

12. Five of these forty-two boxes can be observed through the window in the illustration of the Baker and his uncle; unfortunately the picture is not clear enough to make out the name painted on two of the boxes. For the meaning of these boxes and the probable name of their owner, see Fit 3, note 32. Observe, in the picture of the Baker on the upper deck, that he is sitting on what appears to be one of his boxes. If so, all were *not* left behind on the beach. Perhaps the box belongs to one of the other crew members. For comments on the number "42," see note 32.

13. The illustration for this scene deserves careful study. Above deck, left to right, are the Bellman (with a wart on his nose), the Baker (wearing his seven coats and three pairs of boots), and the Barrister. Below deck, left to right: the Billiard-marker, the Banker, the Bonnet-maker (he is making a lady's bonnet), and the Broker.

The Banker's balance scale is for weighing gold, and the loose silver mentioned in Fit 4, stanza 11. Such scales were used in Victorian banks for just this purpose.

The Broker is holding his malacca walking cane so that the tip of its imitation amber handle just touches his lips. This was such a common affectation of Victorian fops that canes were commonly called toothpicks. The malacca, made from the dark brown stem of a palm, was usually cloudy or mottled. All of which clarifies the couplet in Canto IV of Pope's *Rape of the Lock:*

    Sir Plume, of amber snuff-box vain,
    And the nice conduct of a clouded cane.

London dandies with cane handles at their lips can be seen in numerous cartoons of the period (see p. 6, for example), and in the illustrations for many Victorian novels. The practice, with its obvious homosexual symbolism, was not restricted to the malacca. William May Egley's 1859 painting *Omnibus Life in London* (Tate Gallery) shows a pensive, fashionably-dressed young man with the handle of a short carrying cane touching his lips.

Correspondent Keith H. Peterson called my attention to the following passage from P. G. Wodehouse's story "Jeeves and the Unbidden Guest":

"Motty, who was sucking the knob of his stick, uncorked himself.

" 'Yes, mother,' he said, and corked himself up again."

9   He would answer to "Hi!" or to any loud cry,
          Such as "Fry me!" or "Fritter my wig!"[14]
      To "What-you-may-call-um!" or "What-was-his-name!"[15]
          But especially "Thing-um-a-jig!"

10   While, for those who preferred a more forcible word,
          He had different names from these:
      His intimate friends called him "Candle-ends,"
          And his enemies "Toasted-cheese."[16]

11   "His form is ungainly – his intellect small –"
          (So the Bellman would often remark)
      "But his courage is perfect! And that, after all,
          Is the thing that one needs with a Snark."

14. Edward B. Jackson of New Zealand wrote to suggest that the Baker's willingness to answer to any loud cry may have been suggested to Carroll by one of Gabriel Oak's dogs, described in Chapter 5 of Thomas Hardy's novel *Far from the Madding Crowd*. The book was published two years before the *Snark*.

"So earnest and yet so wrong-headed was this young dog (he had no name in particular, and answered with perfect readiness to any pleasant interjection), that. . . ." The passage goes on to say that if you sent the dog to chase sheep, it would go on chasing forever unless you stopped it.

"Fry me" and "fritter my wig" are expressions that probably were invented by Carroll; at least I have found no evidence that they were common slang expressions of the time. However, *The Oxford English Dictionary* quotes an old Cornish proverb, "Fry me for a fool and you'll lose your fat in the frying" (citing a reference in *Notes and Queries*, a publication that Carroll read), so it is possible that Carroll had this proverb in mind.

"Fritter my wig" evidently means to mix a wig with batter and fry it in oil or lard to make wig fritters. An alternate meaning: to tear a wig into small pieces. In Carroll's time, sailors referred to shredded sails as frittered.

15. Joseph Brogunier wrote to me about the significance of "was" in "What-was-his-name." Both the Baker and the other crew members seem to be anticipating the Baker's vanishing.

16. J. A. Lindon, a British word-puzzle expert, calls my attention to the curious fact that "Candle-ends" (stumps of burned-down candles), "Toasted-cheese," "Fry me," and "Fritter my wig" all refer to objects that are heated. A baker, of course, uses heat in baking, but I incline to the view that the nicknames reflect the crew's awareness that the Baker was perpetually overheated. Although the ship travelled in "tropical climes" (see Fit 2, stanza 7), and note that a hot climate is also suggested by Hope's scanty attire, the Baker insisted on wearing seven coats and three pairs of boots. This would surely keep him as warm as toasted cheese. Evidently he dreaded the loss of his body heat as much as he dreaded the loss of his existence. The name *Candle-ends* may imply that the Baker is about to burn himself out.

Lindon also points out that both phrases occur in Carroll's long poem, *Phantasmagoria*: "candle-ends" in Canto 2, stanza 7, and "toasted cheese" in Canto 3, stanza 13.

Christie Davies, a Welsh sociologist at the University of Reading, sent me an interesting letter in which he argues that "Toasted-cheese" and "Candle-ends" suggest that the Baker was a Welshman from the Cardiganshire county of West Wales. He enclosed several documents to prove that the English once used "toasted-cheese" as a mocking epithet for their Welsh neighbors because toasted cheese (the so-called Welsh rarebit) was a favorite Welsh food. "The English found this dish hilarious," Davies writes, "much as they laugh at the Scotch for eating porridge or the French for eating frogs and snails."

Why Cardiganshire? Because the "Cardis," who were often tradesmen in the Oxford area, were regarded by the British as unusually stingy. Indeed, they were defined as "Scotchmen robbed of their generosity." They would naturally, writes Davies, "devote a ludicrous degree of time and energy to the Gladstonian activity of saving all candle-ends."

12   He would joke with hyænas,[17] returning their stare
         With an impudent wag of the head:
      And he once went a walk, paw-in-paw, with a bear,
         "Just to keep up its spirits," he said.

13   He came as a Baker: but owned, when too late –
         And it drove the poor Bellman half-mad –
      He could only bake Bridecake[18] – for which, I may state,
         No materials were to be had.

14   The last of the crew needs especial remark,
         Though he looked an incredible dunce:
      He had just one idea – but, that one being "Snark,"
         The good Bellman engaged him at once.

15   He came as a Butcher:[19] but gravely declared,
         When the ship had been sailing a week,
      He could only kill Beavers. The Bellman looked scared,
         And was almost too frightened to speak:

16   But at length he explained, in a tremulous tone,
         There was only one Beaver on board;
      And that was a tame one he had of his own,
         Whose death would be deeply deplored.

17. The species of hyena referred to here is clearly the striped hyena, or laughing hyena, so called because its howl resembles demonic laughter. The Baker later wagged his head at a much more dangerous beast (see Fit 8, stanza 3).

18. Wedding cake.

19. This completes Carroll's description of the ten crew members: Bellman, Boots, Bonnet-maker, Barrister, Broker, Billiard-marker, Banker, Beaver, Baker, and Butcher. To the obvious question of why these names all start with *B*, including also Boojum and Bandersnatch, there are several possible answers. One is suggested in the introduction. Perhaps a better one is suggested by the March Hare at the Mad Tea Party. When Alice asked why the three little (Liddell) sisters drew pictures only of objects that begin with *M*, the March Hare replied, "Why not?"

A 1922 letter of Holiday's closes with the following postscript: "I asked Lewis Carroll when first I read his M.S. why he made all the members of the crew have occupations beginning with B. He replied, 'Why not?' "

Carroll used the pseudonym "B.B." in signing some of his early poems. No one knows why, but R. B. Shaberman and Denis Crutch, in their *Under the Quizzing Glass* (London: Magpie Press, 1972), make some interesting observations on these initials. In *The Game of Logic*, after having listed such "things" as Buns, Babies, Beetles, Battledores, and their respective attributes, baked, beautiful, black, and broken, Carroll gives (page 11) the following example of a universal proposition:

"Barzillai Beckalegg is an honest man."

"You think I invented that name, now don't you?" Carroll adds. "But I didn't. It's on a carrier's cart, somewhere down in Cornwall."

Ann Clark, in her 1979 biography of Carroll, defends two other possibilities: Bobby Burns and Beau Brummell.

17   The Beaver, who happened to hear the remark,
           Protested, with tears in its eyes,
     That not even the rapture of hunting the Snark
           Could atone for that dismal surprise!

18   It strongly advised that the Butcher should be
           Conveyed in a separate ship:
     But the Bellman declared that would never agree
           With the plans he had made for the trip:

19   Navigation was always a difficult art,
           Though with only one ship and one bell:
     And he feared he must really decline, for his part,
           Undertaking another as well.

20   The Beaver's best course was, no doubt, to procure
           A second-hand dagger-proof coat –
     So the Baker advised it – and next, to insure
           Its life in some Office of note:[20]

21   This the Banker suggested, and offered for hire[21]
           (On moderate terms), or for sale,
     Two excellent Policies, one Against Fire,
           And one Against Damage From Hail.

22   Yet still, ever after that sorrowful day,
           Whenever the Butcher was by,
     The Beaver kept looking the opposite way,[22]
           And appeared unaccountably shy.

20. According to *The Oxford English Dictionary* (see entry 8B for "office") a life insurance company in England, in Carroll's time, was often referred to simply as an "office." "Office of note" means a company of good repute.

21. Hire: rent.

22. In Holiday's illustration for this scene on the ship's bow, note the Butcher's beaver cap. That is not a dagger hanging from his waist; it is a steel for sharpening knives. The Beaver is making lace by the pillow method. A pattern drawn on paper or parchment is placed on the pillow, pins are inserted, and the threads woven by means of small bobbins.

FIT THE SECOND

THE BELLMAN'S SPEECH

1 T H E Bellman himself they all praised to the skies –
  Such a carriage, such ease and such grace!
 Such solemnity, too! One could see he was wise,
  The moment one looked in his face!

2 He had bought a large map representing the sea,
  Without the least vestige of land:
 And the crew were much pleased when they found it to be
  A map they could all understand.

3 "What's the good of Mercator's[23] North Poles and Equators,
  Tropics, Zones, and Meridian Lines?"
 So the Bellman would cry: and the crew would reply
  "They are merely conventional signs!

4 "Other maps are such shapes, with their islands and capes!
  But we've got our brave Captain to thank"
 (So the crew would protest) "that he's bought us the best –
  A perfect and absolute blank!"[24]

---

23. Gerhardus Mercator, sixteenth-century Flemish mathematician and cartographer. He devised the method, known as "Mercator's projection," of projecting a spherical map of the earth on a flat rectangle so that the parallels and meridians become straight lines, and the poles become the rectangle's top and bottom edges.

24. In contrast, a map in Carroll's *Sylvie and Bruno Concluded*, Chapter 11, has *everything* on it. The German Professor explains how his country's cartographers experimented with larger and larger maps until they finally made one with a scale of a mile to the mile. "It has never been spread out, yet," he says. "The farmers objected: they said it would cover the whole country, and shut out the sunlight! So now we use the country itself, as its own map, and I assure you it does nearly as well."

OCEAN-CHART.

5 This was charming, no doubt: but they shortly found out
    That the Captain they trusted so well
Had only one notion for crossing the ocean,
    And that was to tingle his bell.[25]

6 He was thoughtful and grave – but the orders he gave
    Were enough to bewilder a crew.
When he cried, "Steer to starboard, but keep her head larboard!"
    What on earth was the helmsman to do?

7 Then the bowsprit got mixed with the rudder sometimes:[26]
    A thing, as the Bellman remarked,
That frequently happens in tropical climes,
    When a vessel is, so to speak, "snarked."

8 But the principal failing occurred in the sailing,
    And the Bellman, perplexed and distressed,
Said he *had* hoped, at least, when the wind blew due East,
    That the ship would *not* travel due West!

9 But the danger was past – they had landed at last,
    With their boxes, portmanteaus, and bags:
Yet at first sight the crew were not pleased with the view,
    Which consisted of chasms and crags.

---

25. This use of the word *tingle* was common enough in the eighteenth century but already rare in Carroll's day. Perhaps, as correspondent James T. de Kay has observed, Carroll chose this word to evoke subtly the spine-tingling terror that will soon overtake the crew.

Edward Guiliano, in a talk on the *Snark* published in *Lewis Carroll: A Celebration*, stressed the roll of the Bellman's bell in constantly reminding the reader of the inescapable passage of time as the crew moves toward its destiny. Bells were used on ships and in schools, as well as by town criers, to mark time, and they are tolled by churches to indicate death. The bell is in every illustration of the original book except the blank map on which time is meaningless. Holiday's rendering of the Bellman, Guiliano notes, suggests a wise father-time figure.

"This poem," Guiliano concluded his talk, "which on the literal level has so many humorous moments, turns out to be the saddest of Carroll's writing. The ending is not at all funny. One character vanishes, and another, the Bellman, remains a grave and depressing figure. He has, after all, but one notion of navigation, and that is to tingle his bell."

26. The bowsprit can be seen clearly in two of Holiday's illustrations. In his preface Carroll explains exactly why the bowsprit occasionally got mixed with the rudder. This confusion is often cited by Freudian critics of Carroll, though they are a bit vague as to just what to make of it.

The confusion of bowsprit and rudder may also be a way of saying that the ship occasionally sailed backward, as Carroll's preface tells us it did. Denis Crutch has pointed out (*Jabberwocky*, Autumn 1976) that the Bellman's order, in the previous stanza, to steer to starboard but keep the ship's head to port, is a maneuver that could be executed only by going backward and in a circle. It would explain, Crutch says, why half the time the ship went west when the wind blew due east. "It is my belief," he concludes, "that they merely circumnavigated their own island, ending near where they began."

10   The Bellman perceived that their spirits were low,
        And repeated in musical tone
    Some jokes he had kept for a season of woe –
        But the crew would do nothing but groan.

11   He served out some grog with a liberal hand,
        And bade them sit down on the beach:
    And they could not but own that their Captain looked grand,
        As he stood and delivered his speech.

12   "Friends, Romans, and countrymen, lend me your ears!"[27]
        (They were all of them fond of quotations:
    So they drank to his health, and they gave him three cheers,
        While he served out additional rations).

13   "We have sailed many months, we have sailed many weeks,
        (Four weeks to the month you may mark),
    But never as yet ('tis your Captain who speaks)
        Have we caught the least glimpse of a Snark!

14   "We have sailed many weeks, we have sailed many days,
        (Seven days to the week I allow),
    But a Snark, on the which we might lovingly gaze,
        We have never beheld till now!

15   "Come, listen, my men, while I tell you again
        The five unmistakable marks
    By which you may know, wheresoever you go,
        The warranted genuine Snarks.

16   "Let us take them in order. The first is the taste,
        Which is meagre and hollow, but crisp:
    Like a coat that is rather too tight in the waist,
        With a flavour of Will-o-the-wisp.

27. Surely no reader will fail to recognize this opening line (with an added "and") of Mark Antony's oration at Caesar's funeral, in Shakespeare's *Julius Caesar*.

17   "Its habit of getting up late you'll agree
        That it carries too far, when I say
    That it frequently breakfasts at five-o'clock tea,
        And dines on the following day.

18   "The third is its slowness in taking a jest.
        Should you happen to venture on one,
    It will sigh like a thing that is deeply distressed:
        And it always looks grave at a pun.

19   "The fourth is its fondness for bathing-machines,[28]
        Which it constantly carries about,
    And believes that they add to the beauty of scenes –
        A sentiment open to doubt.

28. Bathing machines were individual wooden locker rooms on wheels. While the modest Victorian bather changed to bathing clothes, horses (surrounded by flies) would pull the machine into several feet of water. He or she would then emerge through a door facing the sea, screened by a large awning attached to the machine. At many beaches a guide or "dipper" would forcibly assist the reluctant bather to make the icy plunge.

In one of Carroll's playful letters to Gertrude Chataway he proposes visiting her at Sandown, the summer resort where they first met. If she is unable to find a room for him, he expects her to give him *her* room and to spend the night by herself on the beach. "If you . . . feel a little chilly, of course you could go into a bathing machine, which everybody knows is *very* comfortable to sleep in—you know they make the floor of soft wood on purpose. I send you seven kisses (to last a week). . . ."

There are many references to bathing machines in Victorian literature. The Lord Chancellor, in the Gilbert and Sullivan operetta *Iolanthe*, sings about "lying awake with a dismal headache" and dreaming of crossing the channel in rough weather on a steamer from Harwich that is "something between a large bathing machine and a very small second-class carriage."

The following ode to the bathing machine appeared anonymously in *Punch*, 1 September 1883:

BEHOLD an old relic of old-fashioned days,
  Recalling the coaches, the hoy, and postchaise!
It has not advanced in a timber or wheel,
  Since first it was fashioned by Benjamin Beale.

It is not æsthetic, nor yet picturesque,
  'Tis heavy and cumbrous, expensive, grotesque—
And I feel very certain there never was seen
  Such an old-fashioned thing as a Bathing Machine!

The windows won't open, the doors never fit,
  The floor is strewn over with pebbles and grit;
A looking-glass too, with a silverless back,
  A pinless pincushion, a broken boot-jack:

It smells of old seaweed, 'tis mouldy and grim,
  'Tis sloppy and stuffy, 'tis dismal and dim—
'Tis a deer-cart, a fish-van, or something between;
  Oh, a hideous hutch is the Bathing Machine!

The driver says "Right!" and he raps at the door;
  He starts with a jerk, and you sit on the floor!
It creaks and it rattles, you rise and you fall,
  And bound to and fro like a mad tennis-ball!

Again there's a lurch, and you nearly fall flat,
  And first sprain your ankle, then tread on your hat—
While you're bumped and you're battered, bruised
    blue, black, and green,
  In that horrid contrivance, the Bathing Machine!

For more on bathing machines, see Chapter 2, note 6, of *Alice's Adventures in Wonderland*, in *The Annotated Alice*; and *The English Seaside* by H. G. Stokes, 1947, pages 17–25. The pages of *Punch* contain scores of cartoons about bathing machines, including the variety that dotted the French coast (for example, see p. 9).

20   "The fifth is ambition. It next will be right
          To describe each particular batch:
      Distinguishing those that have feathers, and bite,
          From those that have whiskers, and scratch.

21   "For, although common Snarks do no manner of harm,
          Yet, I feel it my duty to say,
      Some are Boojums —"[29] The Bellman broke off in alarm,
          For the Baker had fainted away.

29. In Chapter 24 of *Sylvie and Bruno Concluded*, the second half of Carroll's long, sentimental fantasy novel (the first half was published thirteen years after the *Snark*), the following dialogue occurs:

"The Professor sighed, and gave it up. 'Do you know what a Boojum is?'

" '*I* know!' cried Bruno. 'It's the thing what wrenches people out of their boots!'

" 'He means "bootjack," ' Sylvie explained in a whisper.

" 'You can't wrench people out of *boots*,' the Professor mildly observed.

"Bruno laughed saucily. 'Oo *can*, though! Unless they're *welly* tight in.'

" 'Once upon a time there was a Boojum—' the Professor began, but stopped suddenly. 'I forget the rest of the Fable,' he said. 'And there was a lesson to be learned from it. I'm afraid I forget *that*, too.' "

Various attempts have been made to explain the word *Boojum*. Eric Partridge in his essay on "The Nonsense Words in Edward Lear and Lewis Carroll" (*Here, There and Everywhere*, London, 1950) suggests that it packs together *Boo!* and *fee, fo, fi, fum!* Phyllis Greenacre points out that in addition to suggesting *Boo!* it also suggests *boohoo*. One thinks also of *boogieman*, though in Carroll's England it was pronounced with a long "o" and spelled *bogy* or *bogey*. The Old Bogy was the Devil, and a bogy was an evil goblin or anything that aroused terror. The Bogyman was supposed to "get" little children if they misbehaved.

Thanks to the tireless efforts of physicist N. David Mermin, the word *boojum* has now entered the language of physics. It is a singularity that can form in superfluid helium-3, and that works its way to the surface where it softly and suddenly vanishes. See "Let Us Now Praise Famous Boojums," by M. Mitchell Waldrop, in *Science*, Volume 212, 19 June 1981, page 1378. A few years earlier the word *snark* was adopted

in graph theory as the name for a certain rare species of graphs that have three lines meeting at each point. See my *Scientific American* column on mathematical games, April 1976, and the section on snarks in *Edge-Colourings of Graphs*, by S. Fiorini and R. J. Wilson (Pitman, 1977), pages 47–50.

J. A. Lindon notes that *Boojum* is a syllable reversal of *Jumbo*, and that the elephant is one of those few animals for which one can confuse rudder and bowsprit.

Boojum is now a common vernacular name for a slithy, queer-shaped tree that thrives only in the central desert of Mexico's Baja California. Joseph Wood Krutch, in his book *The Forgotten Peninsula* (1961), devotes an entire chapter to the boojum. What does it look like? Answers Krutch: like nothing else on earth. Natives call it a *cirio* (wax candle) because it resembles a candle, though its body is covered with what from a distance seems to be a rough hairy growth but on closer inspection proves to be a stubble of short twigs. "Perhaps only a botanist could love it," writes Krutch. Fully grown specimens reach a height of fifty feet, sometimes drooping over in an arch until the tip touches the ground. Standing in a forest of boojums, Krutch found the effect hallucinatory, like a surrealist dream.

The name *boojum* was given to the tree by the British ecologist Godfrey Sykes when he explored the Baja in 1922. Like Carroll's Banker, Sykes carried with him a telescope. According to his son's account, he focused his telescope on a distant tree, gazed intently for a few moments, then said, "Ho, ho, a boojum, definitely a boojum."

If any reader wishes to learn more about this absurd tree, he can consult an entire book on it that was published in 1975 by the University of Arizona Press: *The Boojum and Its Home*, by Robert R. Humphrey. And if the reader is near Phoenix, Arizona, he will find specimens of boojums in the Botanical Gardens there.

FIT THE THIRD

THE BAKER'S TALE

1   THEY roused him with muffins – they roused him with ice –
        They roused him with mustard and cress –[30]
    They roused him with jam and judicious advice –
        They set him conundrums to guess.

2   When at length he sat up and was able to speak,
        His sad story he offered to tell;
    And the Bellman cried "Silence! Not even a shriek!"
        And excitedly tingled his bell.

3   There was silence supreme! Not a shriek, not a scream,
        Scarcely even a howl or a groan,
    As the man they called "Ho!" told his story of woe
        In an antediluvian tone.[31]

4   "My father and mother were honest, though poor –"
        "Skip all that!" cried the Bellman in haste.
    "If it once becomes dark, there's no chance of a Snark –
        We have hardly a minute to waste!"

30. Mustard-and-cress, a common salad and sandwich ingredient in England, is grown from a mixture of the seeds of white mustard and garden cress. When the shoots are about an inch tall, they are cut with scissors and placed between thin slices of bread to make sandwiches for four o'clock tea.

31. Eric Partridge calls attention to this line as one of those rare instances in which Carroll uses a standard word in a completely whimsical sense. Such words occur often in Lear's verse (e.g., "That intrinsic old man of Peru," "He weareth a runcible hat," "Sweetly susceptible blue," "Propitious old man with a beard").

Several correspondents have disagreed with Partridge. They suggest that "antediluvian" may foreshadow the Baker's tears two stanzas later.

5   "I skip forty years,"[32] said the Baker, in tears,
        "And proceed without further remark
    To the day when you took me aboard of your ship
        To help you in hunting the Snark.

6   "A dear uncle of mine (after whom I was named)
        Remarked, when I bade him farewell –"
    "Oh, skip your dear uncle!" the Bellman exclaimed,
        As he angrily tingled his bell.

7   "He remarked to me then," said that mildest of men,
        " 'If your Snark be a Snark, that is right:
    Fetch it home by all means – you may serve it with greens,
        And it's handy for striking a light.[33]

8   " 'You may seek it with thimbles – and seek it with care;
        You may hunt it with forks and hope;
    You may threaten its life with a railway-share;
        You may charm it with smiles and soap –' "

32. The skipping of 40 years puts the Baker in his early forties. Carroll began writing the *Snark* in 1874 when he was 42. Could the Baker be Carroll himself? J. A. Lindon suggests that the Baker's 42 boxes (Fit 1, stanza 7) are perhaps intended to represent Carroll's 42 years. Each box bore the Baker's name and all were left behind when he joined the Snark-hunting expedition. Note also the mention of Rule 42 in Carroll's preface, and the King's remarks at the trial of the Knave of Hearts (*Alice's Adventures in Wonderland*, Chapter 12): "Rule Forty-two. All persons more than a mile high to leave the court." Curiously, Carroll refers to his age as 42 in his poem *Phantasmagoria* (Canto 1, stanza 16) though at the time this poem was written he was still in his thirties. The number 42 certainly seems to have had some sort of special significance for Carroll.

J. A. Lindon has noticed that if we take the memorable date of 4 July 1862 (on which Carroll began telling Alice Liddell the story of *Alice in Wonderland*) and write it, British style, as 4/7/62, we have a number with 76 in the middle (the publication year of the *Snark*) and 42 on the ends. R. B. Shaberman and Denis Crutch, in *Under the Quizzing Glass*, point out that the first *Alice* book has just 42 illustrations, and the second book would have had the same number had it not been for a last-minute change of plan.

Lindon also recalls that the number of horses and men sent to repair Humpty Dumpty is 4207. Alice's age in the second *Alice* book is 7 years and 6 months, and 6 times 7, Lindon observes, is 42. Indeed, the number 42 calls to mind the common phrase, "all sixes and sevens," but one could go on for pages with this kind of number juggling.

Other passages strengthen the view that Carroll was satirizing himself in the person of the Baker. The Baker's ungainly form and small intellect, his absent-mindedness, his pseudonyms, his tidy packing of boxes, his ways of joking with hyenas and walking with bears, his waggishness, his wakeful nights, his vanishing in the midst of laughter and glee—all add up to a whimsical, funny-sad, self-deprecating portrait.

33. Carroll may have intended this to suggest that the Snark breathes out fire like a dragon, or possibly that the beast's hide is a rough surface on which matches can be struck.

9   ("That's exactly the method," the Bellman bold
          In a hasty parenthesis cried,
       "That's exactly the way I have always been told
          That the capture of Snarks should be tried!")

10   " 'But oh, beamish[34] nephew, beware of the day,
          If your Snark be a Boojum! For then
       You will softly and suddenly vanish away,
          And never be met with again!'

11   "It is this, it is this that oppresses my soul,
          When I think of my uncle's last words:[35]
       And my heart is like nothing so much as a bowl
          Brimming over with quivering curds!

12   "It is this, it is this –" "We have had that before!"
          The Bellman indignantly said.
       And the Baker replied "Let me say it once more.
          It is this, it is this that I dread!

13   "I engage with the Snark – every night after dark –
          In a dreamy delirious fight:
       I serve it with greens in those shadowy scenes,
          And I use it for striking a light:

14   "But if ever I meet with a Boojum, that day,
          In a moment (of this I am sure),
       I shall softly and suddenly vanish away –
          And the notion I cannot endure!"

34. This is the first use in the *Snark* of a nonsense word from "Jabberwocky" (Chapter 1 of *Through the Looking-Glass*). The word is not exactly nonsense: *The Oxford English Dictionary* traces it back to 1530 as a variant of *beaming*.

35. Apparently Holiday interpreted "last words" to mean that the Baker's uncle died after speaking them. At any rate, he pictures the uncle as confined to bed, hands crippled by arthritis, his medicine on a shelf above.

FIT THE FOURTH

THE HUNTING

1   T H E Bellman looked uffish,[36] and wrinkled his brow.
      "If only you'd spoken before!
It's excessively awkward to mention it now,
      With the Snark, so to speak, at the door!

2   "We should all of us grieve, as you well may believe,
      If you never were met with again –
But surely, my man, when the voyage began,
      You might have suggested it then?

3   "It's excessively awkward to mention it now –
      As I think I've already remarked."
And the man they called "Hi!" replied, with a sigh,
      "I informed you the day we embarked.

4   "You may charge me with murder – or want of sense –
      (We are all of us weak at times):
But the slightest approach to a false pretence
      Was never among my crimes!

5   "I said it in Hebrew – I said it in Dutch –
      I said it in German and Greek:
But I wholly forgot (and it vexes me much)
      That English is what you speak!"

36. *Uffish* appears in "Jabberwocky." In a letter to a child-friend, Maud Standen, Carroll says that the word suggests to him "a state of mind when the voice is gruffish, the manner roughish, and the temper huffish."

6   " 'Tis a pitiful tale," said the Bellman, whose face
          Had grown longer at every word:
    "But, now that you've stated the whole of your case,
          More debate would be simply absurd.

7   "The rest of my speech" (he explained to his men)
          "You shall hear when I've leisure to speak it.
    But the Snark is at hand, let me tell you again!
          'Tis your glorious duty to seek it!

8   "To seek it with thimbles, to seek it with care;
          To pursue it with forks and hope;
    To threaten its life with a railway-share;
          To charm it with smiles and soap!

9   "For the Snark's a peculiar creature, that won't
          Be caught in a commonplace way.
    Do all that you know, and try all that you don't:
          Not a chance must be wasted to-day!

10   "For England expects – I forbear to proceed:
          'Tis a maxim tremendous, but trite:[37]
    And you'd best be unpacking the things that you need
          To rig yourselves out for the fight."

11   Then the Banker endorsed a blank cheque (which he crossed),[38]
          And changed his loose silver for notes.
    The Baker with care combed his whiskers and hair,[39]
          And shook the dust out of his coats.

37. The tremendous but trite maxim is, of course, "England expects every man to do his duty." It was a flag signal to the fleet, ordered by Horatio Nelson shortly before he was killed by a musket shot at the battle of Trafalgar in 1805. According to one account of the episode, Nelson first ordered the signal "Nelson confides that every man will do his duty." An officer suggested replacing *Nelson* by *England*, and it was pointed out that *expects* was in the flag code whereas *confides* would have to be spelled out with a flag for each letter. (For details, see *Notes and Queries*, Series 6, Volume 9, pages 261 and 283.)

"If . . . England expects every man to do his duty," Dickens wrote in *Martin Chuzzlewit*, Chapter 43, "England is the most sanguine country on the face of the earth, and will find itself continually disappointed."

38. The practice of crossing checks is still standard throughout the United Kingdom, and is one of the principal ways in which the English system of checking differs from that of the

12   The Boots and the Broker were sharpening a spade
            Each working the grindstone in turn:
      But the Beaver went on making lace, and displayed
            No interest in the concern:

13   Though the Barrister tried to appeal to its pride,
            And vainly proceeded to cite
      A number of cases, in which making laces
            Had been proved an infringement of right.

14   The maker of Bonnets ferociously planned
            A novel arrangement of bows:
      While the Billiard-marker with quivering hand
            Was chalking the tip of his nose.

15   But the Butcher turned nervous, and dressed himself fine,
            With yellow kid gloves and a ruff –
      Said he felt it exactly like going to dine,
            Which the Bellman declared was all "stuff."[40]

16   "Introduce me, now there's a good fellow," he said,
            "If we happen to meet it together!"
      And the Bellman, sagaciously nodding his head,
            Said "That must depend on the weather."

United States. To cross a check "generally," the writer draws two slanting and parallel lines across the face and writes "& Co." between them. This means that the check is not negotiable; it must be deposited to the payee's bank account. To cross a check "specially," the name of the bank where the amount is to be deposited is written across the face of the check. English banks now issue ready-crossed checks, with the parallel lines printed on them, and many people carry checks of both crossed and uncrossed varieties.

39. The Baker appears whiskerless in Holiday's illustrations. Either Holiday failed to note that the Baker combed his whiskers, or Carroll added this stanza after it was too late to alter the art, or there is a small, almost invisible tuft of side whiskers below the Baker's left ear in the illustration that shows him sitting on the deck.

40. *Stuff,* a slang equivalent of *rubbish* or *stuff and nonsense,* was current in Carroll's day. However, as correspondent Thomas Wray pointed out, the primary meaning of *stuff* is a cloth, usually woolen, and often opposed to fine clothes made of silk or linen. "An example of this opposition," he writes, "is found in British legal robes. Silk is used for the gowns of legal barristers, junior barristers wearing stuff gowns. . . . Is not the Bellman disparaging the Butcher's finery by declaring it to be mere stuff?"

17   The Beaver went simply galumphing[41] about,
        At seeing the Butcher so shy:
    And even the Baker, though stupid and stout,
        Made an effort to wink with one eye.

18   "Be a man!" said the Bellman in wrath, as he heard
        The Butcher beginning to sob.
    "Should we meet with a Jubjub,[42] that desperate bird,
        We shall need all our strength for the job!"

41. *Galumphing*, from "Jabberwocky," is one of Carroll's portmanteau words that have entered the dictionary. It is a blend of *gallop* and *triumphant*, meaning (according to *The Oxford English Dictionary*) "to march on exultantly with irregular bounding movements." "Both Carroll and Lear," writes Eric Partridge, "must, in their philological heaven, be chortling at the thought that they have frabjously galumphed their way into the English vocabulary."

42. "Beware the Jubjub bird," so reads a line in the second stanza of "Jabberwocky." Eric Partridge thinks *jubjub* may be a pun on *jug-jug*, an English word expressing one of the notes of the nightingale; perhaps a blend of *jug-jug* and *hubbub*.

FIT THE FIFTH

THE BEAVER'S LESSON

1   T HEY sought it with thimbles, they sought it with care;
They pursued it with forks and hope;[43]
They threatened its life with a railway-share;
They charmed it with smiles and soap.[44]

43. Elspeth Huxley gave the title *With Forks and Hope* to her African notebook, published in the United States by Morrow in 1964.

44. This is the third appearance of this stanza but the first to describe the actual carrying out of the Snark-hunting method advised by the Baker's uncle. (For translations of the stanza into French, Latin, Dutch, Swedish, Danish, German, and Italian, see the annotated bibliography.) The fact that essentially the same stanza occurs altogether six times in the poem has led some to suspect that it may conceal a private, cryptic message. If so, the message has never been decoded.

My theory—the reader may be able to formulate a better one—is that thimbles, forks, a railway share, smiles, and soap are connected with the Snark's five unmistakable marks mentioned in Fit 2. The forks are for eating crisp Snark meat. The railway share appeals to the Snark's ambition to become wealthy and so can be used for baiting a death trap. Smiles are to let the Snark know when a pun has been perpetrated. The soap is of course for the bathing machines that the Snark carries about, and the thimble is used for thumping the side of the creature's head to wake him in time for five-o'clock tea.

The bare-bosomed young woman in Holiday's illustration for this stanza is Hope. (She may also be the ship's wooden figurehead. See the first illustration.) It is amusing to note that when Andrew Lang reviewed the *Snark* in 1876 he failed completely to identify the young lady. "In a sketch of the whole crew," he wrote, "there is a really graceful half-draped female figure with an anchor and a trident, who may or may not be the Bonnet-maker, but who would deeply shock the Banker at her side."

It is not by accident that Holiday placed a sheet anchor on Hope's shoulder. As far back as the sixteenth century, the term *sheet anchor* has been figuratively used for that on which one ultimately relies: one's mainstay, after all else has failed. Artists in England traditionally depicted Hope with such an anchor.

The woman with bowed head is Care. (She is also mentioned in the opening stanza of the poem; the Bellman lands her with the crew.) There are five "forks" in the picture if we count Hope's anchor as a fork. In the upper left corner are the Broker, still sucking his cane, and the Baker. The Barrister is wearing his wig and legal robes. The Banker carries a tuning fork (appropriate, as J. A. Lindon suggests, to a man who deals in notes) and the telescope that he is seen holding in the book's first illustration. The Beaver holds a microscope.

Carroll does not mention either the microscope or telescope. Perhaps the Beaver is searching for microscopic clues, such as a bit of feather or whisker, and the Banker hopes to spot a Snark in the far distance. The instruments are also appropriate, as Lindon has observed, to the habits of the two crew members: a Banker must constantly be looking ahead on his investments, whereas a Beaver is concerned only with what is directly under its nose. (Cf. the railway scene in *Through the Looking-Glass*, in which the Guard looks at Alice first through a telescope, then through a microscope.)

[44]

2   Then the Butcher contrived an ingenious plan
             For making a separate sally;
      And had fixed on a spot unfrequented by man,
             A dismal and desolate valley.

3   But the very same plan to the Beaver occurred:
             It had chosen the very same place:
      Yet neither betrayed, by a sign or a word,
             The disgust that appeared in his face.

4   Each thought he was thinking of nothing but "Snark"
             And the glorious work of the day;
      And each tried to pretend that he did not remark[45]
             That the other was going that way.

5   But the valley grew narrow and narrower still,
             And the evening got darker and colder,
      Till (merely from nervousness, not from goodwill)
             They marched along shoulder to shoulder.

6   Then a scream, shrill and high, rent the shuddering sky,
             And they knew that some danger was near:
      The Beaver turned pale to the tip of its tail,
             And even the Butcher felt queer.

7   He thought of his childhood, left far far behind –
             That blissful and innocent state –
      The sound so exactly recalled to his mind
             A pencil that squeaks on a slate!

8   " 'Tis the voice of the Jubjub!"[46] he suddenly cried.
             (This man, that they used to call "Dunce.")
      "As the Bellman would tell you," he added with pride,
             "I have uttered that sentiment once.

45. *Remark* in the sense of *observe* or *notice*, not in the sense of making a remark.

46. Cf. " 'Tis the voice of the Lobster" (*Alice's Adventures in Wonderland*, Chapter 10), Carroll's parody on Isaac Watts's poem " 'Tis the voice of the sluggard." All three lines derive ultimately from the Biblical phrase (Song of Solomon 2:12) "the voice of the turtle."

9   ""'Tis the note of the Jubjub! Keep count, I entreat;
           You will find I have told it you twice.
        'Tis the song of the Jubjub! The proof is complete,
           If only I've stated it thrice."[47]

10   The Beaver had counted with scrupulous care,
           Attending to every word:
        But it fairly lost heart, and outgrabe[48] in despair,
           When the third repetition occurred.

11   It felt that, in spite of all possible pains,
           It had somehow contrived to lose count,
        And the only thing now was to rack its poor brains
           By reckoning up the amount.

47. Joseph Brogunier called my attention to the importance of "if" in this line. The Butcher is not certain that he has made a statement three times; indeed, there are good grounds for his and the Beaver's doubts. When the Bellman invoked the rule-of-three, he had thrice repeated exactly the same words, "Just the place for a Snark." But the Butcher refers first to the Jubjub's voice, then to its note, and finally to its song. Later, when he tries to prove that he *did* repeat himself thrice, he invokes an irrelevant mathematical argument that begs the question.

Is not all this a striking allegory of Charles Peirce's obsessive preoccupation with monads, dyads, and triads? The Butcher's "queer" feeling (A "queer being" was how William James once described his friend Peirce), when he hears the Jubjub's first scream, is surely an experience of Firstness. But as soon as he recalls the sound's resemblance to a sound heard in childhood, it becomes an experience of Secondness. And when he recognizes the sound as a song, exhibiting continuity in time, he experiences Thirdness.

Can the validity of the three categories be proved? After expressing his beliefs in a triad of modalities (the proof can, must, and shall be done), the Butcher requests paper and ink on which he can write equations and draw existential graphs to show that if you start with Thirdness you can't go any higher. You just keep producing more triads. Note that the Butcher writes with a "pen in each hand." Although Peirce was left-handed, we are told by Paul Weiss (in his article on Peirce in *The Dictionary of American Biography*) that Peirce could "write with both hands—in fact, he was capable of writing a question with one hand and the answer simultaneously with the other."

Peirce, like the Butcher, was convinced that his three categories of Firstness, Secondness, and Thirdness were "exactly and perfectly true." They revealed to him what had previously been "enveloped in absolute mystery," and he would gladly explain his method, in his famous "popular style," if only he had the time, and if his listeners had the brains to understand. There is so much that "remains to be said"! (No book on philosophy was published by Peirce in his lifetime, but he had endless projects for monumental works that he hoped to write.)

Observe the significant reference in stanza 8 to the Butcher having been called "Dunce." This unquestionably is a reference to Duns Scotus, the medieval philosopher Peirce most admired, and whose realism had such a strong influence on Peirce's phenomenology.

The Beaver, in my allegory, is none other than philosopher Charles Hartshorne, co-editor with Weiss of Peirce's *Collected Papers* and the most distinguished living defender of Peirce's three categories. From Peirce's "Lesson" he learns more in ten minutes than he could learn in a lifetime of reading. Although Hartshorne is destined to have many quarrels with Peirce, he need only remember his great encounter with the Jubjub's Firstness, Secondness, and Thirdness to have his admiration and affection for Peirce restored.

"I believe," wrote Hartshorne, "that all things, from atoms to God, are really instances of First, Second, Third, and that no other equally simple doctrine has the power and precision of this one, when purified of its synechistic excesses." See Hartshorne's paper "Charles Peirce's 'One Contribution to Philosophy' and His Most Serious Mistake," in *Studies in the Philosophy of Charles Sanders Peirce*, Second Series, edited by E. C. Moore and R. S. Robin, University of Massachusetts Press, 1964.

48. *Outgrabe* is from the first stanza of "Jabberwocky." Humpty Dumpty explains that *outgribing* "is something between bellowing and whistling, with a kind of sneeze in the middle: however, you'll hear it done, maybe—down in the wood yonder—and, when you've once heard it, you'll be *quite* content."

12 "Two added to one – if that could but be done,"
    It said, "with one's fingers and thumbs!"
   Recollecting with tears how, in earlier years,
    It had taken no pains with its sums.

13 "The thing can be done," said the Butcher, "I think.
    The thing must be done, I am sure.
   The thing shall be done! Bring me paper and ink,
    The best there is time to procure."

14 The Beaver brought paper, portfolio, pens,[49]
    And ink in unfailing supplies:
   While strange creepy creatures came out of their dens,
    And watched them with wondering eyes.

49. J. A. Lindon suggests that the illustration for this scene may have been intended as one of those puzzle pictures in which you try to spot as many objects as you can that begin with a certain letter. Is the letter *B*? The list includes: Butcher, Beaver, Bellman, bell, barrel organs, bats, bugles, band, bottles, books, brace, and bit. Note that in Holiday's original sketch there is a book beneath Colenso's that is titled *Bridge.*

Eric Hyman, taking his cue from the fact that the Beaver brought along "paper, portfolio, pens," wrote to defend the letter *P.* Other *P* words include plumes, pigs, pussy cats, points, pocket, piccolo, and pipes.

The picture has many fascinating details. Note the lizard labelled "income tax" that is rifling the Butcher's pockets. The kittens are playing with the Butcher's yellow kid gloves. The large object in the lower right corner is an ornate ink-stand called a "standish."

Colenso's *Arithmetic*, at the Butcher's feet, was a popular schoolbook of the day. (A copy was listed among Carroll's books that were auctioned after his death.) It was written by Bishop (note the *B*!) John William Colenso, one of the great controversial figures of the Victorian era. He began his career as a mathematical tutor and author of a series of mathematics textbooks widely used throughout England. In 1846 he was appointed Bishop of Natal, a South African province where the native Zulus badgered him with embarrassing questions about the Old Testament. The more Colenso pondered his answers the more he convinced himself that Christianity was lost if it continued to insist on the Bible's historical accuracy. He expressed these heretical views in a series of books, using arithmetical arguments to prove the nonsense of various Old Testament tales. How, for example, could 12,000 Israelites slaughter 200,000 Midianites? This atrocity, the bishop decided, "had happily only been carried out on paper." Such opinions seem mild today, but at the time they touched off a tempest that rocked the English church. Colenso was savagely denounced, socially ostracized, and finally excommunicated, though the courts decided in his favor and he was later reinstated at Natal.

It is appropriate that the second book in Holiday's illustration is *On the Reductio ad Absurdum.* Just as Carroll reduced the sea ballad to absurdity, so Colenso reduced to absurdity the literal interpretation of the Bible. Was Carroll pro or con Colenso? I have been unable to find out. He surely would have sided with the bishop in his attacks on the doctrine of eternal punishment, but it is doubtful if he would have favored Colenso's defence of polygamy among Zulu converts or the degree to which the bishop dismissed Biblical stories as mythology.

For a recent article on Colenso see "The Colenso Controversy," by P. O. G. White in *Theology*, Volume 65, October 1962, pages 402–8.

The winged pigs derive from the old Scottish proverb "Pigs may fly, but it's not likely." "Just about as much right as pigs have to fly," says the Duchess in the first *Alice* book (Chapter 9), and in the second book (Chapter 4) Tweedledee sings:

  And why the sea is boiling hot –
  And whether pigs have wings.

15 So engrossed was the Butcher, he heeded them not,
    As he wrote with a pen in each hand,
   And explained all the while in a popular style
    Which the Beaver could well understand.

16 "Taking Three as the subject to reason about –
    A convenient number to state –
   We add Seven, and Ten, and then multiply out
    By One Thousand diminished by Eight.

17 "The result we proceed to divide, as you see,
    By Nine Hundred and Ninety and Two:
   Then subtract Seventeen, and the answer must be
    Exactly and perfectly true.[50]

18 "The method employed I would gladly explain,
    While I have it so clear in my head,
   If I had but the time and you had but the brain –
    But much yet remains to be said.

19 "In one moment I've seen what has hitherto been
    Enveloped in absolute mystery,
   And without extra charge I will give you at large
    A Lesson in Natural History."[51]

50. It is good to have clearly in mind what is going on here. The Butcher is fairly certain that he has made his statement three times; according to the Bellman's rule-of-three, this proves the truth of his assertion. The Beaver counted the first two statements, but had difficulty adding them to the last one. The Butcher is proving to the Beaver that 2 plus 1 does in fact equal 3. His arithmetical procedure is a sterling example of circular reasoning. It begins with 3, the number he seeks to prove, and ends with 3; but the procedure is such that he is certain to end with whatever number he starts with. If x be the starting number, the procedure can be expressed algebraically as:

$$\frac{(x + 7 + 10)(1000 - 8)}{992} - 17$$

which simplifies to x.

51. Phyllis Greenacre thinks that the ten members of the crew represent the ten children in the Dodgson family, with Charles as the Baker. "The part of the poem in which the Butcher gives the docile Beaver a lesson in natural history," she writes, "is probably [analysts often have difficulty writing "possibly"] but a thinly disguised picture of a consultation among the little Dodgsons regarding the mysterious [sex] life of their awesome parents."

20   In his genial way he proceeded to say
        (Forgetting all laws of propriety,
    And that giving instruction, without introduction,
        Would have caused quite a thrill in Society),

21   "As to temper the Jubjub's a desperate bird,
        Since it lives in perpetual passion:
    Its taste in costume is entirely absurd –
        It is ages ahead of the fashion:

22   "But it knows any friend it has met once before:
        It never will look at a bribe:
    And in charity-meetings it stands at the door,
        And collects – though it does not subscribe.

23   "Its flavour when cooked is more exquisite far
        Than mutton, or oysters, or eggs:
    (Some think it keeps best in an ivory jar,
        And some, in mahogany kegs:)

24   "You boil it in sawdust: you salt it in glue:
        You condense it with locusts and tape:
    Still keeping one principal object in view –
        To preserve its symmetrical shape."[52]

25   The Butcher would gladly have talked till next day,
        But he felt that the Lesson must end,
    And he wept with delight in attempting to say
        He considered the Beaver his friend.

26   While the Beaver confessed, with affectionate looks
        More eloquent even than tears,
    It had learned in ten minutes far more than all books
        Would have taught it in seventy years.

52. H. S. M. Coxeter, professor of mathematics at the University of Toronto, has called my attention to a geometrical interpretation given to this stanza by the English mathematician John Leech. The stanza tells how to saw and glue together the wooden rods for a model of the skeletal framework of a regular polyhedron. For *locusts* read *locuses* or *loci*; for *tape* read *tape measure*.

27   They returned hand-in-hand, and the Bellman, unmanned
                (For a moment) with noble emotion,
          Said "This amply repays all the wearisome days
                We have spent on the billowy ocean!"

28   Such friends, as the Beaver and Butcher became,
                Have seldom if ever been known;
          In winter or summer, 'twas always the same –
                You could never meet either alone.[53]

29   And when quarrels arose – as one frequently finds
                Quarrels will, spite of every endeavour –
          The song of the Jubjub recurred to their minds,
                And cemented their friendship for ever!

---

53. I had always assumed that the Butcher and Beaver became a pair of ship buddies until I read Andrew Lang's review of the *Snark*. "The drawing of the Beaver sitting at her bobbins is very satisfactory," Lang writes, "the natural shyness of the Beaver in the presence of the Butcher being admirably rendered." The thought that the Beaver might be a "she" is rather startling. Carroll always refers to the Beaver alone with neutral pronouns.

The Beaver's lace-making suggests a female, but this is countered by the application of "his" and "he" to the pair, in the fit's third and fourth stanzas. Whichever the case, W. H. Auden, in his book *The Enchafèd Flood*, detects an undercurrent of sexual attraction: ". . . the Beaver and the Butcher, romantic explorers though they are, who have chosen to enter a desolate valley, where the Jubjub bird screams in passion overhead, and the creatures from The Temptation of St. Anthony surround them, escape from the destructive power of sex, sublimating it into arithmetical calculations based on the number 3."

Leigh Mercer called my attention to how the events of this fit contradict the "ever after" in the last stanza of Fit the First.

My statement that Carroll's pronouns do not identify the Beaver's sex was questioned by C. D. Fell in the following poem that appeared in the British journal *Computing*:

I read it through twice, I read it with care,
    I perused it with forks and hope.
I followed its reasons with sympathy rare,
    It charmed me as smiles from a Pope.

Yet with one lone opinion I must disagree
    So I've taken up paper, pen, ink
He says it is plain that the Beaver's a "she";
    Now that is the theory I'll sink.

If you read Fit the Fifth you find him referred
    To not once, not twice, but three times,
By masculine pronouns, so it must be absurd
    To suggest he's a 'she' in these rhymes.

In stanza the third of the fit named before
    You'll find the word 'his' is applied.
You'll find 'he' used twice in verse number four.
    If you read it you'll find I've not lied.

You'll find by addition the total is three
    If, you re-read my references through
So the Beaver is male, you must now agree
    For what's said three times is true.

"I must admit to some prejudice in this matter," Fell added. "My father is the Beaver in the Cambridge Snark Club referred to in the preface to the Martin Gardner edition of the *Snark*."

I must respectfully disagree with Fell. In all three cases the male pronoun is used not in reference to the Beaver alone, but to both the Beaver and Butcher. It was the custom then, even more than today, to use a male pronoun in such contexts rather than the awkward "his or her" and "he or she."

FIT THE SIXTH

THE BARRISTER'S DREAM[54]

1   T H E Y sought it with thimbles, they sought it with care;
              They pursued it with forks and hope;
        They threatened its life with a railway-share;
              They charmed it with smiles and soap.

2   But the Barrister, weary of proving in vain
              That the Beaver's lace-making was wrong,[55]
        Fell asleep, and in dreams saw the creature quite plain
              That his fancy had dwelt on so long.

54. The farcical side of English law had received its classic expression in 1837 in Dickens's story, in *The Pickwick Papers*, of Mr. Pickwick's trial for breach of promise; a trial that may have influenced Carroll's equally celebrated account of the trial of the Knave of Hearts, perhaps also the Barrister's Dream.

Another possible influence on the dream was the trial of the Tichborne claimant. Sir Roger Charles Tichborne, a wealthy young Englishman, was lost at sea in 1854 when the ship on which he sailed went down with all hands. His eccentric dowager mother, Lady Tichborne, refused to believe that her son had drowned. She foolishly advertised for news of Sir Roger and, sure enough, in 1865 an illiterate butcher in Wagga Wagga, New South Wales, responded. Sir Roger had been a slim man with straight black hair. The butcher was extremely fat, with wavy light brown hair. Nevertheless, there was a big emotional recognition scene when mother and claimant finally met in Paris. The trustees of Sir Roger's estate were unconvinced. They brought suit against the claimant in 1871 and the trial turned into one of the longest and funniest of all English court cases. More than a hundred persons swore that the claimant was indeed Sir Roger. Lewis Carroll followed the trial with interest, recording in his Diary on 28 February 1874 the final verdict of guilty and the claimant's sentence of fourteen years for perjury.

It is possible that Carroll intended the Barrister's Dream to be a satire on some of the episodes in the Tichborne case, and there is a plausible conjecture that Holiday's Barrister is a caricature of Edward Vaughan Kenealy, counsel for the claimant (see the cartoon of Kenealy in *Punch*, Volume 68, 1875, page 91). A book on the Tichborne case was in Carroll's library, and he once anagrammed Kenealy's full name as "Ah! We dread an ugly knave."

All this, together with the presence of a Butcher in Carroll's crew, gave rise to a popular interpretation of the poem: that it was throughout intended as a satire on the Tichborne case. (See *The Tichborne Claimant* by Douglas Woodruff, Farrar, Straus and Cudahy, 1957.)

55. See Fit 4, stanza 12.

3   He dreamed that he stood in a shadowy Court,
           Where the Snark, with a glass in its eye,
     Dressed in gown, bands, and wig,[56] was defending a pig
           On the charge of deserting its sty.

4   The Witnesses proved, without error or flaw,
           That the sty was deserted when found:
     And the Judge kept explaining the state of the law
           In a soft under-current of sound.

5   The indictment had never been clearly expressed,
           And it seemed that the Snark had begun,
     And had spoken three hours, before any one guessed
           What the pig was supposed to have done.

6   The Jury had each formed a different view
           (Long before the indictment was read),
     And they all spoke at once, so that none of them knew
           One word that the others had said.

7   "You must know –" said the Judge: but the Snark exclaimed "Fudge![57]
           That statute is obsolete quite!
     Let me tell you, my friends, the whole question depends
           On an ancient manorial right.

56. Note the contrast between the appearance of the Snark in the Barrister's dream—thin, with pointed head, ridged back, three fingers, and thumb—and the actual Snark in Holiday's suppressed picture. Of course the Barrister is only dreaming; also, we must remember that there are several species of Snark.

Bands refers to the traditional pair of projecting cloth strips which you see attached to the Snark's gown below his wig.

57. "Mr. Burchell," writes Oliver Goldsmith in Chapter 11 of *The Vicar of Wakefield*, ". . . sate with his face turned to the fire, and at the conclusion of every sentence would cry out *fudge*, an expression which displeased us all, and in some measure damped the rising spirits of the conversation."

Fudge (meaning "bosh, nonsense") was at one time a common expression of British sailors. According to Isaac Disraeli (in his *Notes on the Navy*): "There was in our time, one Captain Fudge, a commander of a merchant-man; who, upon

his return from a voyage, always brought home a good cargo of lies; insomuch that now, aboard ship, the sailors, when they hear a great lie, cry out '*Fudge!*' "

Thomas Bettler informs me that in the Gilbert and Sullivan operetta *Trial by Jury* (another famous spoof on English courts), the Judge sings:

           Though all my law is fudge,
           Yet I'll never, never budge,
           But I'll live and die a judge!

"Again, it may be remarked," writes Herbert Spencer in *The Philosophy of Style*, "that when oral language is employed, the strongest effects are produced by interjections, which condense entire sentences into syllables. And in other cases, where custom allows us to express thoughts by single words, as in *Beware, Heighho, Fudge*, much force would be lost by expanding them into specific propositions."

8   "In the matter of Treason the pig would appear
        To have aided, but scarcely abetted:
    While the charge of Insolvency fails, it is clear,
        If you grant the plea 'never indebted.'58

9   "The fact of Desertion I will not dispute:
        But its guilt, as I trust, is removed
    (So far as relates to the costs of this suit)
        By the Alibi which has been proved.

10 "My poor client's fate now depends on your votes."
        Here the speaker sat down in his place,
    And directed the Judge to refer to his notes
        And briefly to sum up the case.

11 But the Judge said he never had summed up before;
        So the Snark undertook it instead,
    And summed it so well that it came to far more
        Than the Witnesses ever had said!

12 When the verdict was called for, the Jury declined,
        As the word was so puzzling to spell;
    But they ventured to hope that the Snark wouldn't mind
        Undertaking that duty as well.

13 So the Snark found the verdict, although, as it owned,
        It was spent with the toils of the day:
    When it said the word "GUILTY!" the Jury all groaned,
        And some of them fainted away.

---

58. *Never indebted*, or *nil debet*, is a legal term meaning "he owes nothing." It is the plea of the defendant, in a common-law action of debt, by which he denies completely the allegations of the plaintiff.

R. M. Redheffer and H. P. Young have called my attention to the amusing circular reasoning in the next stanza. Strictly speaking, an "alibi" is an assertion of one's absence from the scene of a crime. The Snark argues that his client is not guilty of desertion because it was somewhere else at the time.

14   Then the Snark pronounced sentence,[59] the Judge being quite
      Too nervous to utter a word:
When it rose to its feet, there was silence like night,
      And the fall of a pin might be heard.

15   "Transportation[60] for life" was the sentence it gave,
      "And *then* to be fined forty pound."
The Jury all cheered, though the Judge said he feared
      That the phrase was not legally sound.

16   But their wild exultation was suddenly checked
      When the jailer informed them, with tears,
Such a sentence would have not the slightest effect,
      As the pig had been dead for some years.

17   The Judge left the Court, looking deeply disgusted:
      But the Snark, though a little aghast,
As the lawyer to whom the defence was intrusted,
      Went bellowing on to the last.

18   Thus the Barrister dreamed, while the bellowing seemed
      To grow every moment more clear:
Till he woke to the knell of a furious bell,
      Which the Bellman rang close at his ear.

59. Cf. the Mouse's tale in Chapter 3 of *Alice's Adventures in Wonderland*, in which Fury (a dog) tells a mouse that he will take him to court and serve as both judge and jury.

60. "Transportation" was the deportation of convicts to a British colony where they were herded into penal gangs and exploited for hard labor. Before the United States won its independence, transported convicts from England provided much of the labor (later taken over by Negro slaves) on the large plantations. Protests from the colonies, chiefly Australia, led to the abandonment of the system, and England began a belated building of adequate prisons. By the time the *Snark* was written, transportation had ceased in England, though it was continued by France and other colonial powers.

FIT THE SEVENTH

THE BANKER'S FATE

1   THEY sought it with thimbles, they sought it with care;
        They pursued it with forks and hope;
They threatened its life with a railway-share;
        They charmed it with smiles and soap.

2   And the Banker, inspired with a courage so new
        It was matter for general remark,
Rushed madly ahead and was lost to their view
        In his zeal to discover the Snark.

3   But while he was seeking with thimbles and care,
        A Bandersnatch[61] swiftly drew nigh
And grabbed at the Banker, who shrieked in despair,
        For he knew it was useless to fly.

4   He offered large discount – he offered a cheque
        (Drawn "to bearer") for seven-pounds-ten:
But the Bandersnatch merely extended its neck
        And grabbed at the Banker again.

---

61. The second stanza of "Jabberwocky" refers to "the frumious Bandersnatch," and the White King (Chapter 7 of *Through the Looking-Glass*) also speaks of the beast. Eric Partridge thinks the word may combine a suggestion of the animal's snatching proclivities with either *bandog* (a ferocious watch-dog) or *bandar* (Hindustani for rhesus monkey).

5   Without rest or pause – while those frumious[62] jaws
        Went savagely snapping around –
    He skipped and he hopped, and he floundered and flopped,
        Till fainting he fell to the ground.

6   The Bandersnatch fled as the others appeared
        Led on by that fear-stricken yell:
    And the Bellman remarked "It is just as I feared!"
        And solemnly tolled on his bell.

7   He was black in the face, and they scarcely could trace
        The least likeness to what he had been:
    While so great was his fright that his waistcoat turned white –[63]
        A wonderful thing to be seen!

8   To the horror of all who were present that day,
        He uprose in full evening dress,
    And with senseless grimaces endeavoured to say
        What his tongue could no longer express.

62. *Frumious*, another "Jabberwocky" word, is fully explained by Carroll in his preface to the *Snark*.

63. Elizabeth Sewell, in her book *The Field of Nonsense*, points out the similarity of this line with a line in an earlier limerick by Edward Lear:

> There was an old man of Port Gregor,
> Whose actions were noted for vigour;
>   He stood on his head,
>   Till his waistcoat turned red,
> That eclectic old man of Port Gregor.

Note that the Banker's black vest turns white, and his white face turns black. As Harold Beaver observes in his essay "Whale or Boojum" we have here a change from reality to a negative image, so familiar to a photography enthusiast like Carroll. The Banker does not entirely vanish; only his mind vanishes. As Beaver notes, the fate of this crew member, whose name differs from the Baker's only by the addition of one letter, prefigures the total disappearance of the Baker in the next fit.

Leigh Mercer suggests that Carroll missed a Carrollian whimsy by not having the Baker's shadow, instead of his vest, turn white.

9 Down he sank in a chair – ran his hands through his hair –
   And chanted in mimsiest[64] tones
  Words whose utter inanity proved his insanity,
   While he rattled a couple of bones.[65]

10 "Leave him here to his fate – it is getting so late!"
   The Bellman exclaimed in a fright.
  "We have lost half the day. Any further delay,
   And we sha'n't catch a Snark before night!"

64. According to Humpty Dumpty, the word *mimsy* (from the first stanza of "Jabberwocky") is a portmanteau word combining *miserable* and *flimsy*.

65. In Holiday's illustration for this scene we see the Banker, black of face and white of waistcoat, rattling a pair of bones in each hand. In Negro minstrels, popular in Victorian England as well as in the United States and on the Continent, bone castanets were traditionally rattled by Mr. Bones (note the *B*), who occupied one of the end chairs. (Mr. Tambo, who played the tambourine, sat in the other end chair.) Alexander L. Taylor, in his study of Carroll (*The White Knight*, 1952), thinks the Banker's fate "may be a weird caricature of extravagant church ritual," but both Carroll and Holiday obviously have in mind nothing more than Mr. Bones.

At the Banker's feet is a piece of sheet music to be played *con imbecillità*. The Butcher is still wearing the ruff and yellow kid gloves that he put on in Fit 4, stanza 15. The scene has the same gibbering nightmarish quality that pervades the final scenes of the two *Alice* books, just before all the dream characters suddenly vanish away.

Note that the Banker has regrown the shock of hair that can be seen on top of his head in Holiday's second picture, but which the first picture shows that he lost before the crew landed.

FIT THE EIGHTH

THE VANISHING

1   THEY sought it with thimbles, they sought it with care;
        They pursued it with forks and hope;
    They threatened its life with a railway-share;
        They charmed it with smiles and soap.

2   They shuddered to think that the chase might fail,
        And the Beaver, excited at last,
    Went bounding along on the tip of its tail,
        For the daylight was nearly past.

3   "There is Thingumbob shouting!" the Bellman said.
        "He is shouting like mad, only hark!
    He is waving his hands, he is wagging his head,
        He has certainly found a Snark!"

4   They gazed in delight, while the Butcher exclaimed
        "He was always a desperate wag!"[66]
    They beheld him – their Baker – their hero unnamed –
        On the top of a neighbouring crag,

66. The Butcher was thought to be a dunce (Fit 5, stanza 8), but recalling how quickly he recognized the voice of the Jubjub, and how he taught the Beaver more in ten minutes than it could have learned from books in seventy years, it is not surprising to find him making a clever pun. (The Baker's habit of wagging his head when confronted by wild animals has already been mentioned in the first fit, stanza 12.) The pun reveals great presence of mind on the Butcher's part. The Boojum was undoubtedly so distressed at being unable to see the point of the joke that it was too embarrassed to confront any of the other crew members before they were all saved by the coming of night.

5   Erect and sublime, for one moment of time.
          In the next, that wild figure they saw
     (As if stung by a spasm) plunge into a chasm,
       While they waited and listened in awe.[67]

6   "It's a Snark!" was the sound that first came to their ears,
         And seemed almost too good to be true.
    Then followed a torrent of laughter and cheers:
      Then the ominous words "It's a Boo –"[68]

7   Then, silence.[69] Some fancied they heard in the air
         A weary and wandering sigh
    That sounded like " jum!" but the others declare
      It was only a breeze that went by.

8   They hunted till darkness came on, but they found
         Not a button, or feather, or mark,
    By which they could tell that they stood on the ground
      Where the Baker had met with the Snark.

9   In the midst of the word he was trying to say,
         In the midst of his laughter and glee,
    He had softly and suddenly vanished away –
      For the Snark *was* a Boojum, you see.

67. "Many children have some fabled ogre," writes Phyllis Greenacre (*Swift and Carroll*, page 240), "often in animal form, or some 'secret,' with which they scare each other and themselves. This is the antithesis of the imaginary companion whose presence is comforting, strengthening or relieving. Psychoanalysis reveals that it is generally some representation of the primal scene, in which the sexual images of the parents are fused into a frightening or awe-inspiring single figure. This is probably [that word again!] the significance of the *Snark*, in which the last 'fit' is an acting out of the primal scene with the Baker first standing 'erect and sublime' and then plunging into the chasm between the crags."

68. Larry Shaw, in a funny article called "The Baker Murder Case" (*Inside and Science Fiction Advertiser*, a fan magazine, September 1956, pages 4–12), argues that the *Snark* is a cleverly disguised tale of the murder of the Baker. On the basis of numerous obscure clues, Shaw proves that the Boots was the Snark, and that the Baker tried to reveal this fact by crying "It's a Boots!" just before the Boots killed him.

69. Holiday's illustration for this scene, showing the Bellman ringing a knell for the passing of the Baker, is a remarkable puzzle picture. Thousands of readers must have glanced at this drawing without noticing (though they may have shivered with subliminal perception) the huge, almost transparent head of the Baker, abject terror on his features, as a gigantic beak (or is it a claw?) seizes his wrist and drags him into the ultimate darkness.

The rocks in the foreground, which resemble the back of a prostrate nude figure, add another eerie touch to the scene. Is it my imagination, or do I see a huge face on the largest boulder when it is viewed on a steep slant, with one eye, from a spot below the picture and to the left? Note also the startling resemblance of this picture to Correggio's *Jupiter and Io*, a painting which depicts the naked Io embraced by the green paw of a cloudy Jupiter as he copulates with her.

❖ ❖

Translations of the *Snark*

THE APPEAL of the *Snark* has not been confined to readers of Carroll's original text, for it has been translated into a number of languages. A bibliographical description of those editions, together with a complete bibliography of English editions, follows in Selwyn H. Goodacre's "The Listing of the *Snark*." A sampling of some of the foreign texts, however, is included here.

La Chasse au Snark. Chapelle-Réanville-Eure, 1929. Translated into French by Louis Aragon.

Aragon wrote this pedestrian translation (it has neither rhyme nor meter) when he was a young Bohemian in Paris, associated with the surrealist movement, and shortly before he completed his transition from Snarxism to Marxism to become the leading literary figure of the French Communist Party.

The first manifesto of the French surrealists, written by André Breton in 1924, spoke of Carroll as a surrealist. In 1931 Aragon contributed an essay on Carroll to the French magazine *Le Surréalisme au service de la révolution*, in which he tried to show that Carroll's nonsense writings, disguised as children's books, actually were politically subversive protests against Victorian bourgeois morality and hypocrisy. The essay is remarkable also for its many factual errors (e.g., the statement that Carroll wore a pointed beard), but there is no evidence that Aragon intended it as a joke. In fact, Breton wrote an article in 1939 to refute Aragon's Marxist interpretation of Carrollian nonsense. (See Philip Thody's essay, "Lewis Carroll and the Surrealists," in

the *Twentieth Century*, Volume 163, May 1958, pages 427–34.)

The following sample stanza from Aragon's translation (as well as the stanzas quoted below from other translations) is the "sought it with thimbles" stanza that begins each of the last four fits.

> Ils le traquèrent avec des gobelets ils le
>   traquèrent avec soin
> Ils le poursuivirent avec des fourches et de
>   l'espoir
> Ils menacèrent sa vie avec une action de chemin
>   de fer
> Ils le charmèrent avec des sourires et du savon

The Hunting of the Snark. London, 1934. Translated into Latin by Percival Robert Brinton, Rector of Hambleden, Bucks, England.

"I have . . . found a certain affinity in character as well as in experience [Brinton writes in his introduction] between the hero of the Aeneid and the hero of 'The Snark.' Both the Bellman and the pious Aeneas were leaders of an adventurous expedition by sea and land: both pursued their quest with simplicity and single-mindedness. Each had devoted followers; each found himself thwarted by a hostile and mysterious power; each has survived to interest later generations in his story."

Mr. Brinton's translation is in Virgilian hexameters:

> Spe simul ac furcis, cura et digitalibus usi
> Quaerebant praedam socii via ferrea monstro
> Letum intentabat: risus sapoque trahebant.

The Hunting of the Snark. Oxford, 1936. Translated into Latin elegiacs by Hubert Digby Watson. Foreword by Gilbert Murray.

The book includes a note by Watson in which he interprets the poem as a search for world peace. "May not 'thimbles' be an allusion to the 'Women's peace crusade' and 'smiles and soap' to the lip-service of those whose practice seldom comes up to their preaching?" He sees the Baker as a "mild-mannered Pacifist who is on very friendly terms with the (Russian) Bear, but suffers a great shock when the Peace which he thinks he has discovered turns out to be an army entitled 'The International Police Force of the New Commonwealth.' "

The Butcher, in Watson's view, is the "truculent warmonger," the Beaver the isolationist who "displays no interest in the concern" but eventually becomes the warmonger's bosom friend. The voice of the Jubjub is the screechings of the yellow press. And so on. He concludes on a hopeful note: the new Bellman of England, Stanley Baldwin, has a name that begins with *B*.

> Cum cura et digiti quaerunt muliebribus armis,
> Cum furcis etiam spe comitante petunt;
> Instrumenta viae ferratae scripta minantur,
> Sapone et fabricant risibus illecebras.

La Chasse au Snark. Paris, 1940. A translation into French rhymed verse by Henri Parisot.

This translation, which Parisot has continually revised, has appeared in several later editions. The following stanza is from the ballad's inclusion in Parisot's translation of *Through the Looking-Glass*, published in Paris by Flammarion, 1969.

> Ils le traquaient, armés d'espoir, de dés à coudre,
> De fourchettes, de soin; ils tentaient de l'occire
> Avec une action de chemin de fer; ou de
> Le charmer avec du savon et des sourires.

La Caccia allo Snarco. Rome, 1945. Translated into Italian by Cesare Vico Lodovici.

> Lo cercarono con diligenza, lo cercarono con ditali,
> lo inseguirono con speranza e con forchette;
> gli insidiarono la vita con un'Azione delle "Meridionali":
> lo incantarono con sorrisi e saponette.

Snarkjakten. Stockholm, 1959. A Swedish translation by Lars Forssell.

> De sökte med fingerborg, listigt fördrev
> med såpa och smaskratt dess hopp.
> Av aktieposter de bildade drev,
> med gaffelskaft drev de den opp.

Snarkejagten. Copenhagen, 1963. Translated into Danish by Christopher Maaløe.

> Så søgte de snarken med gaffel og kiv
> for at slå den med stumhed og stylter
> og true dens liv med et regulativ.
> De lokked med smil og med sylter.

Die Jagd nach dem Schnark. Frankfurt, 1968. Translated into German by Klaus Reichert.

> Du suchst es mit Sorgfalt—und suchst es mit Salz;
> Du jagst es mit Hoffnung und Gabeln;
> Du bedrohst seinen Kopf mit der Auerhahnbalz;
> Du bestrickst es mit Seife und Fabeln.

NOTE: A German work with the startling title *Die Fahrt der Snark* (Berlin, 1930) turns out to be a translation of Jack London's book *The Cruise of the Snark*, 1908. This is an account of a voyage that London and his wife made around the world in a small boat which London built himself and named the *Snark* "because we could not think of any other name."

De Jacht op de Trek. The Hague, 1977. Translated into Dutch by Erdwin Spits.

> Zij spoorden met vingerhoed, spoorden met gratie;
> Joegen hem voort met vorken en hoop;
> Zij bedreigden hem met een NS-obligatie;
> Bekoorden met glimlach en zeep.

De Jacht op de Strok. Amsterdam, 1977. Translated into Dutch by Evert Geradts.

> Zij zochten 't met zorg en een vingerhoed;
> Ze jaagden 't met vorken en hoop;
> Ze brachten 't in 't nauw met Onroerend Goed;
> Een glimlach met zeep deed 'n hoop.

Contemporary Reviews of the *Snark*

Andrew Lang. *The Academy*, Volume 9, 8 April 1876, pages 326–27.

A generally unfavorable review of both text and pictures. After quoting the stanza about the Snark's slowness in taking a jest and its habit of looking grave at puns, Lang adds: "To tell the truth, a painful truth it is, this quality of the snark has communicated itself to the reviewer."

Unsigned. *The Athenaeum.* Volume 67, 8 April 1876, page 495.

"It may be that the author of *Alice's Adventures in Wonderland* is still suffering from the attack of Claimant on the brain, which some time ago numbed or distracted so many intellects. Or it may be that he has merely been inspired by a wild desire to reduce to idiocy as many readers, and more especially, reviewers as possible. At all events, he has published what we may consider the most bewildering of modern poems. . . ."

The two reviews listed above, and four others from 1876 journals, are reprinted in full in Morton N. Cohen's article, "Hark the Snark," in *Lewis Carroll Observed*, edited by Edward Guiliano, Clarkson N. Potter, 1976.

The additional four reviews are from *The Spectator*, 22 April ("tiresome nonsense"); *The Saturday Review*, 15 April ("peculiar humor"); *The Graphic*, 15 April ("glorious piece of nonsense"); and *Vanity Fair*, 29 April ("rubbish").

About the *Snark*

"The Hunting of the Snark." By "Frumious." *The Wykehamist*, May 1876, pages 2–3. An anonymous commentary in rhymed couplets, reprinted by Morton N. Cohen in "Hark the Snark," in *Lewis Carroll Observed*, edited by Edward Guiliano, Clarkson N. Potter, 1976.

"The Snark's Significance." *The Academy*, 29 January 1898, pages 128–30. Short articles by Henry Holiday, M.H.T., and St. J.E.C.II.

"A Commentary on the *Snark*." Snarkophilus Snobbs (F. C. S. Schiller). *Mind!* (a parody issue of *Mind*, published by the editors as a special Christmas number, 1901), pages 87–101.

"The Hunting of the Snark." Devereux Court. *The Cornhill Magazine*, Volume 30, March 1911, pages 360–65.

"Finding of the Snark." Arthur Ruhl. *Saturday Review of Literature*, Volume 9, 18 March 1933, pages 490–91.

"1874–76—The Hunting of the Snark." Chapter 10, *The Diaries of Lewis Carroll*. Edited by Roger Lancelyn Green. Oxford University Press, 1954.

"The Baker Murder Case." Larry T. Shaw. *Inside and Science Fiction Advertiser*, September 1956, pages 4–12.

"The Hunting of the Snark." Richard Howard in *Master Poems of the English Language*. Edited by Oscar Williams. Trident, 1966, pages 773–76.

"Ironic Voyages." Chapter 4, *Nil: Episodes in the Literary Conquest of Void during the Nineteenth Century*. Robert Martin Adams, Oxford University Press, 1966.

"Snark Hunting: Lewis Carroll on Collectivism." E. Merrill Root, *American Opinion*, April 1966, pages 73–82.

"What Is a Boojum? Nonsense and Modernism." Michael Holquist, *Yale French Studies*, Volume 43, 1969, pages 145–64. Reprinted in *Alice in Wonderland*, edited by Donald J. Gray, Norton, 1971.

"On the Hunting of the Snark as a Romantic Ballad." J. R. Christopher. *Orcrist, a Journal of Fantasy in the Arts* (Bulletin of the University of Wisconsin J. R. R. Tolkien Society), Summer 1973, pages 30–32.

"Hark the Snark." Morton N. Cohen in *Lewis Carroll Observed*, edited by Edward Guiliano, Clarkson N. Potter, 1976.

"Whale or Boojum: An Agony." Harold Beaver in *Lewis Carroll Observed*, edited by Edward Guiliano, Clarkson N. Potter, 1976.

Jabberwocky, Volume 5, Autumn 1976, an issue devoted to the *Snark*, with articles by Denis Crutch,

Selwyn Goodacre, Brian Sibley, and Ellis Hillman, and reviews by Sibley and J. N. S. Davis of newly illustrated editions of the *Snark*.

"The Snark Was a Boojum." Haydée Faimberg. *International Review of Psycho-Analysis*, Volume 4, 1977, pages 243–49.

About Lewis Carroll

The Life and Letters of Lewis Carroll. Stuart Dodgson Collingwood, Unwin, 1898.

The Story of Lewis Carroll. Isa Bowman, J. M. Dent, 1899.

Lewis Carroll. Walter de la Mare, Cambridge, 1930.

The Life of Lewis Carroll. Langford Reed, W. & G. Foyle, 1932.

Carroll's "Alice." Harry Morgan Ayres, Columbia, 1936.

Victoria through the Looking-Glass. Florence Becker Lennon, Simon & Schuster, 1945. Collier paperback, 1962.

The Story of Lewis Carroll. Roger Lancelyn Green, Methuen, 1949.

Lewis Carroll: Photographer. Helmut Gernsheim, Chanticleer Press, 1949.

The White Knight. Alexander L. Taylor, Oliver and Boyd, 1952.

Lewis Carroll. Derek Hudson, Constable, 1954.

Swift and Carroll. Phyllis Greenacre, International Universities Press, 1955.

Lewis Carroll. Number 96 of a series of booklets entitled *Writers and Their Work.* Derek Hudson, Longmans, Green, 1958.

Lewis Carroll. Roger Lancelyn Green, Bodley Head, 1960.

The Snark Was a Boojum. James Plysted Wood. Illustrated by David Levine. Pantheon, 1966.

Language and Lewis Carroll. Robert D. Sutherland, Mouton, The Hague, 1970.

The Letters of Lewis Carroll. Edited by Morton N. Cohen with the assistance of Roger Lancelyn Green, Oxford University Press, 1979.

About Henry Holiday

"Henry Holiday and His Art." Angus M. MacKay. *Westminster Review*, Volume 158, London, 1902, pages 391–400.

"The Decorative Work of Mr. Henry Holiday." Unsigned. *International Studio*, Volume 37, New York, 1909, pages 106–15.

Reminiscences of My Life. Henry Holiday. William Heinemann, 1914.

"Henry Holiday." A. L. Baldry. *Walker's Quarterly*, Numbers 31–32, London, 1930, pages 1–80.

RECITATIONS AND MUSICAL VERSIONS

Jean Shepherd liked to recite the *Snark* every few years on his New York City radio show. The last time I heard him do this was in 1964. He said his mother used to read the poem to him when he was a child, and that whenever he asked her what a Snark was her reply would be: "It's all in the story." Shep's comment, after he read the final stanza, was: "And that, friends, ain't Uncle Wiggily."

Boris Karloff recorded the *Snark* on a long-playing record released by Caedmon Company in 1959.

On Christmas Eve 1963 the ballad was read by

Alec Guinness on the BBC Third Programme, and has since been rebroadcast many times.

The entire ballad, except for the Barrister's Dream, was set to music by Max Saunders and broadcast several times on the BBC Third Programme in the early fifties. The "sought it with thimbles" stanza was sung as a chorus by a choir of ten men, and the rest of the poem was sung or recited by Michael Flanders to an orchestral accompaniment. Douglas Cleverdon was the producer.

In September 1971 the Whitney Museum, New York City, gave twelve performances of the *Snark*, set to music by Edwin Roberts. The producer was Berta Walker, and the director, Bill Tchakirides. The opera was recorded and broadcast by radio station WBAI on several later occasions.

Laurence Goeghegan's play, based on the *Snark*, was first produced in Bingley, Yorkshire, in 1949. A musical version, with music by Kenneth Paine, was presented in the Tower Theatre, London, in the winter of 1971–72, by the Tavistock Repertory Company.

SNARK CLUBS

Snark clubs have flourished at both Oxford and Cambridge, and the Cambridge group still meets in London. The Oxford club, I am told by Michael H. Harmer, the Bellman (secretary) of the Cambridge group, was founded in 1879 at New College. Known as The Snarks, it met regularly during the eighties and nineties but apparently had its last official meeting in 1914 on the eve of the First World War. In 1952 someone found the club's address book and there was a dinner in London attended by about thirty-five guests, but that was the last gathering of the crew. John Galsworthy and A. P. Herbert were among the distinguished members. The *Observer*, in its color supplement, 8 January 1967, page 6, printed an 1888 photograph of five members of The Snarks, showing young Galsworthy in the center, sporting a monocle.

The Cambridge group was founded in 1934 by a group of medical students and has been meeting once a year ever since for dinner and a reading of the Agony. It has, at any one time, exactly ten members, each corresponding to a member of Carroll's Snark-hunting crew. The club's eleven rules are so delightfully Snarkish that, with the Bellman's permission, I reproduce them below:

1. That the Club be called the *Snark Club*.
2. That the object of the Club be the glorification of the Snark and its creator.
3. That an Annual Dinner shall be held.
4. That at each Annual Dinner the *Agony* be read complete.
5. That the fine for nonattendance at the Dinner be a *cheque drawn to bearer for seven pounds ten*, which shall be *crossed*.
6. That any member of the Crew who shall be separated from the scene of the Dinner by not less than *one thousand diminished by eight* nautical miles, be exempt from the fine mentioned in Rule 5.
7. That members be posted in the Agony Column of *The Times* newspaper after nonattendance at the Dinner exceeding two consecutive years.
8.
9. That members be replaced as they *softly and suddenly vanish away*.
10. That the Bellman be responsible for the upkeep of the bell, and that it be his peculiar privilege to tingle same.
11. That *Strange Creepy Creatures* may be admitted as additional members of the Crew from time to time, provided the total number available for Snark service at any one time shall not exceed ten.

THE FOLLOWING commentary, by the pragmatist philosopher F. C. S. Schiller, originally appeared in *Mind!*, a parody issue of *Mind*, a British philosophical journal. The parody was published in 1901 as a special Christmas number and is believed to have been written almost entirely by Schiller. The year 1901 was a time when the great bugaboo of pragmatism was the Hegelian concept of the Absolute, a concept no longer fashionable in philosophic circles, though it continues to be smuggled into Protestant theology by German theologians with Hegelian pasts.

The frontispiece of *Mind!* is a "Portrait of Its Immanence the Absolute," printed on pink paper, to symbolize the pink of perfection, and protected by a tipped-in sheet of transparent tissue. The editors note the portrait's striking resemblance to the Bellman's map in *The Hunting of the Snark*. Beneath the absolutely blank pink portrait are instructions for use: "Turn the eye of faith, fondly but firmly, on the centre of the page, wink the other, and gaze fixedly until you see It."

It was this comic issue of *Mind* that provided Bertrand Russell with what he once insisted was the only instance he had ever encountered in which someone actually thought in a formal syllogism. A German philosopher had been much puzzled by the magazine's burlesque advertisements. Finally he reasoned: Everything in this magazine is a joke, the advertisements are in this magazine, therefore the advertisements must be jokes. Footnotes to the commentary are Schiller's except for those that I have added and initialed.—M. G.

A Commentary on the *Snark*
by Snarkophilus Snobbs
[F. C. S. Schiller]

It is a recognized maxim of literary ethics that none but the dead can deserve a commentary, seeing that they can no longer either explain themselves or perturb the explanations of those who devote themselves to the congenial, and frequently not unprofitable, task of making plain what was previously obscure, and profound what was previously plain. Hence it is easily understood that the demise of the late lamented Lewis Carroll has opened a superb field to the labors of the critical commentator, and that the classical beauties of the two *Alice*s are not likely long to remain unprovided with those aids to comprehension which the cultivated reader so greatly needs.

The purpose of the present article, however, is a more ambitious one. Most of Lewis Carroll's non-mathematical writings are such that even the dullest of grown-ups can detect, more or less vaguely, their import; but *The Hunting of the Snark* may be said to have hitherto baffled the adult understanding. It is to lovers of Lewis Carroll what *Sordello* is to lovers of Robert Browning, or *The Shaving of Shagpat* to Meredithians. In other words, it has frequently been considered magnificent but not sense. The author himself anticipated the possibility of such criticism and defends himself against it in his preface, by appealing to the "strong moral purpose" of his poem, to the arithmetical principles it inculcates, to "its noble teachings in Natural History." But prefatory explanations are rightly disregarded by the public, and it must be admitted that in Lewis Carroll's case they do but little to elucidate the *Mystery of the Snark*, which, it has been calculated,[1] has been responsible for $49\frac{1}{2}$ per cent of the cases of insanity and nervous breakdown which have occurred during the last ten years.

It is clear then that a commentary on *The Hunting of the Snark* is the greatest desideratum of English literature at present; and this the author of the present essay flatters himself that he has provided. Not that he would wish the commentary itself to be regarded as exhaustive or as anything more than a *vindemiatio prima* of so fruitful a subject: but he would distinctly advance the claim to have discovered the key to the real meaning and philosophical significance of this most remarkable product of human imagination.

What then is the meaning of the *Snark*? Or that we may not appear to beg the question let us first ask—how do we know that the *Snark* has a meaning? The answer is simple; Lewis Carroll assures us that it not

1. See the Colney Hatch[2] *Contributions to Sociology* for 1899, p. 983.
2. The Colney Hatch Pauper Lunatic Asylum, in Middlesex, was the largest of the mental institutions then serving the London area.—M.G.

only has a meaning but even a moral purpose. Hence we may proceed with his assurance and our own.

I will not weary you with an autobiographical narrative of the way in which I discovered the solution of the Snark's mystery; suffice it to say that insight came to me suddenly, as unto Buddha under the Bô-tree, as I was sitting under an Arrowroot in a western prairie. The theory of the Snark which I then excogitated has stood the test of time, and of a voyage across the Atlantic, in the course of which I was more than tempted to throw overboard all my most cherished convictions, and I have little doubt that when you have heard my evidence you will share my belief.

I shall begin by stating the general argument of the Snark and proceed to support it by detailed comment. In the briefest possible manner, then, I assert that the Snark is the Absolute, dear to pholisophers,[3] and that the hunting of the Snark is the pursuit of the Absolute. Even as thus barely stated the theory all but carries instantaneous conviction; it is infinitely more probable than that the Snark should be an electioneering device or a treatise on "society" or a poetical narrative of the discovery of America, to instance a few of the fatuous suggestions with which I have been deluged since I began to inquire into the subject. But further considerations will easily raise the antecedent probability that the Snark is the Absolute to certainty. The Absolute, as I venture to remark for the benefit of any unpholisophical enough still to enjoy that ignorance thereof which is bliss, is a fiction which is supposed to do for pholisophers everything they can't do for themselves. It performs the same functions in philosophy as infinity in mathematics; when in doubt you send for the Absolute; if something is impossible for us, it is *therefore* possible for the Absolute; what is nonsense to us is *therefore* sense to the Absolute and *vice versa*; what we do not know, the Absolute knows; in short it is the apotheosis of topsyturvydom. Now, Lewis Carroll as a man of sense did not believe in the Absolute, but he recognized that it could best be dealt with in parables.

The Hunting of the Snark, therefore, is intended to describe Humanity in search of the Absolute, and to exhibit the vanity of the pursuit. For no one attains to the Absolute but the Baker, the miserable madman who has left his intelligence behind before embarking. And when he does find the Snark, it turns out to be a Boojum, and he "softly and silently vanished away." That is, the Absolute can be attained only by the loss of personality, which is merged in the Boojum. The Boojum is the Absolute, as the One which absorbs the Many, and danger of this is the "moral purpose" whereof Lewis Carroll speaks so solemnly in his preface. Evidently we are expected to learn the lesson that the Snark will *always* turn out a Boojum, and the dramatic variety of the incidents only serves to lead up to this most thrilling and irreparable catastrophe.

But I proceed to establish this interpretation in detail. (1) We note that the poem has 8 fits. These clearly represent the Time-process in which the Absolute is supposed to be revealed, and at the same time hint that Life as a whole is a *Survival of the Fit*. But why 8 and not 7 or 9? Evidently because by revolving 8 through an angle of 90° it becomes the symbol for Infinity, which is often regarded as an equivalent of the Absolute. (2) The vessel clearly is Humanity and in the crew are represented various human activities by which it is supposed we may aspire to the Absolute. We may dwell a little on the significance of the various members of the crew. They are *ten* in number and severally described as a Bellman, a Butcher, a Banker, a Beaver, a Broker, a Barrister, a Bonnet-maker, a Billiard-marker, a Boots and a Baker. It is obvious that all these names begin with a *B*, and somewhat remarkable that even the Snark turns out a Boojum. This surely indicates that we are here dealing with the most ultimate of all questions, *viz.*, "to be or not to be," and that it is answered in the universal affirmative—*B* at any cost!

Next let us inquire what these personages represent. In the leading figure, that of the *Bellman* we easily recognize *Christianity*, the bell being the characteristically Christian implement, and the hegemony of humanity being equally obvious. Emboldened by this success, it is easy to make out that the *Butcher* is *Mohammedanism*, and the *Banker Judaism*, while the *Beaver* represents the aspirations of the animals towards τὸ Θεῖον.[4] The anonymous *Baker* is, of course, the hero of the story, and the "forty-two boxes all carefully packed with his name painted clearly on each" which he "left behind on the beach" typify the contents of his mind, which he lost before starting on his quest.

The *Barrister* is clearly the type of the *logician* and brought "to arrange their disputes." He too has dreams about the Absolute and wearies himself by proving in vain that the "Beaver's lacemaking was wrong"; as anyone who has studied modern logic can testify, It does dream about the Absolute and is always "proving in vain."

The *Broker* brought "to value their goods" (ἀγαθά)

3. A term for Hegelian philosophers, used throughout the comic issue of *Mind*.—M.G.

4. Cp. Aristotle, *Eth. Nich.*, vii, 13, 6.

is evidently *moral philosophy*. The "*Billiard-marker* whose skill was immense" is certainly *Art*, which would grow too engrossing (= "might perhaps have won more than his share") but for the pecuniary considerations represented by the Banker (Judaism) who "had the whole of their cash in his care."

In the *Boots* we can hardly hesitate to recognize *Literature*, which serves to put literary polish upon the outer integuments of the other intellectual pursuits.

The *Bonnet-maker* finally is manifestly the *Fashion*, without which it would have been madness to embark upon so vast an undertaking.

Having thus satisfactorily accounted for the *dramatis personae* I proceed to comment on the action.

F. 1, st. 1.

> "Just the place for a Snark!" the Bellman cried,
> As he landed his crew with care;
> Supporting each man on the top of the tide
> By a finger entwined in his hair.

The meaning evidently is that Christianity "touches the highest part of man and supports us from above."

F. 1, st. 12.

> He would joke with hyænas

It is well known that few animals have a keener sense of humor than hyenas and that no animal can raise a heartier laugh than the right sort of hyena.

> And he once went a walk, paw-in-paw with a
> bear

The learned Prof. Grubwitz has discovered a characteristically Teutonic difficulty here. In his monumental commentary on the *Shaving of Shagpat*, he points out that *as human* the Baker had no paws and could not possibly therefore have offered a paw to a bear. Hence he infers that the text is corrupt. The "w" of the second "paw" is evidently, he thinks, due to the dittograph initial letter of the succeeding "with." The original "papa" having thus been corrupted into a "papaw" (a tropical tree not addicted to locomotion), an ingenious scribe inserted "w-in" giving a specious but mistaken meaning. The original reading was "papa with a bear," and indicates that a forebear or ancestor was intended. So far Grubwitz, who if he had been more familiar with English slang would doubtless have dealt with the text in a more forbearing and less overbearing manner. Anyhow the difficulty is gratuitous, for it must be admitted that the whole stanza is calculated to give anyone paws.

> "Just to keep up its spirits," he said.

It was probably depressed because it could only make a bare living.

In the second Fit the first point of importance would seem to be the Bellman's map. This is manifestly intended for a description of the *Summum Bonum* or Absolute Good, which represents one of the favorite methods of attaining the Absolute. Moreover, as Aristotle shows, a knowledge of the *Summum Bonum* is of great value to humanity in crossing the ocean of life, although its τέλος is οὐ γνῶσις ἀλλὰ πρᾶξις.

F. 2, st. 3.

> "What's the good of Mercator's North Poles and
> Equators,
> Tropics, Zones and Meridian Lines?"

These terms evidently ridicule the attempt made in various ways to fill in the conception of the *Summum Bonum*, but I confess I cannot identify the chief philosophic notions in their geographical disguises.

F. 2, st. 6.

> When he cried, "Steer to starboard, but keep her
> head larboard!"
> What on earth was the helmsman to do?

The question in the first place is quite irrelevant, as the helmsman was not on earth but at sea and likely to remain there. Still, bearing in mind the effect of this remarkable nautical maneuver, we may perhaps make bold to answer: "He should have turned tail!" For the effect upon the ship would be to make it toss and, as the Bellman obviously preferred the head, the helmsman should have cried "Tails!"

F. 2, st. 9.

> Yet at first sight the crew were not pleased with
> the view,
> Which consisted of chasms and crags.

When Humanity first really catches a glimpse of the local habitation of the Absolute in the writings of the pholisophers, it is disappointed and appalled by its "chasms and crags," *i.e.*, the difficulties and obscurities of these authors' account.

F. 2, st. 10.

> The Bellman perceived that their spirits were low,
> And repeated in musical tone
> Some jokes he had kept for a season of woe—
> But the crew would do nothing but groan.

Tutors have been known to adopt similar methods with a similar effect.

F. 2, st. 15.   We now come to what is perhaps the

most crucial point in our commentary, namely, "the five unmistakable marks, by which you may know, wheresoever you go, the warranted Genuine Snarks. Let us take them in order. The first is its taste, which is meagre and hollow, but crisp: like a coat that is rather too tight in the waist, with a flavour of Will-o'-the-wisp."

1. The taste of the Snark is the taste for the Absolute, which is not emotionally satisfactory, "meagre and hollow, but crisp" and hence attractive to the Baker, while the elusiveness of the Absolute sufficiently explains the "flavour of Will-o'-the-wisp." Its affinity for "a coat that is rather too tight in the waist" applies only to its "meagre and hollow" character; for unless the coat were hollow you could not get into it, while it would, of course, be meagre or scanty if it were "too tight in the waist."

2. "Its habit of getting up late you'll agree
   That it carries too far, when I say
   That it frequently breakfasts at five-o'clock tea
   And dines on the following day."

In this the poet shows, in four lines, what many pholisophers have vainly essayed to prove in as many volumes, namely that the Absolute is not, and cannot be, in Time.

3. "The third is its slowness in taking a jest.
   Should you happen to venture on one,
   It will sigh like a thing that is deeply distressed:
   And it always looks grave at a pun."

This third characteristic of the Absolute is also found in many of its admirers, I am sorry to say. It is best passed over in silence, as our author says elsewhere, without "a shriek or a scream, scarcely even a howl or a groan."

4. "The fourth is its fondness for bathing-machines,
   Which it constantly carries about,
   And believes that they add to the beauty of scenes—
   A sentiment open to doubt."

The "philosophic desperado" in pursuit of Nirvana achieves his fell design by a purificatory plunge into the ocean of Absolute Being. This, however, is not an aesthetic spectacle which "adds to the beauty of scenes," and hence the Snark obligingly carries bathing-machines about in order that in Mr. Gladstone's phrase "essential decency may be preserved."

5. "The fifth is ambition." The Snark's ambition is to become a Boojum, of course. It always succeeds with those who are prepared to meet it halfway. You will doubtless have noticed that the five unmistakable criteria of Snarkhood we have just considered are all of a spiritual character and throw no light upon its material appearance. The reason no doubt is that our author was aware of the protean character of the Absolute's outward appearance, and with true scientific caution did not pretend to give an exhaustive description of the various species of Snark. What, however, he does know he is not loath to tell, and so he bids us distinguish "those that have feathers and bite from those that have whiskers and scratch." In this it is needless to seek for a causal connection between the possession of feathers and mordant habits. The fact is simply mentioned to distinguish these Snarks from birds which have feathers but—since the extinction of the *Archaeopteryx* and *Hesperornis*—have long ceased to wear genuine teeth and to bite, and angels which have feathers but don't bite, not because they are physically, but because they are morally, incapable of so doing. Similarly it would be fanciful to connect the scratching, which is attributed to the second kind of Snark, with the possession of whiskers even in an inchoate condition. But *vide infra* for the doubt about the reading.

Let us consider therefore first the information about the outward characteristics of these Snarks. Some have feathers, some have whiskers. There is no difficulty about the former. We simply compare the well-known poem of Emerson on Brahma, in which the latter points out to those who object to being parts of the Absolute, that "when me they fly I am the wings." If wings, then probably feathers; for the featherless wings of insects are utterly unworthy of any kind of Snark

The mention of Snarks with whiskers on the other hand constitutes a difficulty. For we cannot attribute anything so anthropomorphic to the Absolute. There is, however, evidence of a various reading. The Bodleian MS B_2^n 48971, which is supposed to be in the author's own handwriting, reads *whiskey* instead of *whiskers*. The change is a slight one, but significant. For we may then compare Spinoza's well-known views about the Absolute, which caused him to be euphemistically described as "a God-intoxicated man." It should also be remembered that various narcotics such as bhang, opium, hashish, arrack, etc., have been used to produce the mystic union of the devotee or debauchee with the Absolute, and many hold that whiskey is as good as any of them.

It remains to account for the habit of the Snark in biting and scratching. The learned Grubwitz, to whom allusion has already been made, thinks that these terms are intended to indicate respectively the male and female forms of the Snark (who, in his opinion, represents the university student who is capable of becoming a Boojum—a professor causing all who meet him "softly and silently to vanish away"). The demonstrable absurdity of his general theory of the Snark encourages me to reject also Grubwitz' interpretation in detail, in spite of my respect for his learning. I should prefer, therefore, to explain the biting and scratching more simply as due to the bad temper naturally engendered in so inordinately hunted an animal.

The Third Fit opens, as the reader will doubtless remember, with the attempts made to restore the fainting Baker.

> They roused him with muffins—they roused him
>   with ice—
> They roused him with mustard and cress—
> They roused him with jam and judicious advice—
> They set him conundrums to guess

Such as, probably, *Riddles of the Sphinx*.[5] The other means seem to have been injudicious.

Skipping, with the Bellman, the Baker's father and mother, we come to his "dear uncle," who, *lying* on his deathbed, was able to give the important information which has proved so epoch-making in the history of Snarkology.

And first let us ask who was the "dear uncle"? In answering this question we not only gratify our scientific curiosity but also discover the name of the Baker, our "hero unnamed," as he is subsequently (F. 8, st. 4) called. Now, it must be admitted that we are not told the uncle's name either, but I think that from the account given there can be little doubt but that it ought to have been Hegel. Now a distinguished Oxford pholisopher has proved that what may be and ought to be, that ∴ [therefore] is; and so the inference is practically certain.

F. 3, st. 7.

> "He remarked to me then," said that mildest of
>   men,
> " 'If your Snark be a Snark, that is right:
> Fetch it home by all means—you may serve it
>   with greens' "—T. H. Green's[6] to wit—
> " 'And it's handy for striking a light.' "

It is well known that Hegel thought that the *wrong* kind of Absolute (that of the other professors) was "like the night in which all cows are black." It follows

5. The title of F. C. S. Schiller's best-known book.—M.G.
6. Thomas Hill Green was a distinguished Neo-Hegelian philosopher at Balliol College, Oxford.—M.G.

that the right kind—his own—would conversely serve as an illuminant.

F. 3, st. 8.

> " 'You may seek it with thimbles—and seek it
>   with care;
> You may hunt it with forks and hope;
> You may threaten its life with a railway-share;
> You may charm it with smiles and soap—' "

"You may seek it with thimbles"—this passage is repeated in F. 4, st. 8, by the Bellman, whose subsequent remark in st. 10, "To rig yourselves out for the fight," explains its meaning. Evidently Lewis Carroll here meant subtly to suggest that the pursuit of the Absolute was a form of intellectual *thimble-rigging*.

"You may hunt it with forks and hope." Just as only the brave can deserve the fair, so only the *forktunate* can *hope* to attain the Absolute. There is no justification for depicting Care and Hope as allegorical females joining in the hunt, as the illustrator has done. Altogether the serious student cannot be too emphatically warned against this plausible impostor's pictures; they have neither historic authority nor philosophic profundity. He attributes, *e.g.*, a Semitic physiognomy to the Broker instead of to the Banker; he persistently represents the Baker as clean-shaven and bald, in spite of the statement (in F. 4, st. 11) that "The Baker with care combed his whiskers and hair," and his picture of the Snark exhibits neither feathers nor whiskers! "You may threaten its life with a railway-share." This alludes to the deleterious effect of modern enlightenment and modern improvements on the vitality of the Absolute. "You may charm it with smiles and soap." *I.e.*, adulation and ascetic practices, soap being the substance most abhorrent to Fakirs and Indian sages generally, and therefore suggesting the highest degree of asceticism.

But after all, the momentous revelation of the Baker's uncle is neither his account of the methods of hunting the Snark—they are commonplace enough and he evidently did not choose to divulge his own patent of the Dialectical Method—nor yet his account of the use to which the Absolute may be put—it is trivial enough in all conscience—but rather the possibility—nay, as in the light of subsequent events we must call it, the certainty—that the Snark is a Boojum. No wonder that even the dauntless Baker could not endure the thought that if he met with a Boojum he would "softly and suddenly vanish away," and that the Bellman "looked uffish, and wrinkled his brow." He was of course bound to conceal his emotions and to take an uffishial view of the dilemma. So his reproaches are temperate—

"But surely, my man, when the voyage began,
    You might have suggested it then?"

"It's excessively awkward to mention it now—"

F. 4, st. 5.
    "I said it in Hebrew—I said it in Dutch—
    I said it in German and Greek:
    But I wholly forgot (and it vexes me much)
    That English is what you speak!"

The accounts of the Absolute in German and Greek are famous, while the Hebrew and Dutch probably both refer to Spinoza, who was a Dutch Jew, though he wrote in bad Latin. The forgetting to speak (and write) English is a common symptom in the pursuit of the Absolute.

F. 4, st. 14.
    While the Billiard-marker with quivering hand
    Was chalking the tip of his nose.

Art, when brought face to face with the imminence of the Absolute, recoils upon itself.

The argument of the Fifth Fit is broadly this, that the Butcher and the Beaver both hit upon the same method of approaching the Absolute, by way of the higher mathematics, and so become reconciled. Into the reason of this coincidence, and the rationality of this method it boots not to inquire, the more so as it proved abortive, and neither of them was destined to discover the Snark. That they were brought together, however, by their common fear of the *Jubjub Bird* is interesting, and could doubtless be explained if we could determine the meaning of that volatile creature.

Let us ask, then, what is the Jubjub? In reply I shall dismiss, with the brevity which is the soul both of wit and contempt, the preposterous suggestion that the Jubjub is the pelican. But I am free to confess that I have spent many a sleepless night over the Jubjub. Philologically, indeed it was not difficult to discover that Jubjub is a "portmanteau bird," compounded of *jabber* and *jujube*, but even this did not seem at first to give much of a clue to the problem. Finally, however, it struck me that the author had, with the true prescience and generosity of genius, himself stated the solution of the riddle in the line immediately preceding his description of the Jubjub. It is—

Would have caused quite a thrill in Society

It flashed across me that the Jubjub was Society itself, and if I may quote the account of the Jubjub's habits it will be seen how perfectly this solution covers the facts.

"As to temper the Jubjub's a desperate bird,
    Since it lives in perpetual passion:"

This describes the desperate struggle and rush which prevails in Society.

"Its taste in costume is entirely absurd—
    It is ages ahead of the fashion:"

How profoundly true this is! To be in Society this is what we must aim at; we can never be in fashion unless we are ahead of the fashion.

"But it knows any friend it has met *once* before:"

It is most important in Society to remember the people you have met even once, alike whether you intend to recognize them or to cut them; otherwise vexatious mistakes will occur. There is subtle sarcasm also in the use of the term "friend" to describe such chance acquaintances.

"It never will look at a bribe:"

Such is its anxiety to pocket it.

"And in charity-meetings it stands at the door,
    And collects—though it does not subscribe."

No one who has ever had anything to do with charity bazaars can fail to recognize this!

"Its flavour when cooked is more exquisite far
    Than mutton, or oysters, or eggs:"

The taste for Society is of all the most engrossing.

("Some think it keeps best in an ivory jar,
    And some, in mahogany kegs:")

Some think Society appears to best advantage in an ivory jar, *i.e.*, a "crush" of *décolletées* women, others at a dinner party over the mahogany board.

"You boil it in sawdust: you salt it in glue:"

Dust is American slang for money, so *sawdust* is put *metri gratia* for sordid-dust. That is, Society is boiled, *i.e.*, raised to the effervescence of the greatest excitement, by filthy lucre. "You salt it in glue." *Salt* is short for "to captivate by putting salt on its tail," *glue* is put metaphorically for *adhesiveness*, and the whole, therefore, means that Society is captured by pertinacity.

"You condense it with locusts and tape:"

I.e., lest it should become too thin, you thicken it with parasitic "diners out" to amuse it, and officials (addicted to red tape) to lend it solemnity.

"Still keeping one principal object in view—
    To preserve its symmetrical shape."

The importance of keeping the proper "form" of Society intact is too obvious to need comment. It is hardly necessary to add also that the reluctance of the Mohammedan and the animal to face a society in which the female sex dominates to such an extent fully explains their common fear of the Jubjub. Lastly it is clear that a word compounded of *jabber* and *jujubes*, the latter being used metaphorically for all unwholesome delights, Turkish and otherwise, is a very judicious description of Society.

The Sixth Fit is occupied with the interlude of the Barrister's dream, which seems to have been prophetic in character and throws further light on the Absolute. That Logic should dream of the Absolute will not of course surprise those who have followed the recent aberrations of the subject. Let us consider then this dream of Logic's.

F. 6, st. 3.

> He dreamed that he stood in a shadowy Court,
> Where the Snark, with a glass in its eye,
> Dressed in gown, bands, and wig, was defending a pig
> On the charge of deserting its sty.

The pig was probably *Epicuri de grege porcus*, and the charge of deserting its sty was a charge of pig-sticking or *suicide*. For, as the divine Plato excellently shows in the *Phaedo* (62 B), to commit suicide is to desert one's post, and so to desert the *four* posts of the pigsty must be still worse.

F. 6, st. 4.

> The Witnesses proved, without error or flaw,
> That the sty was deserted when found:
> And the Judge kept explaining the state of the law
> In a soft under-current of sound.

The Judge is *Conscience*, the exponent of the Moral Law, noted for its still small voice.

F. 6, st. 6.

> The Jury had each formed a different view
> (Long before the indictment was read),
> And they all spoke at once, so that none of them knew
> One word that the others had said.

The Jury is *Public Opinion* which was evidently (as so often) very much perplexed by the pigculiarities of the case.

F. 6, st. 7.

> "You must know——" said the Judge: but the Snark exclaimed "Fudge!

> That statute is obsolete quite!
> Let me tell you, my friends, the whole question depends
> On an ancient manorial right." ·

The question was whether the pig was free, or *ascriptus harae*, justly "penned in its pen." In other words, does being born involve a moral obligation to remain alive?

F. 6, st. 8.

> "In the matter of Treason the pig would appear
> To have aided, but scarcely abetted:"

For a soldier to desert his post is, or may be, treason; hence the charge of treason against the suicide.

> "While the charge of Insolvency fails, it is clear,
> If you grant the plea 'never indebted.' "

The suicide is accused of insolvency, of failing to meet the obligations which life imposes on him. His reply is "never indebted," he owes life nothing, he received no "stipend" and will not be "sued for a debt he never did contract."

F. 6, st. 9.

> "The fact of Desertion I will not dispute:
> But its guilt, as I trust, is removed
> (So far as relates to the costs of this suit)
> By the *Alibi* which has been proved."

You prove an *alibi* by not being there. The pig's defence was that it was not there or not all there; in other words, not *compos mentis*. That is, the old excuse of temporary insanity!

F. 6, st. 11.

> But the Judge said he never had summed up before;
> So the Snark undertook it instead,

Conscience has to pronounce judgment upon the particular case, but this particular case has never occurred before; hence Conscience finds itself unable to decide and leaves the matter to the Absolute. The attitude of Public Opinion is similar: "when the verdict was called for, the Jury declined," and "ventured to hope that the Snark wouldn't mind undertaking that duty as well."

In the end the Absolute not only has to defend the offender and take his guilt upon Itself, but also, as ἓν καὶ πᾶν, to assume all the other functions as well, to find the verdict and to pronounce the sentence. Its readiness to do this is suspicious, and suggests the idea that it was acting collusively throughout in pretending to defend the pig.

"So the Snark *found* the verdict," *where* we are not told, but *what* we might have anticipated.

> When it said the word "GUILTY!" the Jury all
>   groaned,
> And some of them fainted away.

The verdict involved a shock to enlightened Public Opinion, like that of the Dreyfus case. The sentence after that seemed comparatively light and so was received with approval.

> "Transportation for life" was the sentence it gave,
> "And *then* to be fined forty pound."
> The Jury all cheered, though the Judge said he
>   feared
> That the phrase was not legally sound.

The sentence was of course absurd, for the suicide had already transported himself out of jurisdiction.

F. 6, st. 16.

> But their wild exultation was suddenly checked
> When the jailer informed them, with tears,
> Such a sentence would have not the slightest
>   effect,
> As the pig had been dead for some years.

The jailer, whose duty it is to keep the pigs in their styes, is the *doctor*. After all, you can do nothing with a *successful* suicide.

F. 6, st. 17.

> The Judge left the Court, looking deeply disgusted:
> But the Snark, though a little aghast,
> As the lawyer to whom the defence was intrusted,
> Went bellowing on to the last.

Though such events shock the Conscience, the Absolute is unabashed.

The Seventh Fit is devoted to the Banker's fate and is perhaps the most prophetic of any. For no discerning reader of this commentary can fail to recognize that it forecasts the encounter of Judaism with Anti-Semiticism. Let us follow the description of this disgraceful episode in contemporary history.

F. 7, st. 3.

> A Bandersnatch swiftly drew nigh
> And grabbed at the Banker, who shrieked in
>   despair,
> For he knew it was useless to fly.
>
> He offered large discount—he offered a cheque
> (Drawn to "bearer") for seven-pounds-ten:
> But the Bandersnatch merely extended its neck
> And grabbed at the Banker again.

The Anti-Semitic Bandersnatch shows that it cannot be bribed by insufficient "ransom," and that two can play at a game of grab.

> Without rest or pause—while those frumious jaws
> Went savagely snapping around—
> He skipped and he hopped, and he floundered
>   and flopped,
> Till fainting he fell to the ground.

After the Anti-Semitic rioters had been driven off, it was found that the Banker—

> . . . was black in the face, and they scarcely
>   could trace
> The least likeness to what he had been:
> While so great was his fright that his waistcoat
>   turned white—
> A wonderful thing to be seen!

This alludes to the wonderful affinity Judaism has for clothing, and we may parallel this passage by referring to Shakespeare's (?) *Merchant of Venice*, Act ii, Scene 1. There an insult offered to his "Jewish gaberdine" produces a powerful emotional effect upon Shylock. Here conversely the ill treatment of their wearer calls forth a sympathetic compensatory effect on the part of the clothes.

In the Eighth Fit the tragedy reaches its consummation and comment is almost needless.

It must be *read*, not without tears, and every line in it confirms the view we have taken of the Snark.

F. 8, st. 5.

> Erect and sublime, for one moment of time.

I.e., before becoming a moment in the timeless Absolute.

F. 8, st. 9.

> In the midst of the word he was trying to say,
> In the midst of his laughter and glee,
> He had softly and silently vanished away—[7]
> For the Snark *was* a Boojum, you see.

One can't help feeling a little sorry for the Baker personally, but nevertheless the verdict of Philosophy must be: "So perish all who brave the Snark again!"

---

7. This line is persistently misquoted by Snobbs; the word is *suddenly*, not *silently*.—M.G.

J. A. LINDON, whose name has been mentioned many times in the notes, is the author of the following fit. "It is rather disappointing," he writes in a letter, "that we hear so little of some of the other members of the crew. Further, one feels that the violence of the Banker's Fate detracts from the drama of the ending, the Vanishing, which follows it. So, just for amusement, I have concocted an extra fit, which we can imagine as coming between these two concluding fits. It is of average length and (as befits interpolation, and especially one at that point) it is not violent or particularly dramatic. Nobody meets a decisive fate, and neither the balance of the tale nor the general status quo is altered."

Mr. Lindon's fit fits so neatly into the spirit of Carroll's agony that I think it provides this fitful commentary with a most fitting conclusion.

The Clue

by J. A. Lindon

They sought it with thimbles, they sought it
    with care;
  They pursued it with forks and hope;
They threatened its life with a railway-share;
  They charmed it with smiles and soap.

But the Billiard-marker, who'd left on the ship
  All the cannons he'd recently made,
Had wandered apart, with the red in his grip,
  To a spot of convenient shade.

Where, baulked of all hope, he was potting
    the soap
  With the butt of his thimble-tipped cue.
(In the glummering[1] dark, with no sign of a
    Snark,
  There was not very much he could do.)

But as he bent, aiming to pocket his care,
  There came a sharp sound in the woods;
And out, all dishevelled, a bow in his hair,
  Flew the maker of Bonnets and Hoods.

He was red with exertion, and blue with the cold,
  He was white with some terror he'd seen;
As the low setting sun turned his feathers to gold
  And his ears a bright emerald green.

He struggled to speak, but emitted a squeak
  Like a bone that has come out of joint.
What on earth had occurred? He had seen—
    he had heard—
  Not a thing could he do but to point.

The Billiard-marker cajoled him with nods,
  He spun him a kiss off the cush;
He played him a thousand up, giving him odds
  Of nine hundred, not barring the "push."

But no word could he say, merely gestured away
  With a frantic but eloquent poke;
So, with tables[2] and chalk, they set off at a walk,
  For the thing was too grave for a joke.

The sunlight was gilding the tops of the crags,
  The gulfs were all shadowed in blue,
As they heard from afar, like the tearing of rags,
  A sound that they both of them knew.

" 'Tis a Snark!" cried the Billiard-marker with
    glee,
  " 'Tis the voice of a Snark!" he exclaimed;
" 'Tis a Snark! Now the times I have told you
    are three!"
  And with "jump" for a hazard he aimed.

The maker of Hoods, quite approving of that,
  Here showed him a print on the ground:
It was long, it was large, it was dim, it was flat,
  It was gray, it was new, it was round.

" 'Tis the trail of a Snark!" cried the man who
    would mark
  Up the score and put chalk on the cues.

1. *Glummering*—the sort of gloomy glimmering that makes you glum.

2. There was really only one table, but it had a second playing surface underneath, in case it rained. The bowsprit generally wobbled on wet days, because the Billiard-marker used all the ship's glue to keep the balls in position.

"More than one has been past—when you meet
them at last,
Snarks are often discovered in twos."

With forks at the ready, impaling their soap,
With threatening shares and a smile,
They followed the tracks with ebullient hope
Through the fortieth part of a mile.

Then the maker of Bonnets beribboned his heels,
Explaining by signs how he'd seen
Other marks, which had surely been made by
the wheels
Of a Snarked-about bathing-machine.

They had come to a place among lowering crags,
And the sound they were seeking was there:
Like a swishing and scraping, or tearing of rags—
'Twas the noise of the Snark in its lair!

They rounded a rock, full of joy at the catch,
And there were the creatures quite plain:

One was turning a grindstone, with whirring
and scratch,
And sucking the crook of his cane.

The other had rolled up the sleeves of his shirt
And with scraper and brush well aloft,
He was slaving away at removing the dirt
From a shoe that the Broker had doffed.

Like gold in the sun shone the crags every one,
Dark-shadowed lay boulders and roots;
From afar in a dell came the sound of the bell;
They had only been following—*Boots*.

NOTE: Lindon has since written a full-scale parody of the entire *Snark* ballad. See "The Hunting of the Slype: A Travesty in Late Bits," in *The Worm Runner's Digest*, Volume 11, Number 2, December 1969, pp. 84–97.

THE
DESIGNS FOR
THE SNARK

Charles Mitchell

THE DESIGNS FOR THE SNARK

❖ ❖

Charles Mitchell

In 1864 William Burges began his redecoration, in the fashion of a miniature Sistine Chapel, of Wyatt's earlier remanagement of Worcester College Chapel in Oxford. He asked Henry Holiday (1839–1927) to paint a series of half-length prophets along the top of the walls and panels of Adam and Eve on the ceiling.[1] Millais had already been commissioned to make designs for the windows, and one of them, an *Annunciation*, was in fact executed. Burges, however, rejected it and engaged Holiday to redesign all seven windows, which are still *in situ*. The first four were already installed by the spring of 1865. This was about the time when Mr. Dodgson, who admired the Pre-Raphaelites and had quite recently met Millais,[2] may very well have become acquainted with Holiday's work, though there is no explicit record of this. The first recorded evidence of their meeting comes in 1870, when Holiday was invited to complete the redecoration of Worcester Chapel with its present frieze round the walls, illustrating the *Te Deum*. During his long stay in Oxford, Holiday consorted with many Oxford worthies: not only Daniel, later Provost of the College and a notable figure in the history of printing, but also the Kitchins (whose daughter Alexandra—"Xie"—was one of Dodgson's childfriends),[3] Mark Pattison, Sir John Stainer, Walter Pater, an earlier acquaintance, Max Müller, and others, including Dodgson.[4] "It was an agreeable surprise," Holiday recalled from this period, "when one morning Lewis Carroll (the Rev. C. L. Dodgson) came to see me and my work, in company with a friend of his and mine. We became friends on the spot and continued so till his death."[5] Their friendship, cemented by a common passion for photography, ripened rapidly. On 6 July 1870 Dodgson left Christ Church with his camera for a few days' visit to the Holidays at their house in Marlborough Road, St. John's Wood, where he took some twenty portraits.[6]

His next recorded meeting with Holiday, though they no doubt met in the interval, occurred on 15 January 1874, when he noted: "went off to Belsize Road, where I called on the Holidays, and found him, Mrs. Holiday, and Winnie [their daughter]. He showed me the drawings he is doing for me (suggestions for groups of two children—nude studies —for me to try to reproduce in photographs from

---

1. Henry Holiday, *Reminiscences of My Life* (London: Heinemann, 1914), pp. 105–6. I am indebted to J. Mordaunt Crook for further information on the project, which is described in his *William Burges and the High Victorian Dream* (London: John Murray, 1981).

2. *The Diaries of Lewis Carroll*, ed. Roger Lancelyn Green (1954; reprinted at Westport, Conn.: Greenwood Press, 1971), p. 213; cf. Jeffrey Stern, "Lewis Carroll the Pre-Raphaelite: 'Fainting in Coils,'" in *Lewis Carroll Observed*, ed. Edward Guiliano (New York: Clarkson N. Potter, 1976), pp. 161–80.

3. Cf. *Lewis Carroll and the Kitchins*, edited with an introduction and notes by Morton N. Cohen (New York: Argosy Bookstore, 1980).

4. Cf. *The Letters of Lewis Carroll*, ed. Morton N. Cohen with the assistance of Roger Lancelyn Green (New York: Oxford University Press, 1979), p. 228, note 2.

5. Holiday, *Reminiscences*, p. 165.

6. *Diaries*, p. 289.

life), which are quite exquisite."[7] And on the following day he recorded: "Told Holiday of an idea his drawings suggested to me, that he might illustrate a child's book for me. If *only* he can draw grotesques, it would be all I should desire—the grace and beauty of the pictures would quite rival Tenniel, I think."[8] His caution was justified. Although Holiday, a close friend of Burne-Jones and an exponent of what has been called the "classical revival" in the sixties,[9] could be relied upon to draw with learned elegance and precision, he had not as yet produced anything to prove his ability to match Dodgson's calculatedly grotesque fantasy. The "child's book" Dodgson had in mind was *Sylvie and Bruno*, for he noted on 4 February 1874: "Received from Holiday the five drawings of children he has done for me, as well as a very lovely drawing for *Sylvie and Bruno*."[10]

I

The genesis of the *Snark* dates from 18 July 1874, the day the last line of the poem occurred to Dodgson—in a moment of escape from the bedside of his dying cousin and godson, Charles Wilcox[11]—during a country walk near Guildford in Surrey.[12] Nearly thirteen years later he recalled the event and its sequel in vivid detail: "I was walking on a hillside, alone, one bright summer day, when suddenly there came into my head one line of verse—one solitary line—'For the Snark *was* a Boojum, you see.' I knew not what it meant, then: I know

not what it means, now; but I wrote it down: and, some time afterwards, the rest of the stanza occurred to me, that being its last line: and so by degrees, at odd moments during the next year or two, the rest of the poem pieced itself together, that being its last stanza."[13] The final four-line stanza, beginning "In the midst of the word . . . ," was completed on 22 July 1874, four days after the Guildford walk.[14]

On the genesis of the illustrations, Holiday said in his *Reminiscences* that Dodgson paid him a visit at Oak-Tree House, Hampstead, in 1875, when he drew Marion Terry lying in chain mail on the lawn. He then went on to say that shortly after this visit Carroll "wrote to me asking if I would design three illustrations to *The Hunting of the Snark*, in three cantos, of which he sent me the MS. It was a new kind of work and interested me. I began them at once, and sent him the first sketches, but he had in the meantime written another canto, and asked for a drawing for it; I sent this, but meantime he had written a new canto and wanted another illustration; and this went on till he pulled up at the eighth canto, making, with the frontispiece, nine illustrations."[15] Writing as an old man of seventy-five or so, forty years after the event, Holiday was here a little muddled in his dating. It is true that Dodgson did spend a week with the Holidays in July 1875, and that on 12 July he did photograph "Polly" Terry in armor.[16] But, in fact, he invited Holiday to illustrate the *Snark* in the previous year, for he recorded in his Diary on 23 November 1874: "Ruskin came, by my request, for a talk about the pictures Holiday is doing for the 'Boojum'—one (the scene on board) has been cut on wood [by Joseph Swain (1820–1909), who cut all the *Snark*'s illustrations]. He much disheartened me by holding out

7. *Diaries*, p. 326. On Dodgson's photography of this kind see Morton N. Cohen, *Lewis Carroll's Photographs of Nude Children* (Philadelphia: Rosenbach Foundation, 1978).

8. *Diaries*, p. 326.

9. Cf. Philip Hook, "The Classical Revival in English Painting," *The Connoisseur*, 191 (1976), pp. 122ff.

10. *Diaries*, p. 327. Cf. Selwyn H. Goodacre, "*The Hunting of the Snark*: A History of the Publication," *Jabberwocky*, the Journal of the Lewis Carroll Society, 5, no. 4 (Autumn 1976), p. 110. I am much indebted to this paper. The "very lovely drawing" was reproduced by Stuart Dodgson Collingwood, *The Life and Letters of Lewis Carroll* (New York: Century, 1899), p. 264.

11. Cf. Morton N. Cohen, "Hark the Snark," in *Lewis Carroll Observed*, pp. 92–95.

12. Cf. *Diaries*, pp. 334–35.

13. Lewis Carroll, "*Alice* on the Stage," *The Theatre* (April 1887), reprinted in *The Lewis Carroll Picture Book*, ed. Stuart Dodgson Collingwood (London: T. Fisher Unwin, 1899), pp. 163–74 (p. 167). Cf. *Letters*, p. 234, note 1, with a working bibliography on the *Snark*.

14. *Diaries*, p. 346.

15. Holiday, *Reminiscences*, pp. 244–45.

16. *Diaries*, p. 341.

no hopes that Holiday would be able to illustrate a book satisfactorily."[17]

In 1898, sixteen years before the appearance of his *Reminiscences*, Holiday published a fuller account of the evolution of the *Snark* and his involvement in it. He recalled how, starting with a notion of only its last line, Dodgson "wrote three stanzas of his poem (or 'fits' of his 'agony,' as he called them), and asked if I would design three illustrations to them, explaining that the composition would some day be introduced in a book he was contemplating;[18] but as this latter would certainly not be ready for a considerable time, he thought of printing the poem for private circulation in the first instance." And he went on: "While I was making sketches for these illustrations, he sent me a fourth 'fit,' asking for another drawing; shortly after came a fifth 'fit,' with a similar request, and this was followed by a sixth, seventh, and eighth. His mind not being occupied with any other book at the time, this theme seemed continually to be suggesting new developments; and having extended the 'agony' thus far beyond his original intentions, Mr. Dodgson decided to publish it at once as an independent work, without waiting for *Sylvie and Bruno*, of which it was to have formed a feature."[19] In the same account Holiday also recalled that at the time he had rather regretted Dodgson's successive expansions of the poem, feeling that they involved a disproportion between its scale and substance. The "Walrus and the Carpenter," he felt, was "happier in its proportion." But on rereading it in 1898 he found it funny all through and wanted nothing cut out.[20]

For a closer account of how the *Snark* was made we must turn from Holiday's late recollections to the contemporary evidence of Dodgson's own letters and diaries, and particularly to his correspondence with Alexander Macmillan who published the book in 1876. These letters are unusually copi-

ous for a special reason: Dodgson did not bring out the book in the normal way. Instead, as with his *Alice*s and other fictions, he brought it out on commission; that is to say, he himself bore the financial risk, employing Macmillan as his agent and publisher. He engaged and paid Holiday on his own account, and sometimes dealt even with Swain, the engraver, and with Clay, the printer, directly. It was this arrangement that permitted him to be so fastidious over every detail of the book's production and so exigent in his often last-minute demands on the ever patient and courteous Alexander Macmillan.[21] These primary records nevertheless, though numerous, are still tantalizingly fragmentary. The letters between Dodgson and Macmillan do not begin as a connected series until October 1875, and even so they are incomplete, while—most frustratingly of all—nobody has yet traced the fundamentally important letters between Dodgson and Holiday, which would have made plain much that must remain—alas!—a matter for inference and conjecture.[22]

17. *Diaries*, p. 334.

18. I.e., *Sylvie and Bruno*, published without the *Snark* in 1889, with forty-six illustrations by Harry Furniss.

19. Henry Holiday, "The Snark's Significance," *The Academy* (29 January 1898), p. 129.

20. Ibid.

21. Charles Morgan, *The House of Macmillan (1843–1943)* (New York: Macmillan, 1944), pp. 79–81 and 107ff.; cf. Morton N. Cohen, "Lewis Carroll and the House of Macmillan," *Browning Institute Studies*, 7 (New York: The Browning Institute, Inc., and The Graduate School & University Center, CUNY, 1979), pp. 36–37, note 7 and *passim*.

22. Dr. Green's edition of the *Diaries* is selective, but in view of his carefully stated principles of editing (*Diaries*, p. xiii), I have assumed that he excluded no references to the *Snark* or to Holiday. I have not seen the surviving originals which are now in the British Library, London. I also confidently assume that Professor Cohen omitted no such references in his meticulous edition of Dodgson's letters, except for what comes in the letters to Macmillan's, which he proposes to edit separately.

Dodgson's original letters to Macmillan's of 1864–98 (hereafter RDM) belong to the Rosenbach Museum and Library in Philadelphia, together with microfilms of the corresponding letters from Macmillan's to Dodgson (hereafter BLMD) which are now in the British Library (Add.mss.55397ff.). Only a selection of the former is published in Morton N. Cohen's *Letters*. I have consulted RDM and the microfilms of BLMD. Another portion of the Macmillan archive is in the Library of the University of Reading, England. This I have not consulted, but I am assured by Dr. J. A. Edwards, Archivist of the University, that it contains nothing *à propos*. Mr. Richard Garnett kindly gave me information about the whereabouts of the Macmillan archive.

On 24 March 1970 an anonymous vendor sold at Sotheby's, London, a large number of letters to Mr. and Mrs. Holiday

The progress of the *Snark* and its pictures during the eleven months or so after Ruskin visited Dodgson in November 1874 is unrecorded (though a good deal of the poem, we know, was already written by that time), save for one illuminating reference. On 23 December 1874 Macmillan mentioned in a letter to Dodgson an illustrator "who could rival Tenniel, for your purposes."[23] It sounds as if Dodgson was worried about Ruskin's criticism of Holiday's drawings, and was casting about for a possible alternative artist. The picture begins to come clearly into focus the following autumn. On 24 October 1875 Dodgson noted in his Diary: "A sudden idea occurred, about which I wrote to Holiday and Macmillan, of publishing the *Snark* poem this Christmas—also of writing an acrostic on Gertrude Chataway (which I did the same night) the four stanzas to begin with 'Girt, rude, chat, away' ''; and next day he added: "Finished the verses and sent them to Mrs. Chataway, asking leave to print them. I think they might do for a dedication to the book, which I think of calling *The Hunting of the Snark*. It also occurs to me that such a publication would give me a good opportunity of circulating ... a new 'Christmas Greeting' to my 40,000 child-readers."[24]

These are the bald records of one of the most emotionally exciting moments in Dodgson's life. A month previously, on 29 September, he had met Gertrude, a clergyman's nearly nine-year-old daughter, with her parents and three sisters, while he was holidaying by the seaside at Sandown in the Isle of Wight; and the little girl at once cap-tivated his heart, as he captivated hers.[25] It was a friendship for life. Next day he went for a walk with her and her sister Alice (to whom he gave a copy of *Through the Looking-Glass*). Two days later he drew her in her paddling blouse and bathing drawers. Three days after that she brought along her friend Violet Martineau to be shown some of his photographs. Next day she was among the party when he made a trip round the island. On the 11th she and her friends came to his lodgings where he told them a story. And just before he left Sandown for his family home at Guildford she came again with another new friend, Sybil Blackwell, to say good-bye. On the 13th, back in Christ Church, he immediately wrote Gertrude, from a brimming heart, one of his most brilliantly contrived and amusing birthday letters;[26] and in his letter of the 25th to Mrs. Chataway, asking permission to print his double acrostic to Gertrude "if I should have occasion to do so," he thanked her "for the society, so liberally granted to me at all times and seasons, of one of the sweetest children it has ever been my happiness to meet."[27] There can be no doubt, as Dr. Selwyn Goodacre first suggested,[28] that it was Dodgson's encounter with Gertrude Chataway, with all the tender feelings it aroused, that galvanized his inventive imagination and stimulated him to press on with the *Snark* as a separate publication. It was now *her* book.

On 26 October Macmillan sent Dodgson an encouraging letter: "By all means let us have the little Poem at once, and please let me know how the illustrations stand. Are any of them engraved? or drawn on the wood? There is no time to lose. But I think it worth doing."[29] But then came a snag. Only two days later, having looked into the matter, Macmillan told him: "Swain says it is quite impossible to cut the blocks he has in hand under three months, and even would hesitate to promise

and their daughter Winifred in lots 490–94, and 496–508. These comprised letters to the Holidays from Ruskin, Holman Hunt, William Morris, Sir Edward Burne-Jones, Lady Burne-Jones, Edward Bellamy, Walter Crane, Lord Leighton, Robert Browning, Mr. Gladstone, Alma-Tadema, Philip Burne-Jones, William De Morgan, George Meredith, Frank Salisbury, Arthur Rackham, G. F. Watts, Joachim, Bernard Shaw, Thomas Hardy, H. G. Wells, and others, and also (lot 497) two letters (not to do with the *Snark*) from Dodgson to Winifred Holiday. The anonymous vendor, whom I have not been able to identify, may well have known where the Dodgson-Holiday letters about the *Snark* now are.

23. BLMD.
24. *Diaries*, pp. 344–45.

25. Cf. her recollections in Collingwood, *Life and Letters*, pp. 379–80.
26. *Diaries*, pp. 343–44; *Letters*, pp. 230–31.
27. *Letters*, pp. 231–33.
28. Goodacre, "*The Hunting*," p. 110.
29. BLMD.

that. So clearly it would not do to attempt it [i.e., an illustrated Christmas book]. What do you say to giving us your poem in the Christmas Number of our Magazine. I think that might serve your purpose in keeping yourself fresh before the public. Our editor will be delighted—so will Yours ever faithfully Alex. Macmillan."[30] Next day Dodgson noted in his Diary: "Heard from Macmillan that Swain cannot finish the blocks under three months, so my first plan must be given up."[31]

His next plan was to postpone publication of the poem until Easter 1876, when it could be properly illustrated. He at once informed Macmillan accordingly, saying that he did not want any prior publication in *Macmillan's Magazine*. To this Macmillan replied on 30 October: "The publication of your poem in the Christmas Number would not in the least interfere with the publication of an illustrated edition at Easter. I think it would rather help than hinder, if as I have no doubt it amused and attracted. It would serve too I think to fulfill the purpose your idea of a Christmas publication aimed at. Won't you send it to me to look at? I will not let it go beyond our own circle, that is Mr. Gure, Mr. Craik and myself."[32] Dodgson was not persuaded, and the poem never appeared in the magazine.

On the same day, 30 October, Holiday arrived in Oxford for a Saturday-to-Monday visit at Christ Church, no doubt to discuss the *Snark*.[33] It was probably then that Dodgson thought of a way of saving his idea of a Christmas publication after all. "It occurs to me," he wrote in his Diary next day, "that as *one* block (the 'landing') is done,[34] it might be worth while to publish at Christmas, using it as the frontispiece: this would have the advantage of keeping the other five pictures, to come out *new*,

if the poem is ever introduced into a story [i.e., *Sylvie and Bruno*]."[35]

This new proposal he at once communicated to Macmillan, who replied on the Monday, 1 November: "(1). If you can send us your poem by the end of this week, you can have proofs early next week and then you can make your corrections in it for final form. (2). I think we ought not to attempt anything about *pictorial* covers. Do it simply in paper cover—red I rather advise and sell for 1/–. (3). We will see Swain about the block [i.e., *The Landing*] and as soon as we get your copy we will be able to arrange the page and frontispiece. If it is to be done at all we should decide on our course *now* as there will not be the least time to consult or devise new ideas. I think a shilling book of this kind might have a considerable sale."[36]

Dodgson almost met Macmillan's request for the text within the week. On 2 November—delivering the text piecemeal—he sent Macmillan fourteen stanzas of the poem which, as he confidently noted in his Diary on the same day, he thought they would "now publish this Christmas, with frontispiece only."[37] These verses Macmillan acknowledged on 3 November, promising proofs on the following day[38]—such was the speed of printing and the efficiency of the mails in those Victorian days. On the 5th he sent Macmillan the "text of *Snark* to the end of 'Fit 3,' "[39] which was tersely acknowledged on the 6th: "Fresh MS received. Your instructions will be attended to. Price we will write you about again. Also number."[40] And on the 6th he composed four new stanzas, the second, third, fifth, and sixth of the present Fit 7 (*The Banker's Fate*), thus, as he recorded, "completing the poem which now consists of 88 stanzas."[41] These he posted to Macmillan on the 7th with a covering letter in which he specified the kind of setup and

30. Ibid.
31. *Diaries*, p. 345.
32. BLMD.
33. *Diaries*, p. 345.
34. This remark does not obviously square with the fact that *The Crew on Board* was already cut by 23 November 1874. But it was not exclusive: it simply means that if the book was to have an appropriate frontispiece *The Landing* was already available for that purpose.

35. *Diaries*, pp. 345–46.
36. BLMD.
37. *Diaries*, p. 346.
38. BLMD.
39. *Diaries*, p. 346.
40. BLMD.
41. *Diaries*, p. 346.

typography he wanted: "I send you the rest of the poem, with the Dedication and Contents and Map. The Preface is not yet written, but we shall want a leaf for it. . . ." He proposed to put the preliminary matter (half title, frontispiece, title page, and preface) in a separate gathering, followed by twenty-one leaves comprising the dedication, the table of contents, the poem, and an advertisement for *Alice* which would go on an extra leaf at the end. He asked for three rather than the usual two sets of proofs. In the postscript of his letter he prescribed: "If you think 'brilliant' type for the dedicatory verses will make the heading look top-heavy, try a larger type: but I want it very small."[42] He added: "I want to write another little Christmas letter, to be slightly gummed into each copy sold this year. Is there time to have it done with a coloured heading? a sprig of holly, say? Mr. Holiday would design one."[43]

Having made these arrangements, Dodgson hastened, that same day, to write to Mrs. Chataway to tell her what he was doing. Seeing that the dedication was to her daughter, she was the first person, after Macmillan, Holiday, Dodgson's family, and Clay, who ought to hear about it. He told her that it would be a very small book, not forty pages long, with "a poem (supposed to be comic)" and a frontispiece by Holiday; and he asked her to keep the title secret in her family circle.[44] That day he recorded in his Diary: "Sent to Macmillan the rest of the MS. of *The Snark*, with the dedicatory verses. Wrote Frances [his sister], and Mrs. Chataway, telling them of the intended publication. No one has yet known of it but Macmillan etc., and Mr. and Mrs. Holiday."[45]

Meanwhile he had been attending to the cover of the book, and contrary to Macmillan's plea of 1 November that it should be kept plain, he wanted to have a picture on it. About this Macmillan wrote on 2 November: "Any design for the cover

to be cut by the time we have named to you must be cut in broad bold style. Besides the prints of it if done in a hurry, as this would be, could not be done effectively if the lines were fine. Swain says that he can let us have the block in a day after Mr. Holiday returns it. Now as he says it is exceedingly fine work [Macmillan was clearly referring here to Holiday], it clearly won't do to hurry this. So I would suggest that you should see a proof of the title page and pass it for press so that we may work it and the frontispiece at once and carefully and leave it to dry quietly and so be ready for letter press and cover. This would materially facilitate matters."[46]

Here, however, they were at cross-purposes. When Macmillan wrote his letter on 2 November, he was assuming that Dodgson wanted the cover to be made of paper. He was wrong. For on the 3rd, in the letter acknowledging receipt of the fourteen stanzas, he wrote: "When you telegraphed about a block I took for granted you meant a woodblock to be printed on *paper*. But if the book is to be done in cloth then the binder must cut in brass and it need not be on wood at all. What we require will be a drawing on paper which the bookbinding artist will see to. This drawing if at all elaborate should be in our hands now, and in any case early next week."[47] Next day, the 4th, Macmillan wrote again about the matter: "Swain has already told Mr. Holiday that his drawing must be made on paper to be cut in brass by our binder. You will see what he can do in that line in Old Christmas, or indeed in your own Alice. But all these things should be arranged at once."[48] Dodgson then consulted Holiday about a proper color for the binding, and told Macmillan in his already quoted letter of 7 November: "Mr. Holiday is sending you a suggestion for *blue* covers: I fancy he is right."

In other matters, too, Dodgson insisted on going beyond the restrictive suggestions so urgently made

---

42. Cf. the tiny script of Dodgson's "fairy letters" to child-friends (*Letters*, pp. 108–9, note 1).

43. RDM.

44. *Letters*, pp. 233–34.

45. *Diaries*, pp. 346–47.

46. BLMD.

47. Ibid.

48. Ibid. Macmillan published Washington Irving's *Old Christmas, from the Sketch Book* in 1875, with illustrations by Randolph Caldecott.

by Macmillan on 1 November. He went ahead with his idea of adding a sprig of holly or some other seasonable decoration to his Christmas letter, about which Macmillan patiently wrote on 12 November: "If you give a coloured border it had better be lithographed, which Cooper could do, if Mr. Holiday will send him a drawing early next week—just as he wants it reproduced *on paper*."[49] Furthermore, Dodgson now wanted gilded pictures on *both* sides of the cover—an idea to which Macmillan objected in this same letter of the 12th as making "a cake which is too thickly coated with sugar." His letter ends: "I sent you a Michael Angelo cover to see if the colour of cloth pleased you. Mr. Holiday and our binder both like it."

What cover-pictures was Macmillan referring to? There can be no doubt, as the subsequent story of the covers shows, that they were the ones we know: those that adorn the regular First Edition of the book and the reprint of May 1876, as well as the miniature facsimile American First Edition pirated in the same year by James Osgood in Boston.[50] Dodgson may well have asked Holiday to design the two covers during their meeting in Christ Church on 30 October – 1 November; and Holiday must then have gone to work on them at once, because, as we shall see in a moment, the brass blocks of both designs were almost finished by 23 November. The front cover displays the Bellman sitting astride the top-gallant yard of a ship ringing his bell, while the topsail below, crossed by halyard and sheets, bears the title: THE / HUNTING / OF THE / SNARK. The back cover depicts a bell-buoy, incorporating the legend IT / WAS / A / BOOJUM, rolling in a turbulent sea. What inspired this second design, incidentally, is recorded by Holiday himself. In 1873 he made a sea-trip round the south coast of England from London to Liverpool. "At Land's End," he related, "I made a sketch which included a bell-buoy, picturesque to eye and ear, with the weird irregular tolling of the bell, and when Dodgson wanted a motive for the back-cover, something that would bear the words 'It was a Boojum,' I bethought me of my bell-buoy, which exactly met his want."[51]

Now we come to a decisive turning-point in the story of the *Snark*'s production. Early in November 1875 Dodgson himself began to wonder whether, rather than planning for a provisional Christmas book soon and a fuller publication later, it would not be better to postpone publication until, once for all, he could produce the thing, as it had now taken clear shape in his mind, exactly as he wanted it. "Heard from Macmillan," he wrote in his Diary on 13 November, "objecting to picture covers on both sides as too much 'sugar for the cake.' This confirmed a doubt I have felt for some days as to the advisability of publishing at all with one picture only. By waiting till Easter, we can have *seven* pictures. I telegraphed him to this effect, and also to Holiday, not to go on designing a border for a Christmas letter till he hears from me."[52] He soon definitely made up his mind to make it an Easter book, and informed Macmillan accordingly. Whereupon Macmillan, *more suo*, proposed a fresh timetable on 23 November: "Easter falls this year about the middle of April. Therefore a book meant for Easter sale should be in the hands of the booksellers in the last week in March. Therefore Clay should have your final proof and the electros of the illustrations during the first week in March. The blocks for the covers are nearly done. I don't think it would be possible for Mr. Holiday to do anything to them now unless we had new blocks cut altogether. Mr. Holiday chose the Michael Angelo colour as what he thought suitable." Then, in response to points which Dodgson probably raised in a lost letter amplifying his telegram announcing his definite change of plan, Macmillan went on: "I think on the whole the illustrations would be

49. Ibid.
50. For editions and reprints see Sidney Herbert Williams and Falconer Madan, *The Lewis Carroll Handbook*, revised and augmented by Roger Lancelyn Green and further revised by Denis Crutch (Folkestone: Dawson and Sons; and Hamden, Connecticut: Archon Books, 1979), pp. 89–92, 122–23, 253–54 (hereafter cited as *Handbook*); and Selwyn H. Goodacre's revised "A Listing of the *Snark*" below.

51. Holiday, *Reminiscences*, p. 246.
52. *Diaries*, p. 247.

best worked separate. I see no good in making the colour of the paper on which they are printed different from the rest of the book. It might be a little thicker, but that would be enough. This, however, and the mode of printing the Easter letter [which Dodgson now proposed to substitute for the Christmas one], might well stand over till late February. Christmas holidays will obliterate all our decisions. Price too we should leave till we are more nearly in possession of all the facts—size etc."[53]

Dodgson gave careful thought to the question of where and how the illustrations should appear in the book. "In the early part of January," he wrote to Macmillan on 21 December, "I hope to get the 'Snark' set up in final form, with the additional matter etc., so as to have ample leisure for verbal corrections before you electrotype. So I would be glad to have the question of pictures settled *now*. The more I think of your proposal to work them off separately, on paper of the same colour as the book, the less I like it. My own expectations would be to find text at the back. There are only two courses which seem to me endurable—one, to have the pictures quite distinct from the text, on a different coloured paper—the other to have them printed along with the book, with text at the back of each picture, as we did with 'Alice.' The latter plan, unless you seriously object, is what I prefer on the whole. If you can tell me you approve of this, I can begin at once arranging the first sheet. We shall have nearly 60 pages altogether, I expect."[54] To this Macmillan responded the next day: "If I suggested that the plates should be *worked* separate it was only as a matter of convenience. But they might easily be worked *with the text*, and yet have not letterpress on the back. I certainly think that the plates, which of course will be a page each, would gain in clearness by the absence of type on the back. We often have printed books so, and I think with good result. At the same time I have no sort of objection to your plan if you prefer it—except that the pictures will certainly

look better, and the book will be so many pages thicker—a very desirable thing, where the cost is so great in proportion to the appearance. Take my way if you can. Of course I think it the best. If not there is no very serious objection to your taking your own."[55]

On 3 January 1876 Dodgson resumed the discussion with another point. "There is one question about the 'Snark,' which I want settled *at once*. I am quite willing to have the pictures worked along with the poem, but without text at the back, if you [are] sure that will look well. But it seems to me that that will oblige us to have all the pictures (except of course the frontispiece) on right-hand pages: now, two of them [*The Butcher and the Beaver* illustrating Fit 1, and *The Vanishing* illustrating Fit 8] refer to concluding verses of cantos. Will this look well? 2/3 of a blank page, and *then* a picture? [Here he made a drawing of this ugly format.] By the other arrangement (of having the text at the back) it would look like this: [another drawing showing an opening with a picture on the left-hand page and the canto ending halfway down the opposite page] the picture is now embedded in the poem, and looks much more natural, I fancy. Please consider this point."[56] Macmillan replied on the 5th: "There is no reason why the cuts to *The Snark* should be on the right hand page more than on the left. They should be so placed that the letterpress to which the picture refers should face it. This is the only condition needful." Five of the pictures in the printed book are in fact on left-hand pages. Macmillan ended his letter with the still-unanswered question: "When can you let us have the copy and plates? If we are to publish at Easter we ought to be making progress now."[57]

Then there was a serious problem about the covers. Dodgson wanted them decorated in gold, which, with Holiday's Bellman and bell-buoy designs, involved large gilded areas. On this Macmillan wrote on 13 January: "The binding of your

53. BLMD.
54. RDM. The printed book is 83 pages long.

55. BLMD.
56. RDM.
57. BLMD.

Snark, if the ornaments are in *gold*, will cost you nearly 1/4 a copy. If you have it black or in blind about half as much. I think to spend so much on the cover is to outdo Falstaff with his *sack* to *bread*. The book will sell quite as well and I really think look better, in plainer dress. Please say if you won't change this."[58] Dodgson's reaction to this plea was not to give up his gold, but to have *two* kinds of binding on sale: one with the Bellman and bell-buoy designs with a good deal of gold, the other with newly designed cover-pictures so as to use less gold.

About this new idea he wrote to Holiday on 15 January.[59] He began his letter by acknowledging the receipt of a number of proofs of the pictures, including one of *The Hunting* (Fit 4) with its beautiful sweet-faced figure of "Hope": "I finished off my letter at Brighton yesterday in a hurry, and omitted to say how pleased I am with the proofs you sent me. They seem to me *most* successfully cut, and I agree with you in thinking the head of 'Hope' a great success; it is quite lovely." Then he broached his new idea. "Now for another piece of designing, if you don't mind undertaking it. Macmillan writes me word that the gorgeous cover [i.e., the heavily gilded Bellman and bell-buoy designs] will cost 1s. 4d. a copy! whereas we can't really afford more than 5d. or 6d., as we must not charge more than 3s. for the book. My idea is this, to have a simpler cover for the 3s. copies, which will, no doubt, be the ones usually sold, but to offer the gorgeous covers also at 4s., which will be bought by the rich and those who wish to give them as presents. What I want you to do is to take 'Alice' as a guide [the first Macmillan edition of *Alice in Wonderland* is bound in red cloth and has gilt roundel-pictures of Alice and the pig on the front and the Cheshire Cat on the back with gilt rules round the edges and gilding on the spine], and design covers requiring about the same amount of gold, or, better, a little less. As 'Alice' and the 'Looking-Glass' have both got grotesque faces outside, I should like *these* to be pretty, as a contrast, and I don't think we can do better than to take the head of 'Hope' for the first side, and 'Care' [another figure in the picture of *The Hunting*] for the second: and, as these are associated with 'forks' and 'thimbles' in the poem, what do you think of surrounding them, one with a border of interlaced forks, the other with a shower of thimbles? And what do you think of putting a bell at each corner of the cover, instead of a single line? The only thing to secure is that the total amount of gold required shall be rather less than on the covers of 'Alice.' All these are merely suggestions: *you* will be a far better judge of the matter than I can be, and perhaps may think of some quite different, and better, design." Holiday, to whose artistic judgment Dodgson so delicately deferred, in fact followed Dodgson's suggestion, for his exquisite roundel-head of "Hope" survives.[60] If he also drew a head of "Care," it has not turned up.

On 15 January, the same day as Dodgson wrote to Holiday, Macmillan wrote again about the covers. He told Dodgson that he had had a long talk with the binder about various ways of doing them, and promised to send specimens the following week; and two days later he wrote again to say that he was trying to "get up some specimen covers, with the gold and black interspersed in such a way as to lessen the cost" which the binder would have ready in four or five days.[61] By this time, the 17th, Dodgson must have told Macmillan's of his latest approach to Holiday, because on that same day he wrote a letter to George Craik, Macmillan's partner, in terms which imply that the firm already knew of it. He began by asking Craik to advertise the *Snark* "to be published on the 1st of April." "Surely," he said, "that is the fittest day for it to appear?" Then he gave directions about the new covers. "When Mr. Holiday has designed the simpler covers I have asked him to do, I suppose they had better begin printing covers at once, as 1000

58. Ibid.
59. Holiday, *The Academy*, p. 129, reprinted in *Letters*, pp. 238–39.

60. See drawing no. 9 (plate XIII) below.
61. BLMD.

must take a long time to prepare. The *colour* had better be red, I think, to match 'Alice.' And don't you think, with such a thin book, it will look best to print the title lengthways [the title on the spine of *Alice in Wonderland* having been printed horizontally], as here drawn? [Here he appended a sketch with the title lengthways on the spine and squiggles indicating "Hope" and "Care" in the centers of the covers.] The 'richly emblazoned' copies I should like done in that dark blue cloth which Mr. Holiday recommended."[62]

On 19 January, back in Christ Church after his Christmas vacation, Dodgson finished the text of the *Snark* in its final form, as he recorded in his Diary: "Wrote stanza 'In the matter of Treason' [Fit 6], completing poem."[63] It was now 141 stanzas long.

Next, having considered the relative prices of the various specimens the binder had prepared, he put his mind once more to the engrossing matter of the covers. Macmillan, who seems to have been out of his office during the second half of January, leaving Craik in charge, did not apparently write again until 2 February, when he told Dodgson that the cost of binding in black would be just about half that of using gold; and he added: "I send all these covers to see if any of them satisfied you. I like the black very much myself and it would enable us to sell the book at 3/6 I think."[64] Dodgson replied the next day with eight questions, including these. Third, with regard to a question he had raised in a lost letter of 15 January, which presumably mentioned his recent proposal to Holiday: "What do you think of the plan of having *two* prices? a simple cover at (say) 3/–, and a richly decorated one at 1/– extra?" Fourth, repeating the suggestion he had made on 17 January to Craik, he said: "I should like it advertised 'will be published on the 1st of April.' Do you approve?" Fifth, he again said that he thought the title on the spine should be printed lengthways, and asked whether

Macmillan approved, adding: "And should it be in plain type, or shall I ask Mr. Holiday to draw fantastic letters for it?" Seventh, referring to a lost letter he wrote on 1 February, he asked: "Can the covers you have sent me be used for binding copies for me to give away?" And eighth, referring to another lost letter of 1 February, he asked: "Could covers be done on red cloth like 'Alice,' but substituting white, grey or cream-colour, for gold? What price would they be?"

Then Dodgson summed up his ideas. "Now as to the covers. I think, for *gold*, the best colour is red—the same red as 'Alice.' It is far more taking than the blue Mr. Holiday advised. *That* would have done beautifully for a volume of poems meant for aesthetic adults. *This* book is meant for children. I don't at all like the mixture of black and gold, and I don't like any of the other covers—except the plain black and grey, which is a nice contrast, and would look well if the black and grey could be interchanged within the border: but that of course cannot be. As it is, with a nigger bellman, a black sail, and scalloped [here he inserted a little drawing of scalloped shape] clouds (caused by converting into *clouds* what should be sky *between* clouds) it won't do at all. My present ideas tend towards—cream-colour on red (the white being *sunk* will protect it from soiling) at 3/— —gold on red at 4/–. What say you?" And he ended: "Clay will be able to go to press long before the end of February. The text is all in type already."[65]

This letter clearly reveals that Dodgson had now drastically reduced his plans for the covers. He still wanted the covers to be of two qualities at different prices, but he now recognized that any gilding on the cheaper binding would be too costly. It had to be either a mixture of black and grey (the combination in fact finally adopted) or, as he inclined to prefer, a mixture of cream and red, while for the dearer binding he now preferred, not Holiday's overly aesthetic blue with gold, but gold with red. Secondly, he had now given up the idea of having roundels of "Hope" and "Care" on the cheaper

62. RDM.
63. *Diaries*, p. 349.
64. BLMD.

65. RDM.

bindings. *Both* qualities of binding were now to display the original designs of the Bellman and the bell-buoy, for which the brass blocks had been ready since late November of the previous year. The only thing still seriously wrong with them was that the printed and unprinted areas of the front cover were illogically reversed. Dodgson presumably told Macmillan about his decision to drop the idea of "Hope" and "Care" roundels in his missing letter of 1 February.

Next day, 4 February, Macmillan sent Dodgson a warning message: "Do you want us to advertise April 1 *now*? You have not got your blocks yet [i.e., those for the illustrations]. Won't it do if we begin to advertise say in the March Mags. Please tell me if you are now sure of getting the blocks in time."[66] Dodgson replied on the 5th with another most informative letter. He began by thanking Macmillan for answering all his questions and by expressing his strong objection to any electrotypes being sent across the Atlantic for the proposed American edition of the book (of which he approved). Then he went on: "I very much like the idea of black and grey done the reverse way. . . . Please have one block cut so at once and let me see the effect. For my own 200 copies I shall want gold on red. I don't want them sent round to the booksellers, but surely there would be no harm by advertising that copies may be had, bound to match 'Alice' and with designs in gold, at 1/– extra? . . . I am sorry that a cream-coloured pigment is so fearfully difficult to obtain. I should have thought you might have advertised for a ton of it and got it in a week. However the black and grey will look nearly as well and will last better. If you approve of advertising for April 1, and don't think the public will regard it as a hoax, you will be the best judge as to when to begin. *I* should have thought about the middle of February[67] but if you

think that too soon, do as you think best." Then about the pictures: "I have no doubt at all that the picture-blocks will be ready by the 20th. 7 of the 9 are cut already (though needing some finishing touches) and the other 2 I believe are in hand. I will ask Mr. Holiday to draw title for back." And finally he said in a caustic postscript: "In cutting the new cover-block they may as well avoid the mistake they made in the present one, of putting a star in front of the rigging!"[68]

Next day, 6 February, Dodgson launched another idea: "Now for a suggestion which has just occurred to me. When you get the lengthways title cut for the back of the book, I want you to print it (or the same words in ordinary type, which would do just as well) on the paper wrapper. The letters had better slope a good deal, so as to be easily read as the book stands upright. The advantage will be that it can stand in bookstalls without being taken out of paper, and so can be kept in cleaner and more saleable condition [here a drawing of the wrapper with lengthways sloping letters]." And as if Macmillan had not extra chores enough, he imposed another: "I should like the same thing done for 'Alice' and the 'Looking-Glass' for the future—and even those on hand, which are already wrapped in plain paper, might be transferred into printed covers:— of course *I* would pay for the trouble of transferring—which may perhaps be a day's work for one of your men."[69] So in addition to his other gifts to typography Dodgson seems to have been the pioneer of the modern printed dust-jacket.[70]

On the night of 10 February Dodgson wrote a new preface for the book;[71] and next day he sent Macmillan two designs of Holiday's for the title

66. BLMD.

67. An accurate prediction. On 12 February Dodgson noted in his Diary: "This evening the *Pall Mall* contained the announcement (in substance what I had told Mr. Greenwood [the editor of *The St. James's Gazette*] a few days ago) of my Easter book" (*Diaries*, p. 350).

68. RDM.

69. Ibid.

70. Goodacre records that the few surviving dust-jackets reproduce the title page on the front and have the title on the spine in roman capitals (see "The Listing" below). An example is illustrated in *The Library*, 5th Series, 26 (June 1971), plate 6. Cf. Morgan, *The House of Macmillan*, p. 110, and Derek Hudson, *Lewis Carroll* (London: Constable, 1954), p. 222.

71. *Diaries*, p. 350.

on the spine, of which he preferred the one with the smaller letters. In spite of all the discussions about it he was still, however, not quite happy about the color of the binding: "Is there any other pigment besides black that could be used? If so, I should like to see specimens. Mr. Holiday wants to give his opinion on the colour for the cheaper cover. I am telling him he had better communicate with you. For the *dearer* covers I hold to 'Alice' red, and gold." In the postscript he said that he was sending his new preface to Clay to be printed smaller than the main text: "I think a book looks very bad when the Preface is more handsomely printed than the text: the contrast should always be the other way."[72]

Meanwhile, as he noted on 5 February in his Diary, he had been at work on the *Easter Greeting*— the thing that later so moved the tender heart of John Henry Newman[73]—which he wanted to slip into the early issues of the *Snark*: "In the afternoon I wrote a large piece of MS. for *An Easter Letter* which I am again thinking of printing to insert in copies of my Easter book. I am afraid the religious allusions will be thought 'out of season' by many, but I do not like to lose the opportunity of saying a few serious words to (perhaps) 20,000 children."[74] The text of this tiny pamphlet was not in fact finished until nearly two months later.

On 19 February Macmillan reported: "The block for the black on grey is being cut. It is a long and expensive process. The only other pigment that can be used is red—which certainly would not do. We are bound I fear to the black and grey you saw—only reversed—if we are to be in time. You have no idea of the work required to get any of these experiments made." He also told Dodgson that, following Holiday's pattern, the lettering on the dust-jacket of the *Snark* would be taken from

the book; that the dust-jackets for *Alice* and *The Looking-Glass* were being printed and would be put on as soon as possible; that the binder was taking the one of Holiday's drawings for the lettering of the spine that would cut most effectively;[75] and that he entirely agreed about the way the preface, of which Dodgson had received a proof, should be printed. On 1 March Dodgson was protesting that he had so far received no more book-covers or any proofs of the illustrations, and he was wondering if the electrotyping of the pictures had yet started.[76]

Next day Macmillan posed him a problem that had to be solved at once if the book was to come out on 1 April: "Swain the engraver pleads for the book being worked from *wood*. If we do 10,000 from these delicate cuttings you will get little more if any use of the blocks. There is a dark block cut [*The Vanishing*, Fit 8] which seems to me impossible to render in ink. Even in proof it is very far from being intelligible. Now what about some [of] the others you have coming? The nine proofs go by this post. The cover will be all right. Decide at once please about electroing or otherwise or we shall all be in a mess."[77] Dodgson's peremptory reply to this the following day, 3 March, was characteristic of his unhurried perfectionism: "*On no account whatever* are the wood-blocks to be used for printing from. That is *one* fixed principle I wish to be borne in mind: and another is:—The date of publishing is not to interfere *in the least* with the goodness of the printing, binding, etc. If necessary, postpone the publishing: but take *full* time to produce a first-rate article. I had rather wait another year, if necessary, than have it fall short of the best we can do. The dark picture will do very well, I think. That it should not look intelligible is one of its merits! The 9 proofs (which arrived safe this morning) complete the thing. There are no more to come. I should like to *see* a specimen of the 'reversed' grey and black cover before it is settled

72. RDM.

73. Cf. Newman's letter to Helen Church, daughter of the Dean of St. Paul's, quoted in Dodgson's letter of 14 May 1876 to Helen Feilden (*Letters*, pp. 250–51).

74. *Diaries*, pp. 349–50. On the *Easter Greeting* see *Handbook*, pp. 92–95, Goodacre, "Lewis Carroll's *Easter Greeting*," *Notes and Queries* (19 July 1972), and *Letters*, p. 250, note 1; on the recipients, *Letters*, pp. 247–48, note 2, 317, 383, 621, note.

75. The spine of the printed book is lettered in large sloping capitals: · THE · HUNTING · OF · THE · SNARK ·

76. RDM.

77. BLMD.

on. Please advertise for April 1 as long as there is a hope of our getting it out by that date."[78] On the same day, crossing letters, Macmillan wrote: "Will you kindly return the thickness copy of the Snark which you had. Till he has this back the binder cannot finish off the new cases he has in hand."[79]

The proofs of the pictures were not entirely to Dodgson's satisfaction, so he asked Swain to make corrections. "Swain tells us," wrote Macmillan on the 7th, "that you have given them instructions for some changes in cutting that will cause two or three days' delay. I would rather get the whole in the Printer's hands before advertising the April 1. Tell me whenever you are *quite* satisfied, and then we will go ahead. The price should be 3/6 and only one style *generally* advertised. We can put a slip in to tell people who want the red cloth and Field of Gold—oh! it should be Field of Cloth of Gold, shouldn't it? and are willing to bob up one more that their wish can be gratified. But I think we will do well to keep one price and style as a rule."[80] Nor had Dodgson, even yet, finally decided on the exact color of the covers of the regular edition. On Friday, 10 March, Macmillan sent him two specimens and observed: "I myself like the lighter one as being the most effective. As it will have a wrapper it will not be more apt to soil than the darker, and the dark cloth, though pretty in itself does not throw up the design half so well. I hope you will be able to let the blocks go to the printer not later than Monday or I fear the chance of April 1 will be small."[81]

But meanwhile Dodgson seems to have raised other queries with further directions, for on Saturday the 11th Macmillan felt constrained to reply: "We really must go straight on now with no pauses if possible to enquire what we can and what we cannot do under certain contingencies, which take no end of time and work to discover. I *think* we can get out by April 1 now the binding is settled. We will carry out your telegram instructions about the lettering on the back. But we could not let you see more proofs of the sheets without actual risk. Surely if you gave the instructions clearly there will be no risk of anything going wrong."[82] To this the unruffled Dodgson rejoined on the 12th: "What you say about 'enquiries we can or cannot do under certain contingencies' puzzles me. I want you to go straight on, without pausing to think of 'contingencies,' only being careful that nothing suffers from hurry, the exact day of publishing being of much less importance than the doing all thoroughly well."[83]

There was also the final positioning of the pictures to attend to, on which Dodgson rather fussily wrote in the same letter, at the same time voicing the perennial complaint of authors: "As to the Dedication, I am nearly in despair: they seem unable to correct one part of it without getting another part wrong." On 15 March Macmillan gently patted the ball back into Dodgson's court, pointing out that he and Holiday had failed to give any indication on the page proofs of where the pictures should go in the book, though he assured him that the omission would cause no delay because the electrotyping would take two days more, by which time they would have "all ready to work off carefully."[84] This was a rare oversight on Dodgson's part, especially since, contrary to common Victorian practice, he no doubt deliberately put no verses or titles under the illustrations, as in the *Alice*s. That was another little problem for his child-readers to puzzle out for themselves.

By 17 March Dodgson himself was having qualms

78. RDM.
79. BLMD.
80. Ibid. Dodgson was much concerned that the dearer copies should not be advertised in the cheaper grey and black ones for fear of embarrassing those who bought the latter as gifts. "This difficulty," he wrote to Macmillan on 17 March, "might be avoided by having the advertisement on a loose fly-leaf—but I fancy the best plan will be to advertise the red and gold copies in the newspapers only, and *not* in the grey and black copies. Could not the advertisement end something like this. 'Copies with the outside designs in gold may be had as follows:—Cloth 4/6—morocco –/– vellum –/–'?" On this point see Goodacre, "*The Hunting*," pp. 112–13.
81. BLMD.

82. Ibid.
83. RDM.
84. BLMD.

about meeting the target date. "We are running it *very* fine for April 1," he wrote to Macmillan, "and I am beginning to be nervous about the pictures not being 'made up' properly, or the sheets being hastily dried. . . . *Please* remember that even as late as April 9 (say) would do perfectly well."[85]

During the later days of March Dodgson was much preoccupied with getting a large number of copies of the *Snark* bound up in a variety of colors and styles for presentation to his special friends. In his letter of 17 March he asked Macmillan: "Have you any technical name for that greenish blue which Mr. Holiday chose for the cover? I shall want you to bind me some copies in it, and it would be convenient to have a name for it when I want to order it"; and on the 21st he wrote: "I am sending you the 2 covers, to be returned to me as they are, after noting the colours. I shall speak of them as 'dark blue' and the 'dark green', unless you can give me more definite names. . . . I want you to bind for me:—100 in red and gold (of course gold on *both* sides), 20 in dark blue and gold, 20 in dark green and gold, 2 in white vellum and gold.[86] An artistic friend suggests that these 2 ought to have 'red gold' edges. Do you know the phrase?" About these 142 presentation copies Dodgson wrote again to Macmillan on 26 March, asking when they

would be ready for him to inscribe: "If you *could* get the two vellum ones done first, and send them to me here [Christ Church], I should be glad—as I should like to send off these two *as soon as possible*. If you *do* send them, you might put a couple of each other colour along with them. But if the vellum cannot be done sooner than the rest, I may as well come to town and write in them: I can come any day, if you will let me know when you can undertake to have them ready for me—the sooner the better."[87]

But still he had not yet completed his *Easter Greeting* which he had begun to compose early in February. This apparent procrastination was probably deliberate like everything else he did. Consistently, from the beginning of the voyage which he had kept on its close-hauled course with such adroit seamanship, he had regarded the *Snark* not as a money-making venture (though he kept a weather eye on that side too), but as a gift to Gertrude Chataway, to the other child-friends of his intimate acquaintance, and to the thousands of anonymous children beyond, whose hearts he had won by his *Alice* books. It looks therefore as if he wanted to see his whole nonsense-poem perfectly in order before he sat back to lay his *ultima manus* on his serious poetic message to his child-friends at large. On 22 March, at 2:30 in the morning, he recorded in his Diary: "I have been sitting up, finishing the MS. of a little 'Easter Letter' to be put into copies of *The Snark*. The book is now printing off."[88]

Four days later, on 26 March, having already received one proof of the *Easter Greeting*, he asked to see another if time allowed. If not, he begged Macmillan to make sure that his corrections of the first proof were properly made, that there were equal margins around the border-line, and that the letterpress on the first page, held up to the light, precisely registered with that of the second. He also requested Macmillan to put copies of the *Greeting* into all copies of the *Snark* that were likely

85. RDM.
86. One vellum copy inscribed "Gertrude Chataway / with the Author's love. / Mar: 29. / 1876" is in the Alfred C. Berol Collection, New York University. The other was bound for Holiday who recorded (*The Academy*, p. 129, and *Reminiscences*, p. 246) the gift and the dedicatory inscription: "Presented to Henry Holiday, / most patient of Artists, / by Charles L. Dodgson, / most exacting, but not / most ungrateful of Authors. / Mar. 29. 1876." Below the dedication there is written in Holiday's hand: "Henry Holiday / June 12, 1923 / with cordial greetings to the / Snarks and Boojums / of the Snark Soc." Holiday's copy is now in the Morris L. Parrish Collection in Princeton University Library. Regarding the epithets Dodgson applied to himself and Holiday cf. the late recollection of Mrs. A. T. Waterhouse, *née* Ruth Gamlen, a child-friend whom Dodgson met in 1892 (cf. *Diaries*, p. 491, and *Letters*, p. 905, note 2), which was published by Derek Hudson (*Lewis Carroll*, p. 316): "He told me a great many stories about the funny little girls he had met upon the beach at Eastbourne, and after dinner we had a most confidential talk about illustrators, how obstinate and tiresome they were, more especially Holiday, who had given him infinite trouble over *The Hunting of the Snark*."

87. RDM.
88. *Diaries*, p. 350.

to sell before the end of April, as well as into both *Alices*, and to keep "a few hundreds" spare.[89] To this Macmillan responded the next day: "You cannot have proof of the Letter without hazard to its getting into the books. We will do our best to have one in each copy of it and *Alice*—and her progeny. The binder has 5000 copies and is binding them, doing your private and peculiars first. . . . I shall hear I suppose tomorrow whether you are coming on Wednesday [29 March]."[90] This letter of Macmillan's must, in fact, have reached Dodgson in Oxford that afternoon, because that same day he sent off a rather donnish reply: "You don't say whether it is Wednesday *morning* or *afternoon* that you mean. Unless you telegraph to the contrary tomorrow, I shall interpret it 'morning' and shall most likely be with you soon after 11, returning here the same day. If the books cannot be warranted to be ready so soon, I had better come on Thursday morning instead." And in the next paragraph we hear, for the first time, of another of Dodgson's last-minute proposals: "I am glad to hear that the tissue-paper is a needless precaution —but that last picture [*The Vanishing*] looks a bit dangerous without it—as also the masses of dead black on page 5 [*The Crew on Board*]."[91]

All went well as first arranged. On Wednesday, 29 March, Dodgson recorded: "Went up to town for the day, and spent from eleven till nearly five at Macmillan's writing in about 80 presentation copies of *The Snark*. . . . Returned to Christ Church by last train, and sat up till long after midnight, recording names of those to whom I have sent

Snarks."[92] For Dodgson, who was prepared to sign the presentation copies a day later, the true publication-date, after all, was All Fools' Day; Macmillan's recorded it as 29 March.[93]

II

I will now survey and catalogue (a) Henry Holiday's known drawings for the *Snark*, (b) the known proofs of Swain's cuts, and (c) the surviving woodblocks of the nine illustrations. These are preserved in Bryn Mawr College Library, in the Library of Princeton University, in two American private collections, and in the Toronto Public Library. The basic publications relating to them are the catalogues of the Carroll Centenary exhibitions mounted in 1932 by Messrs. Bumpus in London and by Columbia University in New York.[94]

(a) *The Drawings*

These are in three batches. The first batch of nine drawings was acquired directly from Holiday (d. 1927)[95] by Harold Hartley (1851–1943) of Brook House, North Stoke, Oxfordshire, who exhibited them with other Carrolliana of his at Bumpus's in 1932. They comprised, in the words of the catalogue, (i) Item 472: "Eight original drawings by Henry Holiday, for illustrations. Fit the First. The Landing. Fit the Second. The Bellman's Speech. Fit the Third. The Baker's Tale. Fit the Fourth. The Hunting. Fit the Fifth. The Beaver's Lesson. Fit the Sixth. The Barrister's Dream. Fit the Seventh. The Banker's Fate. Fit the Eighth. The Vanishing"; (ii) Item 473: "An original drawing by Henry Holiday of an illustration ('The Snark'),

89. RDM.

90. BLMD.

91. RDM. All the pictures in Princeton's vellum-bound copy, inscribed on 29 March 1876, are guarded by tissue-paper. The same is true of the Rosenbach red and gold copy inscribed on 29 March to Kate Terry Lewis, and of the Princeton white and gold copy inscribed on 24 April to Margaret Evelyn Hardy. Bryn Mawr College has a copy of the ordinary buff-colored first issue with tissue-paper over the frontispiece. In the tissue-papered copies I have seen the tissue has foxed the title page, but not the later pages opposite pictures. This indicates that the title page was printed on paper of different make from that used for the bulk of the book.

92. *Diaries*, p. 351.

93. *Handbook*, p. 90.

94. *The Lewis Carroll Centenary in London 1932*, ed. Falconer Madan (London: Messrs. J. and E. Bumpus, Ltd., 1932), pp. 80–82 (hereafter *London Cat.*). *Catalogue of an Exhibition at Columbia University to Commemorate the One Hundredth Anniversary of the Birth of Lewis Carroll (Charles Lutwidge Dodgson) 1832–1898* (New York: Columbia University Press, 1932), pp. 31–33 (hereafter *New York Cat.*).

95. Harold Hartley, "Lewis Carroll and His Artists and Engravers," *London Cat.*, p. 114.

unpublished and never engraved . . .''; (iii) Item 476: "A pencil drawing of 'Hope,' see illustration (the Hunting), by Henry Holiday"; and (iv) Item 477: "A small pencil drawing of 'Hope' with an anchor, by Henry Holiday, intended for a decoration of the cover, but not used.''[96]

These drawings next passed in 1934 or 1935 into the hands of Erwin O. Freund (d. 1948) whose widow exhibited a large selection of her Carroll treasures at the Art Gallery of the University of Miami from December 1950 to January 1951. The exhibition was then noticed in the *Miami Herald* by Doris Reno, who reported that "about 15 of the 20 *Snark* drawings by Henry Holiday" were there receiving their first showing in the United States. She told how Mr. Freund, a special lover of the *Snark*, while on one of his visits to England, had got in touch with Mr. Hartley, then aged eighty-four, who had sold him "his whole collection of Carroll material." On Mrs. Freund's death in 1975 her Carroll Collection passed into private hands; and by courtesy of the present owners the surviving Hartley-Freund *Snark* drawings and proofs—along with the Princeton and Howe-West drawings for the *Snark* to be described later—were exhibited at Bryn Mawr College from 15 March to 15 July 1979.

The particulars of the Hartley-Freund *Snark* drawings are as follows:

1. *The Landing* (frontispiece)   Plate v
Compositional design by Holiday, in graphite pencil on paper, laid down on cardboard. Board, 25.3×17.7 cms.; image, 13.2×8.8 cms., the same size as Swain's cut. Signed in pencil on the image: H.H.; on the board: Henry Holiday.
Several differences from the published cut, notably the inclusion of birds at top left, the omission of the bobstay and hawse-pipes of the ship, and the overlapping of the Banker's arm by the Bellman's leg.

2. *The Crew on Board* (Fit 1)   Plate vi
Compositional design by Holiday, in graphite pencil on paper, laid down on cardboard. Board, 25.3×17.7 cms.; image, 13.1×8.8 cms., almost the same size as Swain's cut (13×8.7 cms.). Signed in pencil on the image: H.H.; on the board: Henry Holiday.

96. *London Cat.*, pp. 80–81.

Notable differences from the published cut are the unbearded Bellman, the less well-defined mast, the indistinct head of the Barrister, the more drastically cut-off head of the Billiard-marker, the indistinct Bonnet-maker, and the aggressively Semitic head of the Broker in the right bottom corner.

3. *The Butcher and the Beaver* (Fit 1)   Plate vii
Compositional design by Holiday, in graphite pencil on paper, laid down on cardboard. Board, 25.3×17.7 cms.; image, 8.8×13.2 cms., nearly the same size as Swain's cut (9×13.2 cms.). Signed in pencil on the image: H.H.; on the board: Henry Holiday.
Considerable differences from the published cut: the Butcher has no peak to his cap and no sleeves, and the coil of rope is on the left rather than behind the ventilator.

4. *The Baker's Tale* (Fit 3)   Plate viii
Compositional design by Holiday, in graphite pencil on paper, laid down on cardboard. Board, 25.3×17.7 cms.; image, 13.2×8.9 cms., practically the same size as Swain's cut (13.2×8.8 cms.). Signed in pencil on the image: H.H.; on the board: Henry Holiday.
Compared to Swain's cut, it omits the Bellman's bell and the latticed window, shows the whole ship, puts the bales in a different position, omits the Uncle's bedhead and the picture, beam, bottle and glass above it, and also the Baker's bag.

5. *The Beaver's Lesson* (Fit 5)   Plate ix
Compositional design by Holiday, in graphite pencil on paper, laid down on cardboard. Board, 25.3×17.7 cms.; image, 13.1×8.8 cms., nearly the same size as Swain's cut (13.2×9 cms.). Signed in pencil on the image: H.H.; on the board: Henry Holiday.
Numerous differences from the published cut: e.g., it omits the "creepy creature" pouring ink on the Butcher's head, the cats at bottom left, and the winged monster's tail to the left; many of the "creepy creatures" are different or undefined, notably the tootling pigs on the right; and the inkwell is in another position. The drawing labels the anti-fundamentalist Bishop Colenso's books "Colenso Arithmetic" and "Bridge," whereas the cut arranges them differently and labels them "Colenso Arithmetic" and "On the Reductio ad Absurdum."

6. *The Barrister's Dream* (Fit 6)   Plate x
Compositional design by Holiday, in graphite pencil on paper, laid down on cardboard. Board, 25.3×17.7 cms.; image, 9×13.1 cms., the same size as Swain's cut.

Signed in pencil on the image: H.H.; on the board: Henry Holiday.

Very considerable differences from Swain's cut, especially in the ominous winglike shape of the Snark's gown, the position of the bell, the size of the Barrister's head, the pose of the Judge, and the poses and expressions of the four members of the Jury at top right. The greatest difference, however, is in tonality. In this drawing the figures beyond the dream-cloud are tonally overemphatic, not contrasting with the head of the sleeping Barrister; in the cut the fact that it is a dream-picture is clearly indicated by the strong contrast between the emphatic Barrister's head and the generally light tonality of the whole scene he dreams about.

7. *The Vanishing* (Fit 8) Plate XI

Compositional design by Holiday, in sepia pen and wash on paper, laid down on cardboard. Board, 25.3×17.7 cms.; image, 13.1×8.9 cms., almost the same size as Swain's cut (13.2×8.9 cms.). Signed in pencil on the image: H.H.; on the board: Henry Holiday.

Generally fairly close to the cut, but less linear; the foliage at bottom left is omitted and the rocks are less emphatic and differently lighted.[97]

8. *The Snark-Boojum* Plate XII

Compositional design by Holiday, in graphite pencil on paper, laid down on cardboard. Board, 25.3×17.8 cms.; image, 13.2×8.8 cms. Signed in pencil on the image: H.H.; on the board: Henry Holiday.

Identical with *London Cat.*, item 473. The drawing was never used because, as Holiday explained,[98] Dodgson did not want the unimaginable Boojum to be

97. Drawings 1–7, all mounted on cardboard of uniform size and make, are undoubtedly identical with those lent by Hartley to Bumpus's exhibition in 1932 as item 472, but the catalogue entry is inaccurate. Contrary to what it says, Fit 1 was illustrated, not by one, but by three pictures (*The Landing*, *The Crew on Board*, *The Butcher and the Beaver*), and Fit 2 has no illustration but the blank map. In Mr. Freund's surviving copy of *London Cat.*, moreover, the initial word "Eight" is corrected in manuscript—apparently not in Freund's hand but perhaps in Hartley's—into "Nine." Hence it would appear that two drawings, *The Hunting* (Fit 4) and *The Banker's Fate* (Fit 7), have gone astray. The identity of *London Cat.*, item 476 ("A pencil drawing of 'Hope' . . ."), is obscure. For though the catalogue distinguishes between this drawing and another of "Hope" (i.e., item 477, which is clearly identical with the Hartley-Freund drawing no. 9 listed below), the former has not turned up. If there *were* two drawings of Hope in the exhibition, it means that three Hartley-Freund *Snark* drawings have gone astray.

98. Holiday, *The Academy*, p. 129.

depicted. Holiday's account is given on p. 4 above. The drawing was twice reproduced at the time of the London exhibition.[99]

9. *Hope* Plate XIII

Head and bust of "Hope" with her anchor set in a circle within a square, with the legend HOPE within the roundel to the left. Graphite pencil on paper, laid down on cardboard and matted; image, 10×7.9 cms. Signed in pencil on the surround: H.H.

Identical with *London Cat.*, item 477. This was Holiday's second design, never used, for the front cover of the book (see p. 91 above).[100]

The second batch of drawings is preserved—along with five of Swain's proofs and the related correspondence—in the Morris L. Parrish Collection in Princeton University Library (MS.AM19267). Its history is well recorded. In a memorandum dated 1 March 1923 Mr. H. C. Smith of Dutton's, the New York publishers, a member of a New York Carrollian club called "The Snarks Ltd.," told the club the story of how, at their general meeting in 1922, "a tall young Boojum suggested the happy idea of trying to find an original drawing for the Snark book," and of how the idea had been more than realized. Smith had enquired of George Sutcliffe, of the London bookbinding firm of Sangorski and Sutcliffe, and Sutcliffe had approached Holiday ("a dear old gentleman still alive and in the best of health," as Smith described him to the club), who responded with a letter which it will be useful to have in full:

Wansfell, 18 Chesterfield Gardens,
Hampstead, N.W. 3
March 13. 22

Dear Sir,

I have been trying to find out the whereabouts of the original "Snark" drawings, and wrote to Mr. Batsford of High Holborn, whose Uncle purchased them in 1907, but he finds no record of the transaction though he has reason to believe they went to America; so I think we can take it that what I now send are the only available drawings remaining from the preparations for the "Snark."

99. In *The Listener* (29 June 1932) and *The Illustrated London News* (9 July 1932).

100. The Hartley-Freund drawings and proofs were traced by James Tanis in 1978.

I enclose a list with prices. I have not given any indication what the different sketches were for because I thought it might afford a little amusement to find them out, but I may say that the drawing of a hand in the top left-hand corner of no. 4 is that of the Banker in the Chase holding a tuning-fork, the arm to the right of that I cannot identify. All the others I think will be discoverable.

I am sending you 5 first proofs and you will notice that the Broker in no. 5 [*The Crew on Board*, Fit 1] is quite different to the one in no. 2. I had intended to give a caricature of a vulgar specimen of the profession, but Lewis Carroll took exception to this and asked me to treat the head in a less aggressive manner, and no. 2 is the result. I consider that no. 5 has much more character, but I understood L. Carroll's objection, and agreed to tone him down.

I was told by a friend who understands these matters, a unique print of this kind was worth 3 times the ordinary proof. I have not charged quite so much as this.

It may interest you and your client to hear that Lewis Carroll at first criticised my introduction of the 2 allegorical figures of "Care" and "Hope" in the Chase [*The Hunting*, Fit 4], and thought I had missed his point of using the word "with" in the 2 senses of the means or instrument and the mental attitude.[101] I answered that on the contrary I had specially noted those two senses and in the same spirit I had added a new one of my own in "company with." He cordially accepted this and said, "By all means let the ladies join the Chase."

Yours sincerely,
Henry Holiday

P.S. I asked Lewis Carroll when first I read his M.S. why he made all the members of the crew have occupations beginning with B. He replied "Why not?"[102]

On 24 March Sutcliffe wrote to tell Smith that he was forwarding Holiday's *Snark* drawings and proofs on approval, hoping that neither set would be broken up; and with them a drawing by Holi-

day for *Sylvie and Bruno*. The Snarks Ltd. immediately bought the *Snark* drawings and prints *en bloc*, but apparently not the drawing for *Sylvie and Bruno*. In June 1923, feeling the postwar pinch which made the time, as he said, "a very hard one for Artists," Holiday sold the club for £25 his treasured vellum-bound copy of the *Snark* presented and dedicated to him by Dodgson. On 1 May 1950 The Snarks Ltd. deposited their Snarkiana in Princeton Library; and on 15 March 1967 the University purchased them.

The Snarks Ltd.'s six *Snark* drawings and five *Snark* proofs were exhibited at Columbia in 1932 (*New York Cat.*, item 75), along with their vellum-bound presentation copy of the book (item 74c).

These are the particulars of the Princeton drawings:

10. *The Landing* (frontispiece)   Plate XIV
Nude life-study for the Bellman in graphite pencil on paper, squared for reduction, 27×14.5 cms., much larger than Swain's cut (13.2×8.8 cms.). Inscribed at top right: "Gaetano G," referring to the model, Gaetano Giuseppi Alfonso Faustino Meo.* Signed in heavier pencil: H. H. Inscribed on the verso by Holiday in heavy pencil: "Study for the Bellman / in *The Landing*."

11. *The Landing* (frontispiece)   Plate XV
Sketch of the whole picture in graphite pencil on paper. Sheet, 17.8×11.4 cms.; image, 13.2×9 cms., the same size as Swain's cut. Signed on the surround in heavy pencil: H.H.

Much more summary than the Hartley-Freund design (no. 1), but showing the Bellman standing apart from the Banker, as in the final cut.

Like the Hartley-Freund drawing, it includes birds (not in the cut) at top left, but in the details of the ship it is less close to the cut than the Hartley-Freund design is.

On the verso is a pencil drawing of two vertical beams fastened together. The sheet bears the number "5" in the top left corner; an inscription (crossed out) reading: "Platform / 1.6 deeper / 1 broader"; the inscription "10 ft. broad / 8-deep"; a rough rectangle below with what appears to be the number "11" crossed out; and a small encircled number "1" in the bottom right corner. The whole is in Holiday's hand

---

101. Holiday tells the same story in *The Academy*, p. 129, and in his *Reminiscences*, p. 245.

102. Princeton MS.AM19267. Holiday probably kept all the original drawings because he engaged to supply Dodgson only with drawn-on blocks. On 22 January 1878 Dodgson wrote to Walter Crane about terms for illustrating *Bruno's Revenge*, a scheme that came to nothing: you "can either draw on the wood at once, or on paper and transfer to wood (at your own expense) keeping the drawings yourself" (Crane, *An Artist's Reminiscences* [London: Methuen and Co., 1907], pp. 185–86).

* Edward Craig most kindly identified for me Gaetano Meo, his grandfather.

except perhaps for the little encircled "1." There is no demonstrable connection between this verso and any of Holiday's designs for the *Snark*.

12. Studies and sketches for *The Crew on Board* (Fit 1), *The Baker's Tale* (Fit 3), *The Hunting* (Fit 4), *The Vanishing* (Fit 8)   Plates XVI–XVII
Cartridge-paper, 30.3×22.5 cms.

(a) Recto: Three sketches and two life-studies in graphite pencil. Inscribed at top left with the number "4" in Holiday's hand, and at the bottom right with a small encircled "6". Signed in pencil: H.H. Top row: (i) Summary compositional sketch of the Baker and the Uncle for *The Baker's Tale* (Fit 3); (ii) life-studies of the Baker's ears for *The Crew on Board* (Fit 1); (iii) summary sketch of (?) the Uncle's left arm for *The Baker's Tale*. Lower part of sheet: (iv) summary compositional sketch of *The Vanishing* (Fit 8); (v) summary sketch (upside down) of what looks a bit like a profile head, which I cannot identify; (vi) a faintly drawn series of titles in vertical rectangles: "Crew / chase / disappearing / Uncle / Bellman / butcher," referring to *The Crew on Board* (Fit 1), *The Hunting* (Fit 4), *The Vanishing* (Fit 8), *The Baker's Tale* (Fit 3), *The Landing* (frontispiece), *The Butcher and the Beaver* (Fit 1).

(b) Verso: Nine life-studies in graphite pencil. Signed in pencil: H.H. Top row: (i) the Banker's left arm in *The Hunting* (Fit 4); (ii) (?) variant study for the same; (iii) right hand of the Baker in *The Crew on Board* (Fit 1). Middle row: (iv) right leg of the Barrister in *The Hunting* (Fit 4); (v) both legs of the Barrister in the same; (vi) left hand of the Baker in *The Crew on Board* (Fit 1). Bottom row: (vii) the figure, without the head, of the Baker in *The Crew on Board* (Fit 1); (viii) the left arm of the Billiard-marker in *The Crew on Board*; (ix) the left arm and head of the same.

13. *The Baker's Tale* (Fit 3)   Plate XVIII
Life-studies in graphite pencil on cartridge-paper, 30.3×22.5 cms. Inscribed at top left in Holiday's hand: "17 Eyre Street Hill / Leather Lane. E.C. / Clutonia Cavia"; at top right: "Gaetano. Martedi. 20." The inscription perhaps refers to the name of the model, his address, and the date of a sitting (cf. drawing no. 10). "Clutonia Cavia" beats me.
Above: (i) the Baker's right hand; (ii) his left hand. Below: (iii) drapery-study of his whole figure.

14. *The Hunting* (Fit 4)   Plate XIX
Nude life-study (or the derivative of such a study)

of "Hope" in graphite pencil on paper, 38 × 16.6 cms. Signed in pencil: H.H. The left leg shows a *pentimento*.

15. *The Beaver's Lesson* (Fit 5) and *The Banker's Fate* (Fit 7)   Plate XX
Life-studies in graphite pencil on paper, 35.5×24.1 cms. Signed in pencil: H.H.
Top row: (i) figure-pose for the Banker in *The Banker's Fate*; (ii) for the Butcher pulling on his gloves in the same. Bottom row: (iii) figure-pose for the Bellman in the same; (iv) the seated Butcher for *The Beaver's Lesson*.

The third batch of drawings, comprising nine finished drawings by Holiday, in various media, for the pictures in *The Snark*, was exhibited by Mr. George Howe of Philadelphia at Columbia University in 1932 (*New York Cat.*, item 76). Mr. Howe acquired them c. 1907 from Messrs. Batsford in London, who presumably bought them from Holiday himself (cf. Holiday's letter to Sutcliffe above at p. 99). They were generously presented to Bryn Mawr College by Mr. Howe's daughter, Mrs. Walter (Helen Howe) West, Jr., in memory of her father, on 31 October 1978. (Mr. Howe also exhibited in 1932 [*New York Cat.*, item 74i] a presentation copy of *The Snark*, containing a fragment of a letter to Holiday and an original sketch by Dodgson, which has not been traced.)

The Howe-West drawings came to Bryn Mawr on cardboard mounts, bound together in a leather-covered binding designed by Holiday, who put it together before 1901. In that year five of the drawings with their mounts (nos. 16, 22, 19, 21, and 20 listed below) were cut out of the volume and lent by the artist, each with a corresponding engraving or proof by Swain, for exhibition at the Victoria and Albert Museum in London.[103] Signs of these excisions and of the subsequent replacement of the drawings into the volume were evident when it came to Bryn Mawr. In December 1978 Mrs. Marilyn Kemp Weidner of Philadelphia dis-

103. *Catalogue of the Loan Exhibition of Modern Illustration Held at the Victoria and Albert Museum, South Kensington 1901* (London: William Clowes and Sons, [1901]), items 548–52. Mr. Ronald Lightbown, Librarian of the Museum, most kindly sent me a photocopy of the catalogue entry.

membered the volume, since the drawings were in a perilous state. She preserved the leather front cover, detached the drawings from their deleterious mounts, cleaned and treated them against future damage, and mounted them on rag boards.

These are the particulars of the Howe-West drawings:

16. *The Landing* (frontispiece)   Plate XXI
Graphite pencil on clay-coated scratch-board. Board, 23.5×15.9 cms.; image, 13.2×9 cms., nearly the same size as Swain's cut (13.2×8.8 cms.). Signed in pencil: H. Holiday.

The drawing omits the ship's bobstay, which appears in the cut.

17. *The Crew on Board* (Fit 1)   Plate XXII
Black ink on paper. Sheet, 29.8×21 cms.; image, 22.7×15.3 cms., much larger than Swain's cut (13×8.7 cms.). Signed in pencil: H. Holiday.

Holiday first designed the figure of the Broker in the bottom right-hand corner in conspicuously Semitic guise, and Swain cut and submitted proofs of this version (see proof 2 [a] below). Subsequently, however, Holiday cut out this section of the drawing, substituting a mitigated drawing of the Broker's head with a davit, block and rope alongside, which he pasted into the sheet. Swain then sawed off the rejected portion of the block and glued in another (see woodblock 2 below) on which he cut the revised image.

The reason why the revision was made is given by Holiday in his letter to Sutcliffe on p. 100 above.

18. *The Butcher and the Beaver* (Fit 1)   Plate XXIII
Black ink on clay-coated scratch-board. Board, 14.1×18.9 cms.; image, 9×13.2 cms., the same size as Swain's cut. Signed in pencil: H. Holiday.

Virtually the same as the cut.

19. *The Baker's Tale* (Fit 3)   Plate XXIV
Black ink on clay-coated scratch-board. Board, 18.4×13.5 cms.; image, 13.1×9 cms., slightly smaller than Swain's cut (13.2×8.8 cms.). Signed in pencil: H. Holiday.

The details are generally very close to those of the cut, but in several passages where the cut is clear, e.g., in the area under the window, the drawing is abraded. There is a hard line at the back of the Baker's head-cloth that does not appear in the cut.

20. *The Hunting* (Fit 4)   Plate XXV
Black ink on paper. Sheet, 24×18.8 cms.; image, 18×12.2 cms., considerably larger than Swain's cut (13.4×8.8 cms.). Signed in pencil: H. Holiday.

Virtually the same as the cut.

21. *The Beaver's Lesson* (Fit 5)   Plate XXVI
Graphite pencil on clay-coated scratch-board. Board, 18.8×12.8 cms.; image, 16.2×11 cms., larger than Swain's cut (13.2×9 cms.). Signed in pencil: H. Holiday.

Virtually the same as the cut.

22. *The Barrister's Dream* (Fit 6)   Plate XXVII
Graphite pencil on clay-coated scratch-board. Board, 12.6×13.9 cms.; image, 11×16.2 cms., larger than Swain's cut (9×13.2 cms.). Signed in pencil: H. Holiday.

Very close to the cut, except that the drawing properly gives the pleading Snark a lighter, dreamlike tonality.

23. *The Banker's Fate* (Fit 7)   Plate XXVIII
Graphite pencil on clay-coated scratch-board. Board, 13.2×18.8 cms.; image, 8.9×13.2 cms., almost the same size as Swain's cut (9×13.2 cms.).

There are no significant differences between the drawing and the cut.

24. *The Vanishing* (Fit 8)   Plate XXIX
A mixture of black ink and bitumen laid on clay-coated scratch-board, the parts to be engraved being scratched out with a point to reveal the white board. Board, 18.8×14.2 cms.; image, 13.1×8.9 cms., practically the same size as Swain's cut (13.2×8.9 cms.). Signature scratched out to show in white: H. Holiday.

Generally very close to the cut, except that in the latter the foliage at bottom left is more crisply defined and the rocks are more brightly lighted. Considerable areas of the black ink and bitumen have flaked away. There are blue-white marks on the larger rocks to indicate where the lighting needed to be heightened by the engraver.[104]

104. Drawings nos. 16, 17, 19, and 20 were published by C. Mitchell in *Bryn Mawr Now*, Bryn Mawr College, 6, no. 2 (November 1978), pp. 4–5 (Corrigenda, ibid., 6, no. 3 [February 1979], p. 11). No. 17 was again reproduced by Nessa Forman, "A Modern-Day Hunt for Carroll's Snark," *The Bulletin*, Philadelphia (3 March 1979), sect. H, p. 10.

(b) *The Proofs*

The known engraver's proofs all belong to the Parrish Collection at Princeton or to the privately owned Hartley-Freund collections. The Princeton set of five,[105] acquired from The Snarks Ltd. (see p. 99 above), was exhibited in the Columbia exhibition in 1932 (*New York Cat.*, item 75). The Hartley-Freund set of ten, acquired from Harold Hartley, was listed in the London exhibition as "Nine burnished and signed proofs of illustrations by Henry Holiday" (*London Cat.*, item 474) and as "A burnished and signed proof of 'The Landing' [*The Crew on Board*], an illustration by Henry Holiday, before alteration" (*London Cat.*, item 475).

They are as follows:

1. *The Landing* (frontispiece)   Plate xxx
   (a) Princeton. Not signed in ms. (b) Hartley-Freund. Signed in ink on the surround: Henry Holiday.

2. *The Crew on Board* (Fit 1)   Plates xxxi–xxxii
   (a) First state with the exaggeratedly Semitic version of the Broker's head: (i) Princeton. Signed "Swain Sc" on the block above the Broker's head, and "H.H." at bottom left of the Broker's head. No ms signature. (ii) Hartley-Freund. Signed in ink on the surround: Henry Holiday.
   (b) Second state as published: (i) Princeton. Signed "Swain Sc" at bottom right and "H H" at bottom left of the revised Broker's head. No ms signature. (ii) Hartley-Freund. Signed in ink on the surround: Henry Holiday.

3. *The Butcher and the Beaver* (Fit 1)   Plate xxxiii
   (a) Princeton. Not signed in ms. (b) Hartley-Freund. Signed in ink on the surround: Henry Holiday.

4. *The Baker's Tale* (Fit 3)   Plate xxxiv
   Hartley-Freund. Signed as in 3(b) above.

5. *The Hunting* (Fit 4)   Plate xxxv
   (a) Princeton. Not signed in ms. (b) Hartley-Freund. Signed as in 3(b) above.

6. *The Beaver's Lesson* (Fit 5)   Plate xxxvi
   Hartley-Freund. Signed as in 3(b) above.

7. *The Barrister's Dream* (Fit 6)   Plate xxxvii
   Hartley-Freund. Signed as in 3(b) above.

8. *The Banker's Fate* (Fit 7)   Plate xxxviii
   Hartley-Freund. Signed as in 3(b) above.

9. *The Vanishing* (Fit 8)   Plate xxxix
   Hartley-Freund. Signed as in 3(b) above.

The Hartley-Freund proofs have been used to illustrate this volume.

(c) *The Woodblocks*   Plates xl–xli

All the nine original woodblocks for the illustrations of the *Snark* are preserved in the Osborne Collection of Early Children's Books, Toronto Public Library, Canada. They were offered to the Library in August 1971 by Frank Hollings, a London bookseller, and they arrived in Toronto in December 1971. The firm then stated: "these are, as far as we know, the only blocks remaining and have come into our hands directly from the Macmillan archives. They have never previously been offered for sale."[106]

Each of the blocks is composed of two pieces of boxwood bolted together; the juncture can be detected in some of the proofs and cuts. All the blocks are inked for the pulling of proofs, but they are in perfect condition because the published cuts were made from electrotypes.

The blocks may be listed as nos. 1–9 according to their order in the book.

The only blocks that call for comment are no. 2 (*The Crew on Board*, Fit 1), where a new segment of boxwood has been glued into the bottom left-hand corner of the block to accommodate the revised version of the Broker's head (cf. p. 100 and notes on drawings 2 and 17); and no. 9 (*The Vanishing*, Fit 8), where the larger rock has been recut to heighten the lighting (cf. note on drawing no. 24).

III

Eschewing higher criticism, I will now try to determine the chronology of the pictures and to define

105. One of the six prints (*The Baker's Tale*) exhibited as a proof in New York in 1932 is not a proof, but page 31 cut out from the book.

106. Warm thanks are due to Mrs. Margaret Crawford Maloney, Head of the Osborne Collection in Toronto, for kindly bringing the blocks to Bryn Mawr and for supplying information about them.

the function of Holiday's various kinds of drawings in their evolution. Then I shall make a few comments on his technique.

Dodgson's diaries and letters, along with Holiday's reminiscences, tell us a certain amount about the composition of the poem and the chronology of its illustrations. The last stanza, we remember, was written in July 1874; and by November of that year, when Dodgson consulted Ruskin about what Holiday was doing for him, he had sufficiently composed enough of the poem to commission three or four pictures, by which time *The Crew on Board* (Fit 1) was already cut. This follows from Holiday's explicit statement, which there is no reason to doubt, even though his account of the continuation of the work is rather slapdash, that Dodgson first asked him to make three pictures for three cantos or fits, and that while he was engaged on these he received a request to illustrate another canto.[107] By the end of October 1875, nearly a year later, six designs in all were done, among which *The Landing* (frontispiece) was cut. In the early days of November Dodgson was putting the finishing touches to his first 88-stanza version of the text. On the 2nd he sent Macmillan fourteen stanzas, which at once went to press. Tempting as it is to identify these with the 14-stanza Fit 3 ("The Baker's Tale"), they were most probably simply the fourteen opening stanzas of Fit 1, because on the 5th Dodgson sent off the next batch of MS to the end of Fit 3. On the 6th he wrote stanzas 2, 3, 5, and 6 of the present Fit 7 ("The Banker's Fate"), which completed the 88 stanzas, and next day he sent Macmillan the rest of the MS including the verses to Gertrude Chataway and the blank ocean chart illustrating Fit 2. He calculated that the book in this form, illustrated only by *The Landing* as a frontispiece, would run to some forty pages. Then on the 13th, a week later, he decided to make it an Easter book, which would allow him seven pictures. Meanwhile Swain could not promise to cut the unspecified blocks he had in hand before the end of January 1876. Towards the middle of that

month he delivered a number of proofs, including *The Hunting* (Fit 4).[108] By 5 February seven blocks were cut, with the last two coming up. We have no record of Dodgson's composition of the extra 53 stanzas of the final 141-stanza version of the poem, except that on 19 January 1876 he completed it by writing "In the matter of Treason...," the eighth stanza in the present Fit 6 ("The Barrister's Dream").

All we know so far about the subjects of the first six pictures is that they included *The Crew on Board*, *The Landing*, and presumably *The Vanishing* (present Fit 8), because it illustrates the first-written stanza of all. Our first step, therefore, is to try to reconstruct the makeup of the 88-stanza *Urtext*; and to do this I resort to a working hypothesis. Let us suppose that the *Urtext* included (1) the present Fit 1 ("The Landing"), (2) the present Fit 2 ("The Bellman's Speech"), (3) the present Fit 3 ("The Baker's Tale"), (4) the present Fit 4 ("The Hunting"), (5) stanzas 2, 3, 5, and 6 of the present Fit 7 ("The Banker's Fate"), and (6) at least the last stanza of the present Fit 8 ("The Vanishing"). Now it is self-evident that component (5) is too short and inconsequential to make a whole fit. So let us further suppose that the fifth and last fit of the *Urtext*, entitled "The Vanishing," started with the first stanza of the present Fit 7 ("They sought it with thimbles . . ."), which was followed by stanzas 2, 3, 5, and 6 of the same; and that the fit then ran straight on to the whole of the present Fit 8 ("The Vanishing"), save for its first stanza ("They sought it with thimbles . . .") which would have been superfluously repetitive. Thus reconstructed the *Urtext*—comprising five fits—makes a perfectly coherent poem proceeding in unbroken sequence of argument from beginning to end; and its stanzas add up to precisely 88!

Now for the makeup of the 141-stanza final version. Let us suppose that when Dodgson decided, in mid-November 1875, to expand the poem, he proceeded as follows. (I am not yet attempting to suggest a chronological order of events.) He kept

107. See p. 85 above.

108. See p. 91 above.

Fits 1–4 as they were. He composed the present Fit 5 ("The Beaver's Lesson") in 29 stanzas, and Fit 6 ("The Barrister's Dream") in 18. To constitute the present Fits 7 ("The Banker's Fate") and 8 ("The Vanishing") he divided the old Fit 5 into two. To make the former he took away stanzas 1, 2, 3, 5, and 6 from the old fit; interpolated the present fourth stanza ("He offered large discount . . ."), which has an adventitious air since the Bandersnatch had already grabbed the Banker once in the third stanza; and rounded the fit off by newly composing the present stanzas 7–10, stanza 7 ("He was black in the face . . .") being one of the last Holiday illustrated.[109] To make a separate Fit 8 ("The Vanishing") he simply prefixed the recurring exordial stanza ("They sought it with thimbles . . .") to the last eight stanzas (beginning "They shuddered to think . . .") of the old Fit 5. It is comforting to observe that the suggested added matter in the final poem adds up nicely to 53 stanzas!

If these suppositions are correct it follows—to spell it out—that the six designs which Holiday finished before the end of October 1875 to illustrate the *Urtext* were *The Landing* (frontispiece), *The Crew on Board* (Fit 1), *The Butcher and the Beaver* (Fit 1), *The Baker's Tale* (Fit 3), *The Hunting* (Fit 4) and *The Vanishing* (old Fit 5); and that to illustrate the subsequently expanded text he designed *The Beaver's Lesson* (new Fit 5), *The Barrister's Dream* (Fit 6), and *The Banker's Fate* (Fit 7).

In what order were they made? For answer we turn to the drawings. No. 12, we remember, shows on the verso life-studies for *The Crew on Board* and *The Hunting*. These are so uniform in character and they sit so tidily together on the page that they look contemporaneous, which means that they were among the first three concurrently ordered ones to be drawn. *The Vanishing*, we have supposed, was ordered first. But Dodgson rejected Holiday's first design for this, *The Snark-Boojum* (no. 8). So, remembering that *The Crew* was cut very early and that it was apparently made at the same time as

109. See p. 107 below.

The Hunting, it is very likely that Holiday executed his first designs in this order: *The Snark-Boojum*, *The Crew on Board* (the first anti-Semitic version), *The Hunting*, and *The Vanishing* (the published version).

What was the fourth picture—on which, we remember, Holiday said he embarked while he was working on the first three? The evidence here is the recto of drawing no. 12. It shows, alongside a life-study of the Baker's ears for the early-designed *Crew on Board*, preliminary compositional sketches of the second version of *The Vanishing* and of *The Baker's Tale*. Thus—if we reasonably suppose that the two preliminary sketches were drawn more or less concurrently with the developed life-studies for *The Crew* and *The Hunting* on both sides of the sheet—it follows that *The Baker's Tale* (life-studies for which occur in the separate drawing no. 13) was in all likelihood the fourth picture Holiday designed.

Which came fifth and sixth? Here our clue is the row of lightly pencilled boxes on the left-hand side of the same sheet, no. 12 recto, in which Holiday jotted down a list of subjects: " Crew / chase / disappearing / Uncle / Bellman / butcher [i.e., *The Crew on Board*, *The Hunting*, the second version of *The Vanishing*, *The Baker's Tale*, *The Landing*, and *The Butcher and the Beaver*]." The first thing that strikes one about this list of titles is that the first four are not in any order of fits, but correspond exactly with the order in which, on other evidence, it seems that the first four designs were completed. They therefore seem to record the chronological order of work done or in hand. The second less obvious point is that close inspection shows the boxes to have been drawn *after* the sketch of *The Vanishing*, because their lines overlap the sketch's faintly drawn frame. Now the list might have been added to the sheet a good time after the other drawings on it were executed, in which case—if we reasonably assume that the last two titles, like the first four, are in deliberate chronological order—we could fairly conclude (a) that *The Landing* and *The Butcher and the Beaver* were the fifth and sixth pictures commissioned and (b) that they were already made or in hand. But it seems more likely that the list was inscribed about the same time as the other drawings on the same side of the sheet (we have Holiday's recollection, for what it is worth, that Dodgson's request for the fifth picture came "shortly after" the request for the fourth).[110] In this case the reasonable inference is that the last two items record the titles of pictures commissioned but not executed. In either case, however, it is clear—if we take Holiday's list seriously—that the last two of the first six pictures Dodgson ordered were *The Landing* and *The Butcher and the Beaver*. But though that was apparently the order in which they were commissioned, it was probably not the order in which Holiday executed them. For the finished design of the latter (no. 18) was drawn, like the first four finished designs (nos. 17, 20, 24, 19), in ink, whereas the finished design of the former (no. 16), like the last three designs (nos. 21–23), was drawn in pencil. Holiday, a most methodical man, is unlikely to have drawn four pictures in ink, then to have drawn *The Landing* in pencil, and then to have switched back with *The Butcher and the Beaver* to ink before continuing his last three designs in pencil.

So what really happened? Dodgson must, in some form, have composed "The Landing," "The Hunting," and "The Vanishing" (old Fit 5) before November 1874, and it was Holiday's pictures for these—together perhaps with his drawing of "The Baker's Tale"—that Dodgson showed Ruskin on the 23rd of that month. "The Landing," with its full cast of characters, was probably the first fit to be written, because *The Crew on Board*, depicting seven of them, was cut by the time of Ruskin's visit. The second fit, the unillustrated "Bellman's Speech," must have been composed before "The Baker's Tale," because its last stanza anticipates the first stanza of the former. The *Urtext*, in short, was written, and the first four pictures were done, by the winter of 1874. Exactly when Dodgson decided to add the two extra illustrations

110. See p. 85 above.

of Fit 1, namely, *The Butcher and the Beaver* and *The Landing*, cannot be determined. But Holiday recalled that the request for the fifth picture came "shortly after" the request for the fourth, so *The Butcher*—and *The Landing* too—may well also date to the year 1874. (We *know* that both were finished, and that *The Landing* was cut, by the end of October 1875.)

Now for the cutting. In his first enthusiasm over the illustration of his new children's poem—which Ruskin did his characteristic best to damp—Dodgson got *The Crew on Board* cut at once; but then, having no plans for immediate publication, he let the thing lie fallow. He kept aside the rest of the completed drawn-on blocks, which Holiday had done *seriatim*, with the idea some day of using them in *Sylvie and Bruno*. But then in October 1875 he met Miss Chataway and his enthusiasm was rekindled. He decided to forge ahead—only to discover that Swain could not cut the required blocks before the end of January 1876.

It was not that Swain was dilatory: the reason why he could not promise to cut the blocks earlier was that he had only just received them. He was probably flooded with orders for Christmas cards and other seasonable urgencies. But before 31 October Dodgson *did* get *The Landing* cut, probably simply because it illustrated the first stanza of the poem. It was therefore conveniently available as a frontispiece for the little book he vainly hoped to get printed that Christmas. The last fact, which perfectly fits the jigsaw puzzle, is that Dodgson did not receive the proofs of *The Hunting* and other pictures until just before 15 January 1876.

Now we come to the three pictures Holiday made to illustrate the fifty-three extra stanzas of the poem: *The Beaver's Lesson* (Fit 5), *The Barrister's Dream* (Fit 6), and *The Banker's Fate* (Fit 7). Concerning their chronology, all we so far know is that on 13 November 1875 Dodgson foresaw seven pictures, if he deferred publication to Easter; and that on 5 February 1876 he told Macmillan that seven of the blocks were cut while the other two, he thought, were in hand. Which picture came seventh? Here

[106]

the clue is drawing no. 15, which shows finely drawn life-studies for *The Beaver's Lesson* and *The Banker's Fate*; and these, like those for *The Crew on Board* and *The Hunting* on sheet no. 12 verso, are so similar in handling and so well distributed on the sheet that they must again have been drawn concurrently. This strongly suggests that they were the subjects of the last two blocks Swain had to finish after 4 February 1876, which would imply that the singly designed picture of *The Barrister's Dream* was the seventh to be commissioned—a conclusion that carries the further implication that when on 13 November 1875 Dodgson foresaw seven pictures, he already contemplated, if he had not yet begun to write, a new fit on the theme of the dreaming Barrister.

It may be objected, however, that "The Barrister's Dream" was the last fit to be written because Dodgson concluded the poem, as he recorded, with the stanza "In the matter of Treason. . . ." But that is no evidence. This last-written eighth stanza of the fit introduces new charges against the poor pig of Treason and Insolvency, whereas the original charge, explicitly taken up in the ninth stanza, was simply of Desertion of his sty. The new stanza was clearly a Baroque interpolation. (Further such embroideries, introduced most probably by Dodgson but possibly by Holiday, are the extra charges of Trespass, Libel, and Contempt— not mentioned in the text—which are inscribed on the Snark's scroll in drawing no. 22 and in the cut.)

I therefore conclude that the last three pictures were done in this order: first *The Barrister's Dream* and then either *The Beaver's Lesson* or *The Banker's Fate*. In fact, *The Banker's Fate* very likely came last of all, because the finished design of *The Beaver's Lesson* (no. 21) was made larger than the cut, thus involving the labor of reduction in transferring it to the block, whereas the drawing of *The Banker* (no. 23), needed perhaps in a hurry, is the same size as the cut.

As for the chronology of Holiday's *parerga*, we have seen that the cover-designs of the book date to November 1875, that the rejected roundel of

"Hope" dates to the latter part of January 1876, and the alternative designs for the lettering on the spine to early February. The decorative border for the superseded Christmas letter which Dodgson suggested to Holiday on 7 November 1875 but countermanded on the 13th was perhaps begun, but the sketch has disappeared.

To complete the record of the early iconography of the book mention should finally be made of the roundels depicting the Bellman (his head taken from the front cover) and the Beaver (whose head was taken from *The Hunting*) that figure on the front and back red-cloth gilded cover of the second reprint of December 1876.[111] No allusion to these occurs in the diaries, but Craik referred to them in letters to Dodgson of 15 and 17 November 1876. They were probably commissioned about then, and Holiday himself no doubt adapted them from his previous designs, though the fact is unrecorded. Craik was reporting on a number of bound and unbound copies of the book which Macmillan's had in stock, and he added: "We can, however, bind the new way when we next require to bind. So it would be well for us to arrange now if we are to do so. We would count on a new edition and raise the price as you suggest."[112]

This decision to drop Holiday's first cover-designs for something that would make the book look more like the highly successful *Alices* arose from a concern Dodgson had had for some time about the way the *Snark* was selling and about Holiday's popular appeal. Only a month or so after the book came out he was asking Craik how he and Macmillan thought it was doing and whether they thought that Holiday was "likely to succeed" as an illustrator of the comic part of his *Phantasmagoria* (which he wanted to reissue with pictures).[113] He emphasized that his question was "not so much a matter of *taste* as a *commercial* one"—whether Craik thought that pictures by Holiday would " 'take'

111. See Goodacre's "Listing" below.
112. BLMD. 17 November 1876.
113. RDM. 12 May 1876.

with the buying public."[114] Craik's opinion was that they might find a better humorous artist, and he suggested Caldecott as a "very promising" alternative.[115] Six months later, rather at a loss to account for the *Snark*'s moderate summer sales, Dodgson again wrote to Craik: "Please keep a look-out among illustrated books, and let me know if you see any artist at all worthy of succeeding to Tenniel's place. I should *much* like to write one more child's book before all writing power leaves me."[116] This time Craik advised Dodgson to look at Walter Crane's *Baby's Opera*: "I think for humour he is superior to Tenniel."[117]

In February 1877, enquiring about Christmas sales of the *Snark*, Dodgson was still wondering: "I am entirely puzzled as to whether to consider it a success or a failure. I hear in some quarters of children being fond of it—but certainly the Reviews condemned it in no measured terms."[118] At all events, the *Snark* was the last book Holiday illustrated and decorated for him.[119]

I turn now to the part played by Holiday's various kinds of drawing in the productive process from first ideas to final cuts. Book-illustration, he said, was for him a new venture;[120] and he had to conform to the normal mid-Victorian practice of the book-illustrator's craft, that is to say, to draw pictures on woodblocks which would be cut by a commercial engraver. Broadly speaking, Holiday seems to have worked up his designs in a way that reflected his academic training as a painter.[121] Having received Dodgson's commission for a picture and digested the text to be illustrated, he doubtless began by trying out ideas for it in more or less

free exploratory doodles and sketches. Most of these are destroyed or lost, but three summary trial sketches of this sort survive in drawing no. 12(a), while in drawing no. 11 (a preliminary sketch of the composition of *The Landing*) we seem to have a more advanced one, apparently of the same class, in the making of which Holiday may have utilized a drawing from a nude male model (drawing no. 10). Then, having decided on his pictorial formulation, he invariably made a compositional design, normally in pencil on paper and about the same size as the intended cut, which established in not very meticulous detail the essential arrangement of the figures in their setting (drawings nos. 1–8). His next step was to make, in pencil on larger paper and usually with the aid of living models posed in the positions established by the compositional design, precisely detailed working studies of whole figures or parts of them (drawings nos. 12–15). Then, finally, he made the finished design, in pencil or ink on board and sometimes larger than the intended cut (drawings nos. 16–24), whose outlines he transferred in reverse to the woodblock, sharpening them up, with the finished design before him, in very hard pencil in the finest detail so that the engraver knew exactly what to reproduce.[122]

How did Dodgson intervene in this procedure? The record shows that he dealt directly with Holiday and Swain, without involving Macmillan, right down to the proof-stage (Macmillan, we remember, did not discover until 2 March 1876 that the dark cut for *The Vanishing* was impossible, as he thought, to print satisfactorily), and that he was a stickler over every detail. We can therefore presume that the missing Dodgson-Holiday correspondence was as meticulous as Dodgson's letters to Macmillan. Fortunately, however, the Rosenbach Museum possesses both preliminary sketches by Dodgson

114. Ibid. 18 May 1876.
115. BLMD. 16 May 1876.
116. RDM. 25 November 1876.
117. BLMD. 27 November 1876.
118. RDM. 4 February 1877.
119. The *Snark* was reprinted with Holiday's pictures in *Rhyme? and Reason?* in 1883.
120. See p. 84 above.
121. He entered the Royal Academy Schools in 1855, having already attended Leigh's school in Newman Street (*Reminiscences*, pp. 28–29).

122. Cf. the description of Tenniel's method in Eleanor M. Garvey and W. H. Bond, *Tenniel's Alice* (Cambridge, Mass.: Department of Printing and Graphic Arts, Harvard University Library, 1978), p. 9. See also W. H. Bond, "The Publication of *Alice's Adventures in Wonderland*," *Harvard Library Bulletin*, 10 (1956), pp. 306ff., especially pp. 307–10 and plates IIa and III.

and the artist and also Dodgson's letters relating to Arthur Frost's protracted illustration, from 1878 onwards, of *Rhyme? and Reason?* (1883). These show exactly how Dodgson intervened in the picture-making; and it is fair to assume that, in his usual logical and consistent way, he was following the procedure he had adopted four years earlier with Holiday (with experience with Tenniel behind him).

Frost's assigned task—to which at every stage Dodgson courteously secured his prior agreement —was to draw comic grotesque pictures of about the same degree of finish as Tenniel's.[123] When ordering a picture Dodgson usually sent Frost a rough drawing of his own (or "scrawl," as he called it) to give him an idea of what he had in mind and which Frost could adopt or adapt if he liked it, or reject if he did not.[124] He asked Frost not to send him drawn-on blocks or to go to the trouble and expense of making finished designs for his approval, but first to send him preliminary "rough sketches" so that he could "suggest any necessary changes" before they went further.[125] This is precisely what happened, as the Rosenbach letters and drawings show. In criticizing Frost's rough specimen drawings Dodgson went into close detail as regards attitudes, facial expression, and costume, and he particularly insisted that Frost should stick to comedy and avoid all vulgarity or anything that might frighten young children.

An excellent example of this kind of collaboration comes in a letter of Dodgson's to Frost of 5 April 1881.[126] Frost had sent him a specimen drawing of the speaker in *Phantasmagoria* with a beseeching little ghost kneeling before him. It shows the man dressed in a nightshirt threatening the ghost with a warming-pan. Dodgson objected that the man was "too *real* in his anger to be funny"; he had "'murder' written in his face" and would "terrify young readers more than amuse them." He also disliked the nightshirt as not at all artistic, though quite proper; he preferred a flowery dressing-gown instead. And further, since he considered the man to be a gentle person who was "worried into unusual violence, which should be preposterous and burlesque," he thought "a pillow or bolster would be more hopelessly useless for exterminating ghosts, and therefore more comic than a warming-pan, which would really be a very deadly weapon." So—though, as he said, "I can't draw"—he enclosed a drawing of the man in a large-flowered dressing-gown whirling a pillow which he hoped would convey better than words what was in his head. Frost adopted the idea, but did not follow the wild gesture of Dodgson's figure, making him more gentle and urbane, dangling the pillow in one hand while he admonishes the frightened ghost with the other.[127]

Guided by this record of Dodgson's dealings with Frost, I shall now try to classify the various *Snark* drawings according to the part they played in the evolution of the nine illustrations for the book, taking these in the order in which they seem to have been made; and at the same time to suggest, whenever possible, the points at which Dodgson is likely to have interposed in their making.

Abbreviations: D=drawing; P=proof; B= woodblock.

1. *The Snark-Boojum* (Fit 5 of the *Urtext*)

D.8 (plate XII) is the compositional design submitted to Dodgson but rejected. It was probably the first of the *Snark* pictures Dodgson ever saw, and was the equivalent—like the other compositional drawings (D.1–7) —of the "rough sketches" Dodgson asked Frost to send him for initial criticism. I shall therefore call them "presentation drawings." D.8 would doubtless have been preceded by tentative exploratory sketches which

123. *Letters*, p. 298. I am much indebted to Miss Suzanne Bolan for pointing out the importance of the Dodgson-Frost correspondence for my argument.

124. Ibid., pp. 308–9; an example on p. 310. In 1863 Dodgson told Tom Taylor that he proposed to send similar drawings to Tenniel to suggest pictures for *Alice in Wonderland* (*Letters*, p. 62).

125. *Letters*, p. 304. On 20 January 1870 Dodgson recorded: "Called on Tenniel, and saw the rough sketches of about ten of the pictures for *Behind the Looking-Glass*" (*Diaries*, p. 286).

126. *Letters*, p. 413.

127. *Letters*, p. 414, reproduces Dodgson's drawing and Frost's print.

are lost. (For other drawings for *The Vanishing* see 4 below.)

2. *The Crew on Board* (Fit 1)

D.2 (plate VI) is the presentation drawing. Detailed life-studies for the Baker's general pose and his hands, based on D.2, appear in D.12(b) (plate XVII), and for his ears in D.12(a) (plate XVI). D.12(b) also includes two lightly drawn life-studies, taken from a youthful model, for the left arm of the Billiard-marker, one showing it straight, the other bent. Holiday has worked over each study with a more emphatic pencil in order to define the exact details of the shirt-sleeve as they should appear in the finished design. The finished design D.17 (plate XXII) shows the Billiard-marker bent-armed, but middle-aged with a pipe in his mouth. Making him middle-aged may well have been Dodgson's idea, since his correspondence with Frost indicates that he was especially concerned about the expressions of his characters, but the pictorial decision to give him a bent arm was no doubt Holiday's, after considering his two try-outs in D.12(b). The clearer definition of the Bonnet-maker in D.17, as compared with his amorphous figure in D.2, was very likely asked for by Dodgson.

Dodgson evidently did not object to the Broker's grossly Semitic features when he received D.2 for first criticism, because the head went through in this offensive form to the first proof-stage (P.2(a) plate XXXI). This means that it was not until he closely scrutinized this proof that he realized that such an uncharitable image would not do, and accordingly asked Holiday to correct it, which Holiday did by pasting the final version of the head into D.17. To make the change Swain, as we have seen, sawed out the rejected section of the already engraved block,[128] glued in another, returned the block to Holiday to draw the new head on, cut the head afresh, and delivered a second proof (P.2(b) plate XXXII). The inserted section of wood is not clearly seen on the front of B.2 (plate XL), but it is clearly visible on the back. P.2(b) exactly corresponds to the revised D.17, except for the addition on the block of Holiday's initials and Swain's signature.

3. *The Hunting* (Fit 4)

The presentation drawing, exhibited in London in 1932 (? item 476), is missing. D.12(b) (plate XVII) includes alternative life-studies of the Banker's left arm and another such pair of the Barrister's legs. D.14

128. Tenniel prescribed such a change in his corrected proof of "Which Dreamed It?" illustrating Chapter 12 of *Through the Looking-Glass* (reproduced by Garvey and Bond, p. 74).

(plate XIX) a bit rickety in its outlines but virtually identical in pose with the more wide-awake and graceful draped figure of "Hope" in the finished design D.20 (plate XXV)—seems to be a study taken from life, or perhaps a copy of one. Not being squared for reduction (cf. 7 below), it may be a presentation drawing sent to Dodgson to see if he liked it.

4. *The Vanishing* (Fit 8)

D.12(a) (plate XVI) includes a preparatory compositional sketch, working towards the presentation drawing of the vanishing Baker which Dodgson asked Holiday to substitute for the rejected presentation drawing of the huge blowfishlike Boojum with the Baker (D.8, plate XII). The Baker's head and expression and the tree in front of his face are already more or less defined as in D.7, D.24 (plates XI and XXIX) and the final cut, but his very lightly sketched-in body has legs with toes turned in—as in the back-view of him in the rejected D.8—and crossed arms, and there is no idea yet of the ringing bell in the top left-hand corner or of the rocks below.

D.7 (plate XI), the presentation drawing, makes the Baker's face, especially in the eyes, less definite than it is in D.12(a), extends and enlarges his right hand and omits his legs; and it introduces the bell and the rocks.

D.24 (plate XXIX) is the finished design, which adds a leafy bush in the left foreground—an essentially compositional addition no doubt due to Holiday, not Dodgson.

The execution of D.7 in sepia (as distinct from the pencil-medium of all the other presentation drawings, D.1–6) and the use of bituminous ink in D.24 clearly indicate that when Dodgson rejected the tonally light D.8 of the Boojum and Baker and ordered an alternative picture, he asked Holiday to make it this time conspicuously dark so as to show that night was coming on, as the text says.

Later on, when the block had been cut, it was decided that the lighting of the rocks in the right foreground needed to be heightened: they are darker in P.9 (plate XXXIX) than in the published cut. So Holiday indicated the required correction in bluish Chinese white on D.24, probably sent the drawing itself to Swain in Bouverie Street to make it, which may perhaps explain why this one is so damaged as compared with the rest of the finished designs. B.9 (plate XLI) clearly shows where Swain did the recutting. This may well have been one of the last-minute tinkerings with the blocks about which Macmillan complained on 7 March 1876.

5. *The Baker's Tale* (Fit 3)

D.12(a) (plate XVI) includes, alongside the kindred early sketch for *The Vanishing*, a preliminary exploratory sketch, very lightly drawn, showing the relative positions of the Baker's and the Uncle's heads without any indication, as yet, of the whole composition and its details. The expression on the Uncle's face and the shape of his ears were modified in the presentation drawing (D.4, plate VIII), but the head of the Baker anticipates it very closely.

D.13 (plate XVIII) shows detailed studies of the Uncle's hands and of his night-shirt and bed-clothes. Despite the remarkable correspondence of hands and drapery as between these studies and D.4, they were probably taken from a living model—possibly the man whose name is written at the top of the sheet—because the Uncle's left hand and bed-clothes extend further to the right than they do in the presentation drawing.

D.19 (plate XXIV) is the finished design. There is no telling which of the many differences in detail between this and the presentation D.4 were due to Dodgson's suggestions or Holiday's invention, but the introduction of the Bellman's arm and bell outside the window may perhaps have been Dodgson's idea because one of the main points of the text is that the Bellman "excitedly" and "angrily" tingled his bell while the Baker was trying to recount his Uncle's tale.

6. *The Butcher and the Beaver* (Fit 1)

D.3 (plate VII) is the presentation drawing, and no detail-studies have been traced.

The finished design, D.18 (plate XXIII), much improves on D.3 by shifting the coil of rope to the center of the middle-ground and by giving the Butcher more clothes in order to bring him, without unduly exaggerating his head, into the front of the picture. These adjustments were probably Holiday's since they tended to make the composition more triangular, recessive, and academic. This was hardly Dodgson's *métier*.

7. *The Landing* (frontispiece)

D.11 (plate XV) is a lightly drawn preparatory compositional sketch, representing a late stage in Holiday's process of working up towards the presentation drawing for Dodgson's inspection. It is tempting to see in the Banker's ridiculously tiny trotting legs a reflection of one of Dodgson's own idea-suggesting sketches or "scrawls," such as he later sent to Frost.

D.1 (plate V) is the presentation drawing. As compared with D.11, it gives the Bellman thigh-high waders instead of wrinkled boots below the knee, elaborates on the waves and the ship, radically changes the Banker's legs into a squatting position, and brings the two figures together so that the Bellman's leg overlaps the Banker's hat.

D.16 (plate XXI) is the finished design. It omits the birds that appear in D.11 and D.1, adds an extra port and hawse-pipes to the ship, sharpens up the details throughout, and much improves the balance of the composition—most likely Holiday's idea—by once more putting a distance between the Bellman and the Banker. This design Holiday transferred to the block, with the addition of a bobstay for the ship, the omission of which neither he nor Dodgson had hitherto noticed. The bobstay was certainly added to the block before Swain cut it, because no extra piece of wood was inserted into the block to accommodate it (cf. B.2). The bobstay duly appears in P.1 (plate XXX).

D.10 (plate XIV) is a nude life-study for the Bellman apparently taken from the same model as the one who posed for a life-study of the Bellman in the picture of *The Banker's Fate* (D.15, plate XX); it calls for rather more searching analysis. Since the pose of the model so closely coincides with the Bellman's in the prepresentation sketch D.11, especially as regards the right arm and torso, and since it would have been so hard for the model to take the pose so precisely from that drawing, the most reasonable inference is that this life-study, squared-up for reduction, was used as the basis for the Bellman's figure in D.11. Then came the presentation drawing D.1, which exactly repeats the position of the Bellman's right arm (except that it is now naked) in the life-study (D.10) and in the prepresentation drawing (D.11), but differs quite a bit from D.11 as regards his left hand and shoulder and the angle of the bell. It was probably at this point that, in order to get these features exactly right in D.16, Holiday went over D.10 with a more emphatic pencil, accentuating not only the right arm and upper right torso, but also the arched left shoulder and the hand holding the bell. These accentuations clearly overlap the earlier squaring. Then lastly, adhering to these newly stabilized details, Holiday made his final design (D.16).

8. *The Barrister's Dream* (Fit 6)

D.6 (plate X) is the presentation drawing, which overemphasizes the winglike figure of the pleading Snark in the dream-world—the sort of error, since it went against the sense of the text, which Dodgson himself would very likely have corrected.

D.22 (plate XXVII), the finished design, clarifies the figures in the dream and alters their poses, and it keeps the real world of the dreaming Barrister and the world of his dream properly distinct by contrasting the tonalities of the two realms.

Swain rather spoilt the effect by somewhat blackening the figures of the Snark and the three Jurymen in the top right-hand corner, as P.7 shows; but neither Dodgson nor Holiday took steps to rectify this.

9. *The Beaver's Lesson* (Fit 5)

D.5 (plate IX) is the presentation drawing. D.15 (plate XX) includes a faintly drawn life-study of the seated Butcher which concentrates with heavier pencil on the hands and legs. These more precise formulations of features that are more summary in D.5 are carried over exactly into the finished design (D.21, plate XXVI), which corresponds with final cut. D.21 differs in many details from D.5, as indicated in the catalogue above, in ways that might have occurred either to Dodgson or to Holiday. Among these a change very likely introduced by Dodgson himself, because he was a logician, was in the title of one of the books ("Reductio ad Absurdum"), unless Holiday was here again being independently ingenious, as he was when he assigned a third meaning to "with" in "The Hunting."[129]

10. *The Banker's Fate* (Fit 7)

The presentation drawing, exhibited in London in 1932 (item 472), is missing. D.15 (plate XX) includes three faintly drawn studies, perhaps taken from life, of the Bellman, the Banker's dress-suit, and the Butcher pulling on his gloves, which are posed as they appear in the finished design and are worked up in whole or part in more emphatic pencil in order to fix particular details in more or less final form. D.23 (plate XXVIII) is the finished design.

Our enquiry into the purposes of Holiday's surviving drawings in the making of the *Snark*'s final pictures has proved sadly unilluminating on the central question of Dodgson's precise contribution to the productive process; but, remembering that he was always very deferential to the professional judgment of his illustrators, I have tried, in the very few instances where it seems possible, to distinguish changes of design attributable to Holiday from those likely to have been introduced by Dodgson. That Dodgson *did* intervene largely and frequently cannot be doubted; but the disappearance of the Dodgson-Holiday correspondence makes it impossible to tell the story of that intervention in any detail. So there, until those letters turn up, I must leave the matter.

129. See p. 100 above.

Now for a few words on Holiday's technical procedures. He consistently executed what I have called his presentation designs, including the rejected *Snark-Boojum* (nos. 1–8), in pencil on paper, about the same size as the intended cuts. The only exception, as we have seen, was the revised picture of *The Vanishing* (no. 7) where the darkness of the scene called for the use of sepia.

When he made his finished designs on board (nos. 16–24), however, he did so in a variety of sizes and media.

His first finished drawing, *The Crew on Board* (no. 17), was executed with the pen in black ink, and it is much bigger than the cut. This was not the long-experienced illustrator Tenniel's way; Tenniel made his finished drawings for the *Alice*s in pencil the same size as the cuts so that they could immediately be transferred in reverse to the block by means of tracing paper. Holiday may perhaps have been moved to adopt a different medium and a larger format by two considerations. He may well have used ink because he wanted to see from the start the effect of a cut that would consist largely of fine black lines; and he probably felt that by working large he could make sure that he prescribed nothing that Swain would find it hard to cut. As a painter accustomed to reducing and enlarging drawings to a required size, he would have seen no difficulty about reducing his design in order to transfer it to the woodblock.

He did the same with his next finished design, *The Hunting* (no. 20), which is again drawn in black ink, this time entirely with the pen; it is again a good deal larger than the cut. But with the third drawing, *The Vanishing* (no. 24), Holiday made his image the same size as the projected cut. Here he was largely using a special medium of scratched bitumen and ink, and could gauge the effect just as well on a small scale, which also had the advantage of allowing him to transfer the image directly on to the block without the extra labor of reduction. The fairly simple designs of *The Baker's Tale* (no. 19) and *The Butcher and the Beaver* (no. 18) are again the same size as the cut, thus again avoiding reduction. But Holiday was still wedded to ink.

With the last four drawings he switched over to pencil, perhaps feeling now that he did not need the aid of inked lines to judge the final effect. *The Landing* (no. 16) is the same size as the cut. *The Barrister's Dream* (no. 22) and *The Beaver's Lesson* (no. 21) are more detailed compositions, which is perhaps why Holiday again decided to draw them larger than the cuts. Once more he wanted to ensure that they would cut without technical difficulty. In the last design, *The Banker's Fate* (no. 23), detailed as it is, Holiday made the image in pencil the same size as the cut. It was needed quickly, and he was confident in his own and Swain's respective skills.

All this shows that though Holiday was a beginner in the art of book-illustration,[130] he was not simply progressively learning Tenniel's way. There may have been an element of experimentation and self-teaching in his changes of medium and size, but he was an independent thinker with a gift for technical innovation.[131] In designing his finished drawings for the *Snark*, he clearly knew at every stage exactly what he was doing, however unorthodox it was.

How did he reduce his oversize designs for reproduction, in reverse, on the blocks? He might have employed any of three methods. He might have had his designs photographically reproduced the required size on the wood—a method that began to be employed in the sixties, with which the Dalziels and Swain became familiar.[132] But Holiday certainly did not use this. Macmillan asked about the drawing of pictures on the wood, and he spoke of Holiday returning blocks, which he would only have had to draw on. In April 1881, when he was in America, Frost asked Dodgson whether, rather than sending drawn-on woodblocks across the Atlantic, he might not send drawings to be photographed on the block. Dodgson assented only after consulting Dalziel and Du Maurier on the feasibility of the idea, which implies that the technique was new to him.[133] Another method would have been to use a camera lucida or an elaborate camera obscura. But Holiday, in the mid-seventies, used neither. He recorded that early in 1885 he devised a camera obscura with an adjustable lens which enabled him to throw a subject on paper any size he wanted—a method, he said, "very superior to the old method of squaring."[134] This well-tried method of squaring was no doubt the one he used to reduce the large *Snark* designs. He would have taken a large piece of squared transparent paper on which he lightly traced the design. Then by eye, but with the guidance of the squares, he would have redrawn the traced design in soft pencil or crayon on another piece of squared transparent paper, framed the same size as the desired cut. This he would then have flipped over to impress the image with a point on the wood, finally sharpening up this reversed image with a hard pencil. Then Swain would take over.

In 1878, two years after his experience of illustrating the *Snark*, Cassell's invited Holiday to do a series of seven articles on wood engraving.[135] The sound exemplars of appropriate design for engraving on wood, he wrote, were the blocks of Thomas Bewick "in which the objects are drawn with light instead of being drawn with darkness. Bewick dis-

130. The *Snark* seems to have been Holiday's first essay in book-illustration. He later designed the covers of three numbers (1893–94) of *Aglaia*, the Journal of the Healthy and Artistic Dress Union, depicting the Graces (reproduced in Walter Crane's *Of the Decorative Illustration of Books Old and New* (London: G. Bell, 1896), p. 157, and in Holiday's *Reminiscences*, p. 405); historiated initials for his own book *Stained Glass as an Art* (London: Macmillan, 1896); and drawings for a series of concert programs (reproduced in *Reminiscences*, pp. 374, 377).

131. In 1863 he invented an instrument for widening binocular vision for landscape-work (*Reminiscences*, pp. 100–102); in 1870 he drew lunar craters with the aid of a telescope (ibid., p. 171); in 1885 he invented a new kind of camera obscura (ibid., p. 299), on which see below; and in 1888 he bought and used the first snapshot camera to come on the market, the "Detective Camera" (ibid., pp. 325ff.).

132. Cf. Geoffrey Wakeman, *Victorian Book Illustration: The Technical Revolution* (Detroit: Gale Research Company, 1973), pp. 76–81.

133. *Letters*, p. 413.

134. See note 131 above.

135. Henry Holiday, "Wood Engraving," *The Magazine of Art*, 1 (1878), pp. 26–29, 85–88, 105–8, 177–79; 2 (1879), pp. 93–95, 123–27.

covered the true powers of the woodblock and gives us for the first time engravings in which white is cut out of black, and where we find no attempt to force the material into the unnatural imitation of cross-hatching, or any other mode of execution for which it is unfitted." The scratched-out parts of drawing no. 24 (plate XXIX) were made, we observe, with precisely Bewick's kind of wood engraving in view.

With this proper method Holiday then went on to contrast the false method used by many contemporary designers for woodcut:

In working with the pen, the obvious way of darkening white ground is by a series of lines; and, if the tint thus given must be still further darkened in parts, this is most simply effected by crossing these lines with others —i.e., by cross-hatching; but on wood the engraver starts with pure black, and has nothing whatever to do with modes of darkening. With pen cross-hatching is a means to an end; on wood it is by fac-similists regarded as an end in itself, which, being quite unattainable on their material, is to be simulated at great cost of labour by the execution of a sufficient number of small white triangles, rhomboids, etc., etc., so disposed as to present the appearance of cross-hatching. . . . Let the reader remember, therefore, at what time he sees the cutting of small triangles, rhomboids, squares, trapezoids, and all kinds of polygons, *not* to fall down and worship, for it is a false image that has been set up.

Nowhere in Swain's cuts for the *Snark* have I been able to detect any such cross-hatching.

Holiday returned to the theme in his *Reminiscences*:[136]

There are only two ways of dealing with wood-engraving. . . . The first is for the artist to treat his line-drawing with a strict view to the process to which it is to be subjected, avoiding cross-hatching and similar modes of execution. The second, and true way, is for the wood-engraver to be an artist himself, as etchers commonly are, and to evolve his own technique.

And he went on: "When I made the *Snark* drawings, I had no Bewick to cut them and had to content myself with the first of the above methods."

This recognition that, so long as art and craft were sundered, the best a Victorian designer could

do was thoroughly to understand the procedures of the commercial craftsman, puts Holiday in the avant-garde of his time. His message, narrowly interpreted, was simply technical and aesthetic; but it had deeper resonances. For in 1877, the year before Holiday's articles in *The Magazine of Art* came out, William Morris, a good friend of Holiday's with whom Mrs. Holiday closely collaborated as an embroidress,[137] began—with greater authority and a passionate desire for social change—to enunciate the cognate doctrines in his first public lecture.[138]

"A novelist," wrote Anthony Trollope, "desires to make his readers so intimately acquainted with his characters that the creatures of his brain should be to them speaking, moving, living, human creatures. This he can never do unless he know those fictitious personages himself. . . . They must be with him as he lies down to sleep, and as he wakes from his dreams."[139] So it was with Lewis Carroll, the poet; and the creatures of his fantasy peopled his mind, as Mrs. Proudie did Trollope's, long after they left his pen.

The last pictures Dodgson selected to illustrate the *Snark*—he did not commission them but bought them ready-made—were not by Holiday; but I refer to them in conclusion because they give us a glimpse of how Dodgson would use pictorial images —and no doubt Holiday's too—to give a new after-life to the creatures of his brain as he wound fresh tales around them for the delight of generations of his child-friends.

Sometime between December 1882 and the early

136. Holiday, *Reminiscences*, p. 258.

137. Cf. J. W. Mackail, *The Life of William Morris* (London: Longmans, Green and Co., 1901), I, pp. 374–75; *The Letters of William Morris to His Family and Friends*, ed. Philip Henderson (London: Longmans, Green and Co., 1950), pp. 86–87, 96–97; Holiday, *Reminiscences*, p. 266, where he quoted Morris as saying: "You know, Holiday, I'd back your wife for heavy sums against all Europe at embroidery."
138. "The Lesser Arts (delivered before the Trades' Guild of Learning, 4 December 1877)," in William Morris, *Hopes and Fears for Art* (London: Longmans, Green and Co., 1929), pp. 1–37. On Holiday's Socialism cf. *Reminiscences*, pp. 318, 348, 349, 351.
139. Anthony Trollope, *An Autobiography* (London: Oxford University Press, 1923), pp. 211–12.

summer of 1883, as Curator of Christ Church Common Room, which was then being reconstructed, Dodgson arranged for William De Morgan to install a splendid set of ruby-luster tiles round its fireplace.[140] Later on he decided to have more red tiles round his own big fireplace in his sitting-room in the corner of Tom Quad, and on 4 March 1887 he visited De Morgan in London to choose them.[141] He chose nineteen. Three that went in the middle of his fireplace depicted a big ship, which he identified with the ship from which the Snark-hunters landed; the rest depicted various strange beasts including what he christened the Beaver from the *Snark*, the Eaglet, Gryphon, Lory, and Dodo from *Alice in Wonderland*, and the Fawn from *Through the Looking-Glass*.[142] During the 1914–18 war Dodgson's fireplace was dismantled, when

three of the tiles were broken.[143] The remainder were then put together to make a fire-screen which is now in the Senior Common Room of the College (plate XLII).

At the time of Dodgson's death in 1898 Enid Stevens (1882–1960), one of his later child-friends, recalled how he would interpret his tiles both literally and allegorically.

Her brief memoir vividly evokes the scene: "As I sat on Mr. Dodgson's knee before the fire [her own portrait hung over the chimney-piece], he used to make the creatures have long and very amusing conversations between themselves. The little creatures on the intervening tiles used to 'squirm' in at intervals. I think they suggested the 'Little birds are feeding,' etc., in *Sylvie and Bruno*."[144] It is a precious recollection.[145]

140. *Diaries*, pp. 412, 415, 417.

141. Ibid., p. 449. Cf. *Letters*, pp. 519–20, note 3.

142. The fireplace is reproduced in *The Lewis Carroll Picture Book*, p. 234. I am indebted to the Rev. Michael Watts, Precentor of Christ Church, and Dr. J. F. A. Mason, Curator of the Common Room, for their courtesy in allowing me to see the tiles in the Common Room and the relics of Dodgson's fireplace. Dodgson's tiles were designed either by De Morgan or his partner Reginald Thompson. Miss Victoria Gill kindly referred me to A. M. W. Stirling, *William De Morgan and His Wife* (New York: Henry Holt, 1922), p. 86, where it says that they would "vie with each other in inventing grotesque beasts and monsters, and laugh like happy schoolboys when either succeeded in evolving some more than usually fantastic creature." Miss Gill has identified green De Morgan tiles of the eagle, the dodo, and the bird spearing a fish (also occurring among Dodgson's tiles) at Wightwick Manor.

143. Roy Harrod, "Dodgson of Christ Church," *The Times Literary Supplement* (11 December 1970), p. 1471.

144. *Picture Book*, pp. 369–71. Cf. *Letters*, p. 825, note 1.

145. I owe special thanks to James Tanis, who has brought so many of Holiday's drawings to light, for inviting me to attempt this essay and for keeping an eye on its writing; to Martin Gardner for welcoming this oblique contribution to the annotation of the *Snark;* to Morton N. Cohen who interrupted the labor of seeing his magistral edition of Dodgson's letters through the press to give me many friendly helps and who generously agreed to my use of the Dodgson-Macmillan correspondence which he proposes to edit; to Selwyn H. Goodacre who gave similar extraordinary aid and warned me of pitfalls; to Suzanne Bolan, Director of the Rosenbach Museum and Library in Philadelphia, who courteously accorded me every possible facility for consulting pertinent manuscripts, books, and microfilms in the Rosenbach Library and gave me expert advice; to Alexander Wainwright, Assistant Curator for Special Collections in Princeton University Library, for allowing me to study Holiday's drawings

and manuscripts in the Parrish Collection; to Richard Garnett of Macmillan London Ltd. for information on the Macmillan Archive; to Daniel Waley, Keeper of MSS in the British Library, for referring me to Sotheby's sale of letters to Holiday in 1970; to Margaret Maloney, Head of the Osborne Collection in Toronto Public Library, for information on Holiday's original woodblocks; to Laura Light who allowed me to consult a paper she wrote on Holiday's *Snark* pictures at Dr. Tanis's instance; and to John Dooley of the Canaday Library, Bryn Mawr College, who castigated my manuscript. I am no less grateful for various help and information to Mary Dunbar, J. A. Edwards, Victoria Gill, Janet Hartley, the late Sir Thomas Kendrick, Susan Lambert, Ronald Lightbown, Ian Lochhead, J. F. A. Mason, David Mitchell, Annette Niemtzow, Joseph Trapp, Robert Wark, Marcia Werner, and the Rev. Michael Watts.

Grateful thanks go as follows for kind permission to quote from copyright materials: to the Trustees of the C. L. Dodgson Estate and the Trustees of the Rosenbach Museum and Library, Philadelphia—Dodgson's letters to Macmillan's and Frost; to Macmillan London Ltd. and the British Library Board—Macmillan's letters to Dodgson; to the Trustees of the C. L. Dodgson Estate, the British Library Board, Dr. Roger Lancelyn Green, and the Oxford University Press, New York—Dodgson's *Diaries*. I am also thankfully indebted for courteous permission to reproduce other material to the following: Bryn Mawr College Library and two anonymous owners—drawings by Holiday and proofs of his *Snark* illustrations; the Curator of the Morris L. Parrish Collection of Victorian Novelists, Princeton University Library—drawings and a letter by Holiday; the Osborne Collection of Early Children's Books, Toronto Public Library—two of the original woodblocks; the Curator of the Common Room (Dr. J. F. A. Mason), Christ Church, Oxford, and Thomas Photos, Headington, Oxford—a photograph of a fire-screen made from tiles from Dodgson's room in Christ Church.

THE PLATES

Gertrude Chataway
Oct 7/75

PLATE I A pencil sketch by Lewis Carroll, of Gertrude Chataway at the seaside
Courtesy of the Dodgson Family Collection in Guildford Muniment Room; used with
permission of the Trustees of the C. L. Dodgson Estate

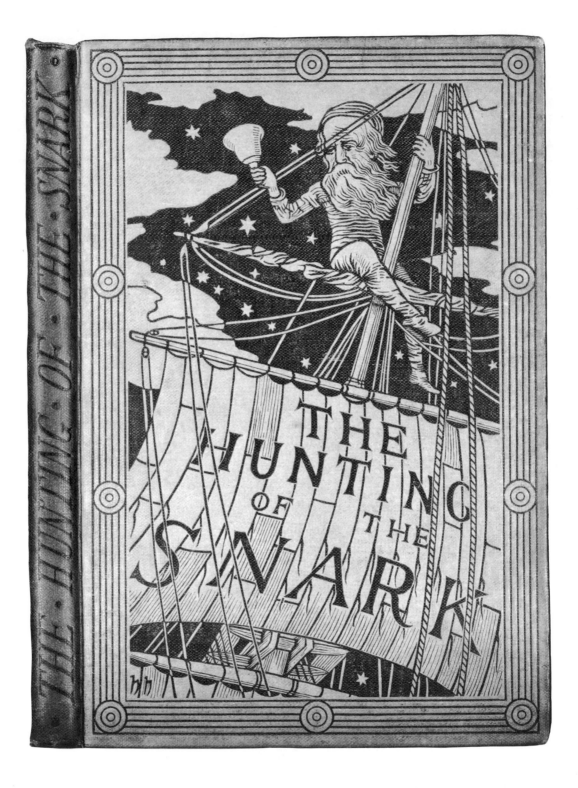

PLATE II Spine and front cover of the First Edition

PLATE III Back cover of the First Edition

PLATE IV Henry Holiday (photograph by Swain after Mendoza)
From A. L. Baldry, "Henry Holiday," *Walker's Quarterly*, nos. 31–32, 1930

Henry Holiday

PLATE V *The Landing* (drawing no. 1)

Henry Holiday

PLATE VI *The Crew on Board* (drawing no. 2)

Henry Holiday

PLATE VII *The Butcher and the Beaver* (drawing no. 3)

Henry Holiday

PLATE VIII *The Baker's Tale* (drawing no. 4)

Henry Holiday

PLATE IX *The Beaver's Lesson* (drawing no. 5)

Henry Holiday

PLATE X *The Barrister's Dream* (drawing no. 6)

Henry Holiday

PLATE XI *The Vanishing* (drawing no. 7)

Henry Holiday

PLATE XII *The Snark-Boojum* (drawing no. 8)

PLATE XIII *Hope* (drawing no. 9)

PLATE XIV *The Landing* (drawing no. 10)

PLATE XV *The Landing* (drawing no. 11)

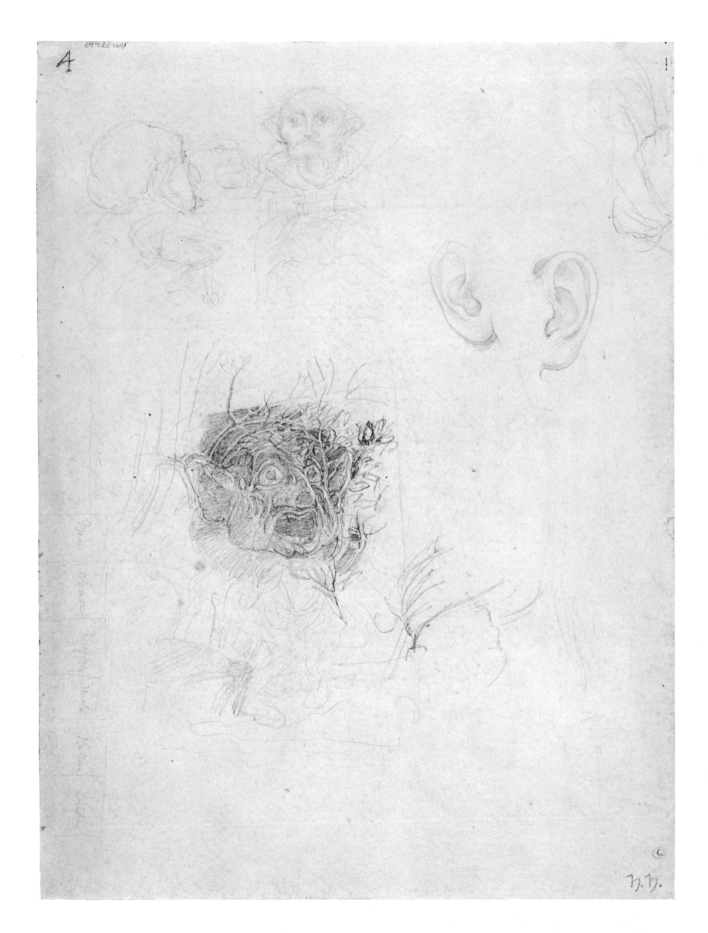

PLATE XVI Studies and sketches for *The Crew on Board, The Baker's Tale, The Vanishing* (drawing no. 12(a) recto)

PLATE XVII Studies and sketches for *The Crew on Board, The Hunting* (drawing no. 12(b) verso)

PLATE XVIII *The Baker's Tale* (drawing no. 13)

PLATE XIX *The Hunting* (drawing no. 14)

PLATE XX *The Beaver's Lesson* and *The Banker's Fate* (drawing no. 15)

PLATE XXI *The Landing* (drawing no. 16)

PLATE XXII *The Crew on Board* (drawing no. 17)

PLATE XXIII *The Butcher and the Beaver* (drawing no. 18)

PLATE XXIV *The Baker's Tale* (drawing no. 19)

PLATE XXV *The Hunting* (drawing no. 20)

PLATE XXVI *The Beaver's Lesson* (drawing no. 21)

PLATE XXVII *The Barrister's Dream* (drawing no. 22)

PLATE XXVIII *The Banker's Fate* (drawing no. 23)

PLATE XXIX *The Vanishing* (drawing no. 24)

Henry Holiday

PLATE XXX *The Landing* (proof no. 1)

Henry Holiday

PLATE XXXI *The Crew on Board* (proof no. 2(a) first state)

PLATE XXXII *The Crew on Board* (proof no. 2(b) second state)

Henry Holiday

PLATE XXXIII *The Butcher and the Beaver* (proof no. 3)

Henry Holiday

PLATE XXXIV   *The Baker's Tale* (proof no. 4)

Henry Holiday

PLATE XXXV *The Hunting* (proof no. 5)

Henry Holiday

PLATE XXXVI *The Beaver's Lesson* (proof no. 6)

Henry Holiday

PLATE XXXVII *The Barrister's Dream* (proof no. 7)

Henry Holiday

PLATE XXXVIII *The Banker's Fate* (proof no. 8)

Henry Holiday

PLATE XXXIX *The Vanishing* (proof no. 9)

PLATE XL *The Crew on Board* (woodblock no. 2)

PLATE XLI *The Vanishing* (woodblock no. 9)

PLATE XLII Fire-screen made from tiles from Dodgson's room in Christ Church

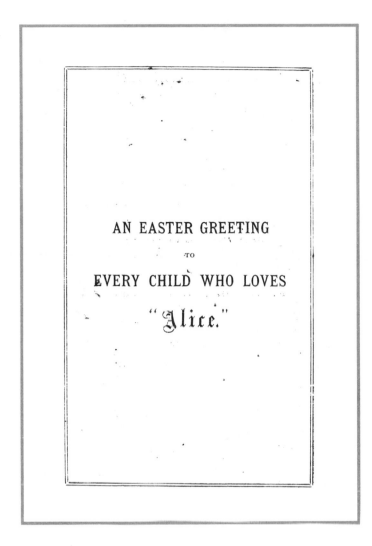

AN EASTER GREETING

·TO·

EVERY CHILD WHO LOVES

"𝕬𝖑𝖎𝖈𝖊."

PLATE XLIII *An Easter Greeting*

DEAR CHILD,

Please to fancy, if you can, that you are reading a real letter, from a real friend whom you have seen, and whose voice you can seem to yourself to hear wishing you, as I do now with all my heart, a happy Easter.

Do you know that delicious dreamy feeling when one first wakes on a summer morning, with the twitter of birds in the air, and the fresh breeze coming in at the open window——when, lying lazily with eyes half shut, one sees as in a dream green boughs waving, or waters rippling in a golden light? It is a pleasure very near to sadness, bringing tears to one's eyes like a beautiful picture or poem. And is not that a Mother's gentle hand that undraws your curtains, and a Mother's sweet voice that summons you to rise? To rise and forget, in the bright sunlight, the ugly dreams that frightened you so when all was dark——to rise and enjoy another happy day, first kneeling to thank that unseen Friend, who sends you the beautiful sun?

Are these strange words from a writer of such tales as "Alice"? And is this a strange letter to find in a book of nonsense? It may be so. Some perhaps may blame me for thus mixing together things grave and gay; others may smile and think it odd that any one should speak of solemn things at all, except in church and on a Sunday: but I think——nay, I am sure——that some children will read this gently and lovingly, and in the spirit in which I have written it.

For I do not believe God means us thus to divide life into two halves——to wear a grave face on Sunday, and to think it out-of-place to even so much as mention Him on a week-day. Do you think He cares to see only kneeling figures, and to hear only tones of prayer——and that He does not also love to see the lambs leaping in the sunlight, and to hear the merry voices of the children, as they roll among the hay? Surely their innocent laughter is as sweet in His ears as the grandest anthem that ever rolled up from the "dim religious light" of some solemn cathedral?

And if I have written anything to add to those stores of innocent and healthy amusement that are laid up in books for the children I love so well, it is surely something I may hope to look back upon without shame and sorrow (as how much of life must then be recalled!) when my turn comes to walk through the valley of shadows.

This Easter sun will rise on you, dear child, "feeling your life in every limb," and eager to rush out into the fresh morning air——and many an Easter-day will come and go, before it finds you feeble and gray-headed, creeping wearily out to bask once more in the sunlight——but it is good, even now, to think sometimes of that great morning when the "Sun of Righteousness shall arise with healing in his wings."

Surely your gladness need not be the less for the thought that you will one day see a brighter dawn than this—— when lovelier sights will meet your eyes than any waving trees or rippling waters——when angel-hands shall undraw your curtains, and sweeter tones than ever loving Mother breathed shall wake you to a new and glorious day ——and when all the sadness, and the sin, that darkened life on this little earth, shall be forgotten like the dreams of a night that is past!

Your affectionate Friend,

LEWIS CARROLL.

EASTER, 1876.

PLATE XLIV *An Easter Greeting*

THE
LISTING OF
THE SNARK

Selwyn H. Goodacre

THE LISTING OF THE SNARK

✤✤

Selwyn H. Goodacre

". . . go on with your list . . ."
(*Through the Looking-Glass*, 1871)

THIS SECTION is a revised and augmented version of the booklet I issued on the centenary of the Snark inspiration, on 18 July 1974. It now covers the years up to and including 1980.

I am once more indebted to my fellow collectors and enthusiasts who have greatly assisted me in supplying details of copies in their possession, and for their further helpful and constructive criticism; particularly I must thank John Davis, Denis Crutch, Brian Sibley, Stan Marx, Joe Brabant, Morton Cohen, Edward Guiliano, Sandor and Mark Burstein, Byron Sewell, David and Maxine Schaefer, Mary Boxen, and Oliver Fancher.

The listing is in four sections: English-Language Editions, Translations, Anthologies containing the entire *Snark*, and "Candle-Ends." The entries are arranged chronologically, but each edition is pursued to its final disappearance, even if the chase extends over forty-two years. Where a description appears meagre and hollow, it simply means that darkness came on before a copy was run to earth.

Finally I again thank my fellow members of the Crew of the Newcastle Snark Club, who originally urged me to join the hunt, and who annually shudder to think that the chase might fail.

English-Language Editions

1876   Macmillan, London. The First Edition, published on 29 March. Dodgson's own copy was dated 30 March 1876, but he inscribed eighty copies for presentation on 29 March. He had earlier thought it should be published on 1 April: "Surely that is the fittest day for it to appear."

The book is fully described in *The Lewis Carroll Handbook* (revised version by Denis Crutch, 1979), but there are two minor errors of description: a. Title page – the comma after GLASS should be a stop. b. The lettering on the spine has stops before THE, and after SNARK

The basic binding is buff cloth boards (which by now are usually found "weathered" to grey). It is just possible that some regular copies of the First Edition were in red cloth boards, with lettering and pictures in gilt. Dodgson arranged for a number of copies to be bound in special covers; on 21 March he asked for "100 in red and gold . . . , 20 in dark blue and gold, 20 in dark green and gold, 2 in white vellum and gold." In 1877 he offered a child-friend the choice of light blue or light green. The Harcourt Amory Catalogue (Harvard) also records a copy in "tan cloth, lettered and ornamented in black," and comments that a lavender color is also known. There is known to be a presentation copy in blue and gilt, which has the bell and sail only on the front cover, with bell buoy on the back. Other variants may well exist, but details are not to hand.

Copies of the First Edition are known in a grey dust-wrapper. It is possible that *all* copies originally had them. The front cover has a reproduction of the title page, the spine has the title in roman uppercase, lettered upwards, the back cover has the advertisements, the text on both covers within a line frame around the edge.

The First Edition consisted of 10,000 copies, and many are found with *An Easter Greeting* (issued Easter 1876) loosely inserted. Again, it is possible that all copies originally had them. Easter Sunday in 1876 was on 16 April.

Early reprints have the number of "thousand" on the title page. The first reprint was in May 1876. Copies are identical to the First Edition, apart from respacing on the title page to accommodate the number of "thousand" (below HENRY HOLIDAY) in thick black lowercase. Copies have been seen with "Eleventh," "Twelfth," "Thirteenth," and "Fourteenth." It is likely that there are also copies with "Fifteenth."

The second reprint was in December 1876. Copies now have the number of "thousand" in uppercase italics, in the same position. It is likely that the reprint includes the "Sixteenth," "Seventeenth," and "Eighteenth" thousands. During the issue of this reprint, the binding style changed from the buff boards to an "Alice-style" binding in red cloth boards, with three parallel lines round the border, and gilt roundels on the front and back covers; the front has the Bellman, the back the Beaver, the latter being slightly smaller in size. Copies of the "Seventeenth Thousand" have been seen in both binding styles. The price rose from 3/6 to 4/6 in 1877, probably coincident with the change of binding.

Stocks remained available for sale until 1883, and were then withdrawn because of the publication of *Rhyme? and Reason?* (which included the full text and pictures of the *Snark*).

In 1890 the *Snark* was readvertised. Remaining bound copies of the "Eighteenth Thousand" in the "Alice-style" covers were sold off first, after which the remaining stocks of unbound sheets were bound in red cloth boards, decorated and lettered in gilt in a return to the design of the First Edition. When these had been cleared, new copies were printed, and advertised as the "19th Thousand," although this was no longer stated on the title page. Instead, the date of reprint appears on the reverse of the title page—thus the first was in "July 1890." Reprints followed in December 1890, 1891, 1893, 1894, 1895, 1896. For the first reprint of 1897, the height was increased slightly (from 18.5 cms. to 18.7 cms.) to match the similar increase in height of the new editions of the *Alice* books of 1897.

Reprinted again in 1897, 1898, 1899, 1900, 1903 (when the endpapers changed from black to white), 1906, 1908, and 1910. Advertisements in other Carroll works give varying numbers of "thousand" for the edition as the years go by, but no great reliance can be placed on these numbers—for example, "20th Thousand" is quoted in 1897 and also in 1908, while other 1908 advertisements state "25th Thousand."

The price remained at 4/6 until 1918 when it rose to 6/–. The edition finally went out of print in 1920, just over forty-two years after it was first published.

Many of the reprints will have had dust-wrappers, but examples are rare. A 1908 reprint example has been seen—speckled yellow paper covered with a close design based on the Macmillan motif in orange. The title is in black, with an elaborate Macmillan motif in black in the center; title, etc., on the spine; the back has the advertisements; flaps blank.

1876   James R. Osgood, Boston. A curious production, presumably pirated, and probably produced by a photographic process from a copy of the English Edition, which it mimics closely apart from being very small. Buff cloth boards, pale yellow endpapers. pp. xiv, 86. Reprinted in 1877.

1890   Macmillan, New York. Possibly timed to coincide with the new reprint in England. Reprinted in 1891.

1897   Van Vechten & Ellis, Warsaw, Wisconsin. A limited edition of ninety-nine numbered copies. Vellum boards, decorated in red and black; edges uncut. The text is printed in black with wide red decorative borders. William H. Ellis contributes "A Word by Way of Palliation," "Explanatory Diagrams and Picturings by Gardner C. Teall." This fine volume was the second book to be issued by the Philosopher Press, "finished on this ninth day of June," but published in November.

There is a cheaper edition, issued at the same time, limited to 333 numbered copies. Beige paper boards, title, etc., and picture within a frame in dark brown on both covers. The text lacks the wide decorative borders. pp. 88. 15.6×12 cms.

1898   Macmillan, New York. Plain red cloth boards, title in gilt on the spine reading up; the covers have a single line round the border in blind. All edges plain, white endpapers, no advertisements. Printed on one side of the leaf only; 52 leaves. The setup of type is from *Rhyme? and Reason?*, and not from the standard edition of the *Snark*. 18.6×12.3 cms.

Reprinted in 1899, 1902 (when the title on the spine reads down), 1908, 1914 (the copy examined is in green cloth, with title and design on front in white, a white line round the border, title, etc., on spine in white, back blank; this may be a variant), 1923, 1927, 1930, 1937. Thus, just about forty-two years in print.

1899   A. L. Burt, New York. The *Snark* occupies pp. 1–48 (with the Holiday illustrations); selections from

Sylvie and Bruno occupy pp. 49–206. pp. 206 plus 2 leaves, and advertisements. Possibly reprinted in 1910, but no details available.

1901   A. L. Burt, New York. No further details available.

1903   Harper and Bros., New York and London. Full title *The Hunting of the Snark & Other Poems and Verses*. Illustrations by Peter Newell in sepia monochrome, frontispiece in color. Cream vellum boards, decorated and lettered in gilt; embossed gilt Bellman on the lower front cover. Top edge gilt, others uncut. The *Snark* is on pp. 5–41, with eight pictures (including the frontispiece). The text pages have a wide decorative border in pale green, by Robert Murray Wright.

Issued in a green dust-wrapper, with the same design on front as the front cover; possibly originally also issued in a cloth board slipcase, in quarter vellum with gilt title. The Harcourt Amory Catalogue, apparently describing this edition, suggests that it should be enclosed in an oilpaper wrapper lettered on the spine, with "Price $3.00 net." pp. xiv, 248. 22 × 14.5 cms.

There are two other issues—in green, or red, ribbed cloth boards.

It seems likely that there was also an issue to match the "Peter Newell Edition" of the *Alice* books—black cloth boards with paste-on color picture and title on the front cover. This could be the 1906 reprint. The Amory catalogue also mentions an issue in blue cloth boards, in "Harper's Young People Series." Text printed without the ornamental borders.

1906   G. P. Putnam & Sons, The Knickerbocker Press, New York and London. In the series "Ariel Booklets." Limp red leather, with title in gilt within an ornamental surround; gilt ornamentation also round the border; back blank; the spine has the title, etc., in gilt. Includes the Holiday illustrations (which are attributed to Swain!); also includes poems from the *Alice* books (with Tenniel pictures) and from other works. pp. xi, 124. 13.8×9.5 cms.

1909   Altemus, Philadelphia. In the series "Slip-in-the-Pocket Classics Series," and listed in the *Publishers' Trade List Annual* for 1909–13, 1916, and 1921, although actual copies simply give the copyright date of 1909. A floral design frames the cover design, the series name is printed on the front cover and spine of the dust-wrapper. Bindings vary; one is known with a paste-on picture of a landscape signed "J. C. Claghorne." Another copy has been seen in green cloth boards, title and author on the front cover in gilt in an

elaborate floral design, title on the spine in gilt, back blank. pp. 120 plus 3 blank leaves at the front and 2 at the back. 13.1 × 10.2 cms.

Also known in the "Langhorne Series"—"Velvet Calf, Gilt Top, Boxed, 75¢."

1910   Macmillan, London. The "Miniature Edition," published in October, in the same format as the "Miniature Editions" of the *Alice* books (published in 1907 and 1908). Red cloth boards; the front cover has the Bellman roundel in gilt a little above center; the back cover is blank; the three parallel lines round both borders are in blind, but in gilt on the spine; title and publisher in gilt on the spine. Issued in a dust-wrapper, very similar in design to the examples found on some of the contemporary reprints of the standard edition (see above)—speckled yellow paper covered with a close design in orange based on the Macmillan motif, with lettering in black; the back cover has the advertisements; flaps blank. pp. xiv, 84, leaf with advertisements. 15.4×9.9 cms.

Reprinted in November 1910, 1911, 1913, 1916, 1920, 1924, 1928, 1931, and 1935. The first-edition style of dust-wrapper was retained at least until the 1916 reprint. The 1931 reprint dust-wrapper is in blue (or red) on a white paper; the front cover has the Bellman roundel, the back the advertisements, the flaps blank. The dust-wrapper for the 1935 reprint is in red on white; the front cover has the illustration for The Baker's Tale, the back is blank, the front flap has the advertisements, the back flap blank.

As with the standard edition, no great reliance can be placed on the number of "thousand" stated in the various advertisements. In November 1910 it reads "10th thousand," 1911 "15th thousand," 1912 "10th thousand"; by 1918 it is consistently "20th thousand," but after this the number is no longer stated.

The price of the first edition was 1s. In 1918 it rose to 1/6; in 1921 to 2s.; in 1942 to 2/6. It was last advertised in 1948, four years short of forty-two years in print.

The 1928 issue was the first where an alternative binding was offered—Écrasé morocco, at 5s. This is pale orange, with a gilt roundel on the front cover of the Baker (from p. 5). A blue morocco binding has also been seen, with covers blank; title, etc., on the spine in gilt. The 1931 and subsequent issues were also offered in "ledura leather-cloth," at 3s. (rising to 3/6 in 1942). This is yellow, with the same roundel in gilt, with 3 slightly elaborated yellow bands in blind around. Title, etc., on the spine in gilt, with embossed ship, back blank.

[1927] Kahoe and Spieth, Yellow Springs, Ohio. Unillustrated. Marbled paper boards, with paper label on the spine with title in black. pp. vi, 58 (last 3 leaves blank). 17.3×11 cms.

[1932] Peter Pauper Press, New Rochelle. Illustrated by Edward A. Wilson. Green, beige and brown decorated paper boards, green cloth spine with title and motifs in gilt. A limited issue of 275 unnumbered copies, printed at the Walpole Printing Office on a green-tinted paper. A picture begins each fit, and has block coloring, the color changing for each fit. pp. 80. 25.1×15.7 cms.

A single leaf prospectus was issued, printed on the same green paper, and carrying one of the pictures. 25.3×15.9 cms.

UNDATED (c. 1930s?) Haldeman-Julius Company, Girard, Kansas. Number 989 in the series "Little Blue Books," edited by E. Haldeman-Julius. Unillustrated. Pale blue paper wrappers, lettered in black. pp. 32. 12.5×8.7 cms.

[1939] Peter Pauper Press, Mount Vernon, New York. Illustrated by Cobbledick. Decorated green paper(?) boards; issued in a slipcase. Pictorial title page in green, sepia, and black. Each page is decorated in green and sepia. pp. 75.

There is another issue, also undated. Limited to 1450 unnumbered copies. Grey paper boards, with darker-grey postage-stamp-size illustrations of the characters. Black on red paper label on the spine with the title. Bottom edges uncut. Pictorial title page in red, grey, and black. Each page decorated, the colors changing in rotation for each fit—grey/red, grey/green, grey/orange, grey/blue. pp. 78. 20.1×13.5 cms.

Issued in a red paper boards slipcase.

1939 Oxford University Press, London. Full title *The Hunting of the Snark and Other Verses*. Number 2 in the series "Chameleon Books." Unillustrated, but the black front endpapers carry a picture of seven of the crew in black line on white, colored with brown, and the back endpapers Alice and characters from the *Alice* books, both by Malcolm Easton. Paper boards decorated with a design of fish in brown and grey; title, etc., in grey on the front and spine. Issued in matching dust-wrapper; the title here is given as *The Hunting of the Snark & Other Lewis Carroll Verses*. The other verses are from the *Alice* books and *Sylvie and Bruno*. pp. 64. 18×12.4 cms.

Reprinted in 1946 and 1949 (where the first edition is said to be 1940).

1941 Chatto & Windus, London. Illustrated by Mervyn Peake. Yellow paper boards, the front cover reproducing in black the title and picture from p. 19, the back cover the illustration from p. 26, with title above, and refrain verse and publisher below; title on the spine in black. Number 26 in the series "Zodiac Books." Published on 20 November 1941, at 1s. pp. 48. 18×11.3 cms.

Second Impression, 1941—pink cloth boards, with title on the spine in gilt. Issued in a grey dust-wrapper, which repeats on the front the title-page design, but without the date; the back has the p. 40 illustration enlarged, with publisher's name; title, etc., on the spine. 20.8×13 cms. The text and pictures are identical to the first edition, except for the title page where both are increased in size. A deluxe issue, published on 16 December 1941, at 5s. 1400 copies were printed, but it was not a limited issue as such.

Third Impression, 1942. Styled "Second Impression" (on the reverse of the title page).

Fourth Impression, 1948. Very similar to the first, but no mention of Zodiac Books. Published "by Lighthouse Books Ltd. and distributed by Chatto & Windus." On p. [47] the *Snark* is listed as Number 4 in a list of six various titles. Name of publisher removed from the back cover; price "2s." added.

Fifth Impression, 1953. Styled "Fourth Impression." Blank yellow paper boards simulating cloth, with title and publisher's device on the spine in silver. Issued in a dust-wrapper which copies the binding of the first edition, but with nothing below the refrain on the back.

Sixth Impression, 1958. Styled "Fifth Impression."

Seventh Impression, 1960. A special issue for the Reprint Society Book Club. Slightly smaller—18.2×12.2 cms.—but text, etc., the same size. The reverse of the title page has "This edition published by the Reprint Society Ltd. by arrangement with Chatto & Windus Ltd. 1960." Limp beige cloth; front cover has in black the title, author, and illustrator, and part of the p. 45 illustration; the back cover has the title, etc., and p. 10 illustration, with note of the Book Society.

Eighth Impression, 1964. Styled "Sixth Impression." As the sixth, with price (5s. net) added on the front flap of the dust-wrapper.

Ninth Impression, 1969. Styled "Fourth Impression," but giving a list of impressions from 1953; standard book number added, and also on the front flap with the new price (10/– net 50p).

Tenth Impression, 1973. Styled "Fifth Impression." The dust-wrapper has the title running down the front free edge, with note of illustrator at the bottom left. The front flap has the title and illustrator, the picture of the Beaver and the price change to 70p net. (This issue is still available, with a stick-on label on the front flap giving 95p as the price. Thus, it is rapidly approaching forty-two years in print.)

[1952] Peter Pauper Press, and Mayflower Publishing Co. and Vision Press, New York. Full title is *The Hunting of the Snark, and Other Nonsense Verses;* the other verses are from the *Alice* books and *Sylvie and Bruno.* Illustrations by Aldren Watson. There appear to be two issues of this volume, but no copies available for description. One is described as in decorated paper boards, in a slipcase, pp. 92; the other as a "Collector's Presentation Edition."

1962 Simon and Schuster, New York (also issued by Bramhall House). *The Annotated Snark,* introduction and notes by Martin Gardner. Buff half-cloth, dark-brown paper boards, with gilt bell on the lower front cover, spine lettered in brown. Cream dust-wrapper, with title, etc., in red, black, and brown, all within a frame of the Bellman's map; the back has laudatory extracts from reviews of *The Annotated Alice.* pp. 112. 25×14.8 cms.

This book, which contains the full text, copious annotations, bibliography, Holiday illustrations, and appendices, has been rightly called "the apotheosis of Snarkolatry." The present volume is the revised and augmented version.

First published in England by Penguin Books Ltd., London, in 1967. It contains a new preface by Martin Gardner, the whole book revised, updated, and new material added. Paper wrappers, with a pictorial cover design by Germano Facetti, utilizing six of the Holiday illustrations. The back cover has a two-verse parody about the book.

Reprinted in 1973, with revisions, and extended bibliography; and new wrappers designed by David Pelham, in pale blue featuring on the front cover in brown the title and the Holiday picture of the Bellman supporting the Banker, the upper half against a turquoise circle; the back cover has the same circle, with parody and text as before. Reprinted in 1975 (where it states that the 1973 revision was in 1974!), and again in 1977 and 1979, with further small corrections.

1966 Pantheon Books, New York. Illustrations by Kelly Oechsli, in line from pen-and-ink drawings, with added color wash. Black half-cloth, buff paper boards; title on the spine in grey. Dust-wrapper in white, with an extra picture on the front cover against a blue background of the ship in sail approaching; the back cover has the ship viewed sailing away. pp. iii, 48. 25.5×17.5 cms.

1966 De Roos, Utrecht. Illustrations by Peter Vos. An edition specially printed for members of De Roos, Utrecht, limited to 175 numbered copies on paper made by Hahnemühle, bound by Proost and Brandt, n.v. Amsterdam. Paper boards with illustration in monochrome extending over both covers; title on the spine in silver. All edges plain. pp. 40. 25.3×17.2 cms.

1970 Heinemann, London. Illustrated by Helen Oxenbury, in color and monochrome. Pictorial paper boards, in green, lettered in white and turquoise, with the picture from p. 29 in a circle, with added color and background; the back cover has the Jubjub from p. 33, again in full color. Matching dust-wrapper, back flap has a photograph of Helen Oxenbury, and reviews. Issued at 22s. (£1.10). pp. 48. 27.8×21.3 cms.

Published the same year in New York, by Watts, at $4.95.

1973 Simon and Schuster, New York. *The Snark Puzzle Book,* by Martin Gardner. Yellow cloth boards, with bird (from the back cover of the First Edition, but in reverse) in black on the upper front cover; title in black on the spine. Pale green dust-wrapper, with title based on the Holiday bell-buoy design, on a turquoise background; title on the spine in brown, green, and black. Includes all the Holiday pictures, and seventy-five "Snarkteasers," with answers provided in the appendix. "Jabberwocky" also included with the Tenniel pictures. pp. 128 (last 2 leaves blank). 23.6×16.7 cms.

1973 Normal, Illinois. Illustrations by Arlene Bennett. Twenty-six unnumbered pages of hand-lettered text, with fourteen pictures ranging from tiny marginalia to half-page illustrations. Limited edition of sixty-five numbered copies, signed by the illustrator; hand-bound under the guidance of Oliver Fancher at Illinois State University.

1974 Catalpa Press, London. Illustrations by Byron Sewell, introduction by Martin Gardner. Black cloth boards, with pocket inside back cover enclosing cards with sections of the crew members' faces, so that they can be re-sorted. A limited issue of 250 numbered copies, signed by the illustrator. It is a highly elaborate version; a section of the sheets are given over to a picture of the vessel and crew in a single concertinaed sheet. There are other special effects, which altogether make a page count misleading, if not impossible. 30.2×21 cms.

Issued at £25. A single-leaf prospectus was issued, 20.8×14.8 cms.

1975　The Whittington Press, Andoversford. Line illustrations by Harold Jones. A limited edition of 750 numbered copies signed by the illustrator, including thirty bound in full leather. Black cloth boards (or leather) with title in gilt on the front cover within an ornamental frame; title, publisher's mascot, and four sets of double lines in gilt on the spine. Top edge gilt, others uncut. A fine and luxurious publication. pp. 48. 29×19 cms. Issued at £15 (£30 for the leather copies).

1975　Michael Dempsey, London. Monochrome illustrations by Ralph Steadman. Plain beige cloth boards; title in black on the spine. Yellow dust-wrapper, with title in illustrator's script with the picture from p. 37. pp. 72. 27.9×26 cms. Issued at £4.50. 150 copies included an etching, numbered and signed by the artist.

Six of the pictures were issued in a portfolio as etchings limited to 65 numbered sets, signed and titled by the artist, at £150. The book was published in New York by Clarkson Potter in 1976, in paper wrappers.

1976　John Minnion, London. Line illustrations by John Minnion. Blue paper wrappers; the front cover has, in black, the title and an extra picture, the back cover another extra picture, with short biographical note. Pictures on every page interwoven with text in the illustrator's own script. A personal tour de force. pp. 39. 29.5×21 cms. Issued at £1.50.

1976　Folio Society, London. Illustrations by Quentin Blake. Cloth boards, with an extra color picture of the chase extending over both covers. Title in gilt on the spine. Text set in Bell type, appropriately. Issued in a pale-blue paper boards slipcase. Available to members of the Society at £3.95. pp. 52. 22.1×15.5 cms.

1980　Windward (W. H. Smith), Leicester. A facsimile of The 1876 First Edition. Cream paper boards, with First-Edition cover designs in black; the spine has the publisher and title in roman uppercase reading upwards, black endpapers. Pale brown dust-wrapper with matching designs in dark brown; the spine has the title reading downwards; the front flap has text about the volume, the back flap a brief Carroll biography. Issued at £2.95. pp. xiv, 83. 18.6×12.3 cms.

Translations

FRENCH

1929　*La Chasse au Snark*, Hours Press (Miss Nancy Cunard), Chapelle-Réanville-Eure. Translated by Louis Aragon, unillustrated. A limited edition of ten copies on Japon, numbered from 1 to 5, with five not for sale; and 250 copies on Alfa, numbered from 1 to 200, with 50 not for sale. Each copy signed by the translator. Red paper boards, with title, etc., in both languages on the front cover in black. pp. 38. 30×22 cms.

Reprinted by P. Seghers, Paris in 1949 and 1962. The latter is in stiff wrappers, with a picture on the front cover in green and purple by Mario Prassinos. pp. 69. 16×13.3 cms.

1940　Librairie José Corti, Paris. Translated by Henri Parisot, unillustrated. A limited edition of 255 unnumbered copies, five on Madagascar, and 250 on Alfa. Stiff white card wrappers, with title, etc., on the front cover in black. pp. 32, (iii). 24.5×15.5 cms.

1945　P. Seghers, Paris. Translated by Henri Parisot. Also includes "Fantasmagorie" and "Poeta Fit Non Nascitur."

1946　*La Chasse au Snark et autres poèmes*, Fontaine, Paris. Translated by Henri Parisot ("revue et corrigée"), illustrations by Gisèle Prassinos. The additional poems are the two above, plus "Le Morse et le Charpentier, Assis sur une Barrière et Jabberwocky."

1948　G.L.M., Paris. Translated by Florence Gilliam and Guy Lévis Mano, illustrated. A limited edition of 1080 copies. Includes the English text. There was a new edition in 1970, published by Le Club Français du Livre. pp. 146.

1950　Éditions Premieres, Paris. A new translation by Henri Parisot, illustrations by Max Ernst. In the series "L'Age d'Or." Issued in a limited edition of 775 numbered copies, Nos. 1–25 on Marais Crevecoeur, with a signed and numbered color etching and an embossed design inscribed "Carte de l'océan" by Ernst, and Nos. 26–775 on Alfama (there were a few copies "hors commerce"). pp. 72. 16.7×13.2 cms.

1952　P. Seghers, Paris. A translation by Henri Parisot is included in his biography of Lewis Carroll (in the series "Poètes d'Aujourd'hui"). One of the Ernst illustrations is included.

1962   Jean-Jacques Pauvert. Translated by Henri Parisot. Illustrations by Henry Holiday. A limited edition of 1999 numbered copies, 1–30 on pur Fil Du Marais, 31–1999 on offset Alfa Bellegarde. Blue paper wrappers with the title, etc., in black on the front with in the center a reproduction of the First Edition cover—front and back on the front and back, in black and white. pp. ix, 82. 18.2 × 13 cms.

1969   Pierre Belfond, Paris. A translation by Henri Parisot is included in *Le rire des Poètes*—an anthology of humorous poetry. Pp. 26–76 is a selection of Carroll verses, including the *Snark*.

1971   Aubier-Flammarion, Paris. Translated by Henri Parisot, the *Snark* is on pp. 248–99 of the volume containing his translation of *Through the Looking-Glass*, and is followed by the suite of illustrations by Max Ernst. The text in English is on the left-hand page, the French on the right. Stiff paper wrappers, the front cover has the title, etc., in brown and black, with a photograph of Dodgson below on the right, with a brown rectangle on the left. The back cover has the opening paragraph from *Looking-Glass* (bilingual) with the Dodgson photograph above. pp. 318. 17.8× 10.9 cms.

Reprinted in 1976, with an extended list of books at the end "dans la même collection." Red stiff paper wrappers, with title, etc., in black and white and with a "butterfly blot" picture. On the back in white is "Lewis Carroll" and "en bilingue." The *Snark* translation is revised again.

In a letter to the present writer, H. Parisot stated that he first translated the *Snark* in 1940, and subsequently reworked it about ten times, before producing his definitive version for the Aubier-Flammarion bilingual edition in 1976.

LATIN

1934   Macmillan, London. Rendered into Latin verse, in Virgilian hexameters, by Percival Robert Brinton D.D. (Rector of Hambleden, Buckinghamshire). Unillustrated. English text is on the left-hand page, Latin on the right. Red paper wrappers, lettered in gilt, back blank. pp. vi, 58. 19.3 × 13 cms.

1936   Shakespeare Head Press, sold by Basil Blackwell, Oxford. Translated into Latin elegiacs by H. D. Watson, with a foreword by Gilbert Murray. Unillustrated. English text is on the left-hand page, Latin on the right. Dark-blue cloth boards; title, etc., on the front in gilt, and on the spine. All edges uncut. The translation was directly inspired by the Brinton trans-

lation above. The volume includes a number of other poems by the translator, along with their Latin translations. pp. xvi, 116. 19× 12.8 cms.

ITALIAN

1945   *La Caccia allo Snarco*, Magi-Spinetti, Rome. Translated by Cesare Vico Lodovici. Illustrations by Ketty Castellucci. pp. 79.

SWEDISH

1959   *Snarkjakten*, Albert Bonniers Förlag, Stockholm. Translated by Lars Forssell. Illustrations by Tove Jansson in line from pen-and-ink drawings. Stiff paper wrappers; the front cover is off-white with an abstract design in pen and ink with added watercolor; title, etc., in black, and also on the spine. The back cover has a drawing from the text. pp. 56. 22 × 14.2 cms. Issued at 9.75 Kr.

DANISH

1963   *Snarkejagten*, Det Schønbergske Forlag, Copenhagen. Translated by Christopher Maaløe. Includes the English text. Paper wrappers; the front cover has a photographic reproduction of a fabric picture of a Snark with a bathing-machine sporting Union Jack wheels. pp. 77. 22.2 × 15.7 cms.

GERMAN

1968   *Die Jagd nach dem Schnark*, Insel Verlag, Frankfurt am Main. Translated by Klaus Reichert. English text on the left-hand page, German on the right. Illustrations by Henry Holiday. Paper boards, the covers designed in the style of the First Edition, but in purple on green, and with the addition of a paper label with the title, etc., and a similar label on the spine. The volume matches the edition of *Alice's Adventures in Wonderland* and *Letters to Child Friends*; all three volumes are in the series "Insel-Bücherei." The *Snark* is "Nr. 934." pp. 96. 18× 11.6 cms.

1968   *Die Jagd nach dem Schnark*, Manus Presse, Stuttgart. Illustrations by Max Ernst, part in color. A limited edition of 130 copies, numbered and signed by Ernst. Issued in portfolio; includes the English text. pp. 100.

SPANISH

1970   *La Caza del Snark*, Calatayud-Dea, Buenos Aires. Apparently a second edition. No details available of first publication, but the volume is illustrated. pp. 75.

DUTCH

1977   *De Jacht op de Trek*, Uitgeverij J. Couvreur, The Hague. Translated by Erdwin Spits. Illustrations by

Inge Vogel. Stiff paper wrappers in metallic green, with title, etc., and pictures in maroon. The front cover has the ship approaching with a large bird in the foreground; the back cover has the ship sailing away. pp. 44. 19.3×13 cms.

1977 *De Jacht op de Strok*, Drukwerk, Amsterdam. Translated by Evert Geradts and with his own illustrations. Paper boards; the covers have a close design of green leaves on a yellow background, title in green on a white background; above is a circular paste-on picture of forks and "Hope" (represented as the upper half of a nude female figure); the back cover has a triangular paste-on picture again of "Hope," but with thimbles. Issued in a cellophane dust-wrapper lettered in black, with author and translator, etc. The book ends with an 8-page "Nawoord" by Geradts, with a photograph. pp. 104. 22.1×13.8 cms.

Anthologies including the *Snark*

Although I hope most examples are included, I cannot claim that this section is comprehensive. Certain volumes which properly belong here have been listed or mentioned earlier: *Rhyme? and Reason?* because of its importance to the narrative of the early history; the Parisot French translations, for the sake of clarity and continuity; and a number because they present the *Snark* as the main feature of the book—1899 Burt, 1903 Newell, 1939 Chameleon, and the 1936 Watson Latin translation.

The books listed here are cited only in their first editions.

1. *Alice's Adventures in Wonderland, Through the Looking-Glass and the Hunting of the Snark* (introduction by Alexander Woollcott): The Modern Library, Boni & Liveright, New York 1924.

2. *Alice in Wonderland, Through the Looking-Glass and Other Comic Pieces*: Everyman's Library, Dent/Dutton, London/New York 1929.

3. *The Collected Verse of Lewis Carroll*: E. P. Dutton & Co., New York 1929.

4. *Alice in Wonderland with the Hunting of the Snark and Poems from Sylvie and Bruno* (ed. Guy N. Pocock): The King's Treasuries of Literature, J. M. Dent, London 1930.

5. *The Lewis Carroll Book* (ed. Richard Herrick): The Dial Press, New York 1931.

6. *Alice's Adventures in Wonderland, Through the Looking-Glass and The Hunting of the Snark* (introduction by Mrs. F. D. Roosevelt): Jacket Library, National House Library Foundation, Washington 1932.

7. *The Collected Verse of Lewis Carroll*: Macmillan, London 1932.

8. *Logical Nonsense: The Works of Lewis Carroll* (ed. Philip C. Blackburn and Lionel White): G. P. Putnam's Sons, New York 1934.

9. *Nonsensibus* . . . by D. B. Wyndham Lewis: Methuen, London 1936.

10. *Alice's Adventures in Wonderland, Through the Looking-Glass and the Hunting of the Snark*: Carlton House, New York, undated but c. 1930s.

11. *The Complete Works of Lewis Carroll* (introduction by Alexander Woollcott): Random House, New York 1936.

12. *Poems selected from the Works of Lewis Carroll*: Macmillan, London 1939.

13. *Poets of the English Language*, Volume 5, Tennyson to Yeats (ed. W. H. Auden and Norman Holmes Pearson): The Viking Press, London 1950.

14. *The Humorous Verse of Lewis Carroll* (ed. J. E. Morpurgo): in the series "Crown Classics," Grey Walls Press, London 1950.

15. *Lewis Carroll's Alice in Wonderland and other Favorites*: Pocket Books, Inc., New York 1951.

16. *Alice's Adventures in Wonderland, Through the Looking-Glass and other Writings* (introduction by Robin Deniston): Collins, London and Glasgow 1954.

17. *The Book of Nonsense by Many Authors* (ed. Roger Lancelyn Green): Children's Illustrated Classics, Dent, London 1956.

18. *The Silver Treasury of Light Verse* (ed. Oscar Williams): A Mentor book, New American Library, New York 1957.

19. Lewis Carroll, *Nonsense Verse*: Pocket Poets, Edward Hulton, London 1959.

20. *The Sapphire Treasury of Stories for Boys and Girls* (ed. Gillian Avery): Gollancz, London 1960.

21. *The World of Victorian Humor* (ed. Harold Orel): Appleton-Century-Crofts, Inc., New York 1961.

22. *Through the Looking-Glass and what Alice found there and The Hunting of the Snark*: Dolphin Books, Doubleday, Garden City, New York 1961.

23. *Alice's Adventures in Wonderland, Through the Looking-Glass, and the Hunting of the Snark*: A Nonesuch Cygnet, the Nonesuch Press, London 1963 (published under the Bodley Head imprint in 1974).

24. *The Oxford Book of Nineteenth Century Verse* (ed. John Hayward): Oxford University Press, London 1964.

25. *The Works of Lewis Carroll* (ed. Roger Lancelyn Green): Spring Books, Paul Hamlyn, London 1965.

26. *Alice in Wonderland* (ed. Donald J. Gray): A Norton Critical Edition, W. W. Norton & Co., New York 1971.

27. *La Caza del Snark* (trans. Ulalume González de León): in *Plural*, No. 2, November 1971.

28. *Gendai-shi-techo*: Shichosha, Tokyo 1972.

29. *Wyprawa na Żmireuzu: Męka w Ośmiu Konwulsjach* (trans. Robert Stiller): in *Literatura na Świecie*, No. 5, 1973.

30. *Riusu kyaroru shishu* (ed. and trans. Yasunari Takashashi and Jun-Nosuke Sawazaki): Chikumashobo, Tokyo 1977.

31. *The Illustrated Lewis Carroll* (ed. Roy Gasson): Jupiter Books, Ltd., London 1978.

32. *El Riesgo del Placer*, by Ulalume González de León: Biblioteca Era Poesia, Mexico 1978.

33. *The Faber Book of Nonsense Verse* (ed. Geoffrey Grigson): Faber, London 1979.

Candle-Ends

1936   *A Rime of Three Worthies*, by Ashley Ohmsted: privately printed, Edgartown, Massachusetts. A limited edition of ten numbered copies, composed at the office of the *Vineyard Gazette* and imprinted in the shop of the Martha's Vineyard Printing Co., Oak Bluffs, Massachusetts. Green half-cloth, decorated paper boards in green and beige on cream. This curiosity is a full-length parody of the *Snark*. It falls well short of the original. pp. 22, plus 4 blank leaves at the beginning, and 3 at the end. 23.9 × 15.5 cms.

1973   Complete manuscript of the *Snark*, transcribed and illustrated by Charles E. Wright. This is unpublished, and is in the possession of J. N. S. Davis. Separate sheets, 35.3×27.8 cms. The transcription in a fine personalized script covers 40 sheets, preceded by the title sheet, and a suite of 14 sheets, each with one of the 13 characters, and the Author. A fine production, that one might think merits publication.

1976   *Fit for a Beaver: "Fit the First" from* THE HUNTING OF THE SNARK, by Lewis Carroll, illustrations by Byron Sewell, Chicken Little's Press, Austin, Texas. A limited edition of thirty numbered and signed copies. Tan paper wrappers, with title and picture on the front cover in black matching the title page. One picture per verse, quite different from the Sewell full-length edition noted above (1974). Printed on one side of the leaf only—27 leaves. 28×21.5 cms.

1976   *The Hunting of the Snark, Fit the First*, by Lewis Carroll, illustrations by Byron W. Sewell, privately printed by Byron Sewell, Austin, Texas. A limited edition of eight numbered and signed copies. Black stiff card wrappers, with title, etc., on the front in gilt. The text, printed from the illustrator's own script, is on one side of the leaf only, apart from the title page, which has the imprint and copyright notice on the reverse. Each verse merits a leaf to itself. The verses are interspersed at intervals with the illustrations which are hand-pulled lithographs in color on German etching paper. Each is mounted on grey card, protected by a tissue guard, and attached at the top only so that the title, limitation note, and signature in pencil can be read on the reverse. The pictures may be described as symbolic in style; the symbolism is more obscure in some than in others. 25 leaves. 27.5 × 21.5 cms.

THE HUNTING OF THE SNARK

Facsimile of the
First Edition

The Hunting of the Snark.

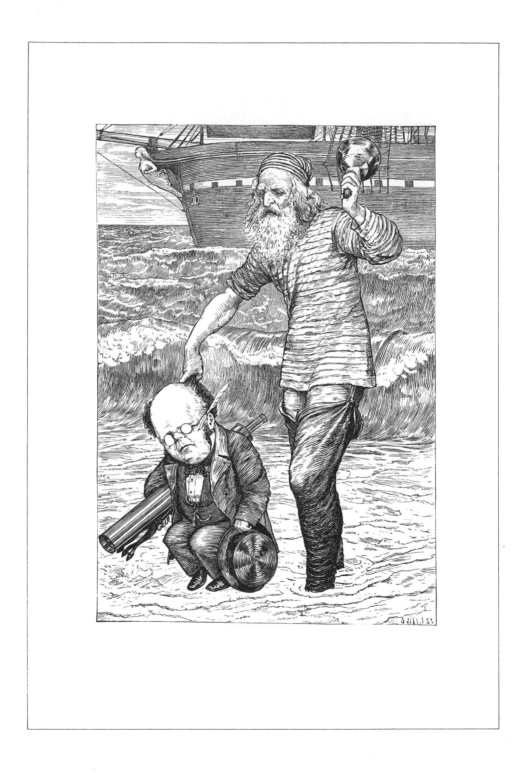

THE HUNTING
OF THE SNARK

an Agony,
in Eight Fits.

BY

LEWIS CARROLL

AUTHOR OF "ALICE'S ADVENTURES IN WONDERLAND," AND "THROUGH THE
LOOKING-GLASS."

WITH NINE ILLUSTRATIONS
BY
HENRY HOLIDAY

London:
MACMILLAN AND CO.
1876.

LONDON :
R. CLAY, SONS, AND TAYLOR, PRINTERS,
BREAD STREET HILL.

Inscribed to a dear Child:
in memory of golden summer hours
and whispers of a summer sea.

Girt with a boyish garb for boyish task,
　　Eager she wields her spade: yet loves as well
Rest on a friendly knee, intent to ask
　　The tale he loves to tell.

Rude spirits of the seething outer strife,
　　Unmeet to read her pure and simple spright,
Deem, if you list, such hours a waste of life,
　　Empty of all delight!

Chat on, sweet Maid, and rescue from annoy
　　Hearts that by wiser talk are unbeguiled.
Ah, happy he who owns that tenderest joy,
　　The heart-love of a child!

Away, fond thoughts, and vex my soul no more!
　　Work claims my wakeful nights, my busy days—
Albeit bright memories of that sunlit shore
　　Yet haunt my dreaming gaze!

PREFACE.

IF——and the thing is wildly possible——the charge of writing nonsense were ever brought against the author of this brief but instructive poem, it would be based, I feel convinced, on the line (in p. 18)

"Then the bowsprit got mixed with the rudder sometimes."

In view of this painful possibility, I will not (as I might) appeal indignantly to my other writings as a proof that I am incapable of such a deed: I will not (as I might) point to the strong moral purpose of this poem itself, to the arithmetical principles so cautiously inculcated in it, or to its noble teachings in Natural History——I will take the more prosaic course of simply explaining how it happened.

The Bellman, who was almost morbidly sensitive about appearances, used to have the bowsprit unshipped once or twice a week to be revarnished, and it more than once happened, when the time came for replacing it, that no one on board could remember which end of the ship it belonged to. They knew it was not of the slightest use to appeal to the Bellman about it——he would only refer to his Naval Code, and read out in pathetic tones Admiralty Instructions which none of them had ever

b

been able to understand——so it generally ended in its being fastened on, anyhow, across the rudder. The helmsman * used to stand by with tears in his eyes: *he* knew it was all wrong, but alas! Rule 42 of the Code, "*No one shall speak to the Man at the Helm,*" had been completed by the Bellman himself with the words "*and the Man at the Helm shall speak to no one.*" So remonstrance was impossible, and no steering could be done till the next varnishing day. During these bewildering intervals the ship usually sailed backwards.

As this poem is to some extent connected with the lay of the Jabberwock, let me take this opportunity of answering a question that has often been asked me, how to pronounce "slithy toves." The "i" in "slithy" is long, as in "writhe"; and "toves" is pronounced so as to rhyme with "groves." Again, the first "o" in "borogoves" is pronounced like the "o" in "borrow." I have heard people try to give it the sound of the "o" in "worry." Such is Human Perversity.

This also seems a fitting occasion to notice the other hard words in that poem. Humpty-Dumpty's theory, of two meanings packed into one word like a portmanteau, seems to me the right explanation for all.

For instance, take the two words "fuming" and "furious." Make up your mind that you will say both

* This office was usually undertaken by the Boots, who found in it a refuge from the Baker's constant complaints about the insufficient blacking of his three pair of boots.

words, but leave it unsettled which you will say first. Now open your mouth and speak. If your thoughts incline ever so little towards " fuming," you will say " fuming-furious ; " if they turn, by even a hair's breadth, towards " furious," you will say " furious-fuming ; " but if you have that rarest of gifts, a perfectly balanced mind, you will say " frumious."

Supposing that, when Pistol uttered the well-known words—

" Under which king, Bezonian ?   Speak or die ! "

Justice Shallow had felt certain that it was either William or Richard, but had not been able to settle which, so that he could not possibly say either name before the other, can it be doubted that, rather than die, he would have gasped out " Rilchiam ! "

b 2

Contents.

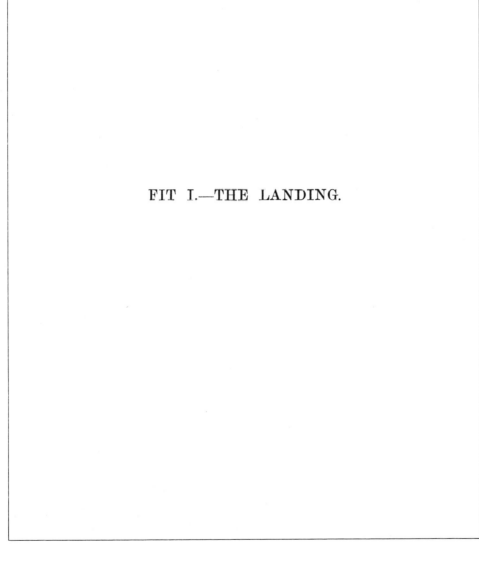

FIT I.—THE LANDING.

Fit the First.

THE LANDING.

"Just the place for a Snark!" the Bellman cried,
    As he landed his crew with care;
Supporting each man on the top of the tide
    By a finger entwined in his hair.

"Just the place for a Snark! I have said it
    twice:
    That alone should encourage the crew.
Just the place for a Snark! I have said it thrice:
    What I tell you three times is true."

B

The crew was complete: it included a Boots—
  A maker of Bonnets and Hoods—
A Barrister, brought to arrange their disputes—
  And a Broker, to value their goods.

A Billiard-marker, whose skill was immense,
  Might perhaps have won more than his share—
But a Banker, engaged at enormous expense,
  Had the whole of their cash in his care.

There was also a Beaver, that paced on the deck,
  Or would sit making lace in the bow:
And had often (the Bellman said) saved them
    from wreck,
  Though none of the sailors knew how.

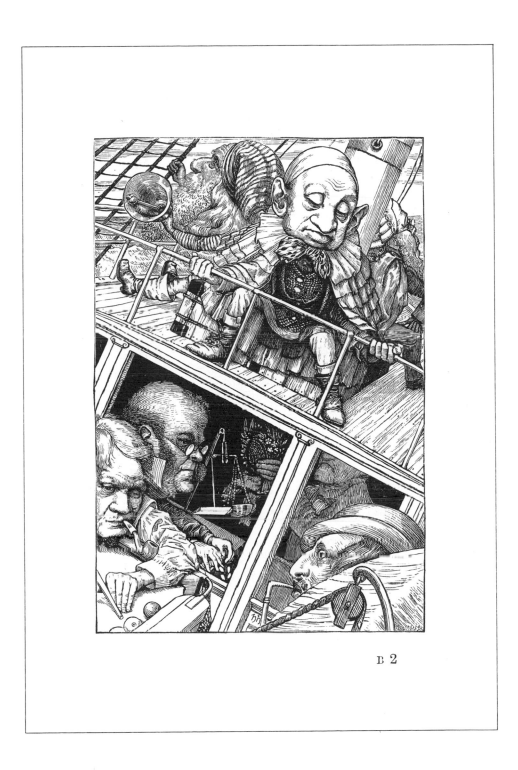

B 2

There was one who was famed for the number of
  things
  He forgot when he entered the ship:
His umbrella, his watch, all his jewels and rings,
  And the clothes he had bought for the trip.

He had forty-two boxes, all carefully packed,
  With his name painted clearly on each :
But, since he omitted to mention the fact,
  They were all left behind on the beach.

The loss of his clothes hardly mattered, because
  He had seven coats on when he came,
With three pair of boots——but the worst of
  it was,
  He had wholly forgotten his name.

He would answer to " Hi ! " or to any loud cry,
  Such as " Fry mé ! " or " Fritter my wig ! "
To " What-you-may-call-um ! " or " What-was-his-
    name ! "
  But especially " Thing-um-a-jig ! "

While, for those who preferred a more forcible
    word,
  He had different names from these :
His intimate friends called him " Candle-ends,"
  And his enemies " Toasted-cheese."

" His form is ungainly——his intellect small——"
  (So the Bellman would often remark)
" But his courage is perfect ! And that, after all,
  Is the thing that one needs with a Snark."

He would joke with hyænas, returning their stare
   With an impudent wag of the head:
And he once went a walk, paw-in-paw, with a
      bear,
   " Just to keep up its spirits," he said.

He came as a Baker: but owned, when too late—
   And it drove the poor Bellman half-mad—
He could only bake Bridecake——for which, I
      may state,
   No materials were to be had.

The last of the crew needs especial remark,
   Though he looked an incredible dunce:
He had just one idea——but, that one being
      " Snark,"
   The good Bellman engaged him at once.

He came as a Butcher: but gravely declared,
　　When the ship had been sailing a week,
He could only kill Beavers. The Bellman looked
　　　scared,
　　And was almost too frightened to speak:

But at length he explained, in a tremulous tone,
　　There was only one Beaver on board;
And that was a tame one he had of his own,
　　Whose death would be deeply deplored.

The Beaver, who happened to hear the remark,
　　Protested, with tears in its eyes,
That not even the rapture of hunting the Snark
　　Could atone for that dismal surprise!

It strongly advised that the Butcher should be
    Conveyed in a separate ship :
But the Bellman declared that would never agree
    With the plans he had made for the trip :

Navigation was always a difficult art,
    Though with only one ship and one bell :
And he feared he must really decline, for his
      part,
    Undertaking another as well.

The Beaver's best course was, no doubt, to procure
    A second-hand dagger-proof coat——
So the Baker advised it——and next, to insure
    Its life in some Office of note :

                C

This the Banker suggested, and offered for hire

(On moderate terms), or for sale,

Two excellent Policies, one Against Fire,

And one Against Damage From Hail.

Yet still, ever after that sorrowful day,

Whenever the Butcher was by,

The Beaver kept looking the opposite way,

And appeared unaccountably shy.

FIT II.—THE BELLMAN'S SPEECH.

Fit the Second.

THE BELLMAN'S SPEECH.

THE Bellman himself they all praised to the
    skies——
    Such a carriage, such ease and such grace!
Such solemnity, too! One could see he was wise,
    The moment one looked in his face!

He had bought a large map representing the sea,
    Without the least vestige of land:
And the crew were much pleased when they
    found it to be
    A map they could all understand.

"What's the good of Mercator's North Poles and
    Equators,
  Tropics, Zones, and Meridian Lines?"
So the Bellman would cry: and the crew would
    reply
  "They are merely conventional signs!

"Other maps are such shapes, with their islands
    and capes!
  But we've got our brave Captain to thank"
(So the crew would protest) "that he's bought us
    the best———
  A perfect and absolute blank!"

This was charming, no doubt: but they shortly
    found out
  That the Captain they trusted so well

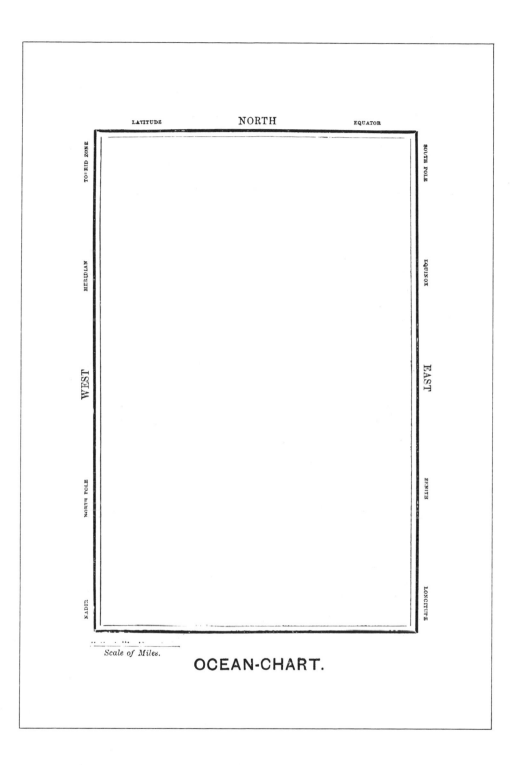

LATITUDE   NORTH   EQUATOR

TORRID ZONE

SOUTH POLE

MERIDIAN

EQUINOX

WEST

EAST

NORTH POLE

ZENITH

NADIR

LONGITUDE

Scale of Miles.

OCEAN-CHART.

Had only one notion for crossing the ocean,
  And that was to tingle his bell.

He was thoughtful and grave——but the orders
    he gave
  Were enough to bewilder a crew.
When he cried "Steer to starboard, but keep her
    head larboard!"
  What on earth was the helmsman to do?

Then the bowsprit got mixed with the rudder
    sometimes :
  A thing, as the Bellman remarked,
That frequently happens in tropical climes,
  When a vessel is, so to speak, "snarked."

But the principal failing occurred in the sailing,
 And the Bellman, perplexed and distressed,
Said he *had* hoped, at least, when the wind blew
  due East,
 That the ship would *not* travel due West!

But the danger was past——they had landed
  at last,
 With their boxes, portmanteaus, and bags:
Yet at first sight the crew were not pleased with
  the view,
 Which consisted of chasms and crags.

The Bellman perceived that their spirits were low,
 And repeated in musical tone

      D

Some jokes he had kept for a season of woe------
    But the crew would do nothing but groan.

He served out some grog with a liberal hand,
    And bade them sit down on the beach:
And they could not but own that their Captain
      looked grand,
    As he stood and delivered his speech.

"Friends, Romans, and countrymen, lend me
      your ears!"
    (They were all of them fond of quotations:
So they drank to his health, and they gave him
      three cheers,
    While he served out additional rations).

"We have sailed many months, we have sailed
    many weeks,
  (Four weeks to the month you may mark),
But never as yet ('tis your Captain who speaks)
  Have we caught the least glimpse of a Snark!

"We have sailed many weeks, we have sailed
    many days,
  (Seven days to the week I allow),
But a Snark, on the which we might lovingly
    gaze,
  We have never beheld till now!

"Come, listen, my men, while I tell you again
  The five unmistakable marks

By which you may know, wheresoever you go,
　The warranted genuine Snarks.

" Let us take them in order.　The first is the taste,
　Which is meagre and hollow, but crisp :
Like a coat that is rather too tight in the waist,
　With a flavour of Will-o-the-wisp.

" Its habit of getting up late you'll agree
　That it carries too far, when I say
That it frequently breakfasts at five-o'clock tea,
　And dines on the following day.

" The third is its slowness in taking a jest.
　Should you happen to venture on one,

It will sigh like a thing that is deeply dis-
    tressed :
And it always looks grave at a pun.

"The fourth is its fondness for bathing-machines,
    Which it constantly carries about,
And believes that they add to the beauty of
    scenes——
A sentiment open to doubt.

"The fifth is ambition. It next will be right
    To describe each particular batch :
Distinguishing those that have feathers, and bite,
    From those that have whiskers, and scratch.

" For, although common Snarks do no manner

of harm,

Yet, I feel it my duty to say,

Some are Boojums———" The Bellman broke off

in alarm,

For the Baker had fainted away.

FIT III.—THE BAKER'S TALE.

Fit the Third.

THE BAKER'S TALE.

They roused him with muffins—they roused him
with ice—
They roused him with mustard and cress—
They roused him with jam and judicious advice—
They set him conundrums to guess.

When at length he sat up and was able to speak,
His sad story he offered to tell;
And the Bellman cried "Silence! Not even a
shriek!"
And excitedly tingled his bell.

E

There was silence supreme! Not a shriek, not a

  scream,

  Scarcely even a howl or a groan,

As the man they called "Ho!" told his story of

  woe

  In an antediluvian tone.

"My father and mother were honest, though

  poor——"

  "Skip all that!" cried the Bellman in haste.

"If it once becomes dark, there's no chance of a

  Snark——

  We have hardly a minute to waste!"

"I skip forty years," said the Baker, in tears,

  "And proceed without further remark

To the day when you took me aboard of your

    ship

  To help you in hunting the Snark.

" A dear uncle of mine (after whom I was named)

  Remarked, when I bade him farewell——"

"Oh, skip your dear uncle!" the Bellman ex-

    claimed,

  As he angrily tingled his bell.

" He remarked to me then," said that mildest of

    men,

   " ' If your Snark be a Snark, that is right :

Fetch it home by all means——you may serve

    it with greens,

  And it's handy for striking a light.

E 2

" 'You may seek it with thimbles—and seek it
　　with care ;
　You may hunt it with forks and hope ;
You may threaten its life with a railway-share ;
　You may charm it with smiles and soap—' "

("That's exactly the method," the Bellman bold
　In a hasty parenthesis cried,
"That's exactly the way I have always been told
　That the capture of Snarks should be tried!")

" 'But oh, beamish nephew, beware of the day,
　If your Snark be a Boojum! For then
You will softly and suddenly vanish away,
　And never be met with again!'

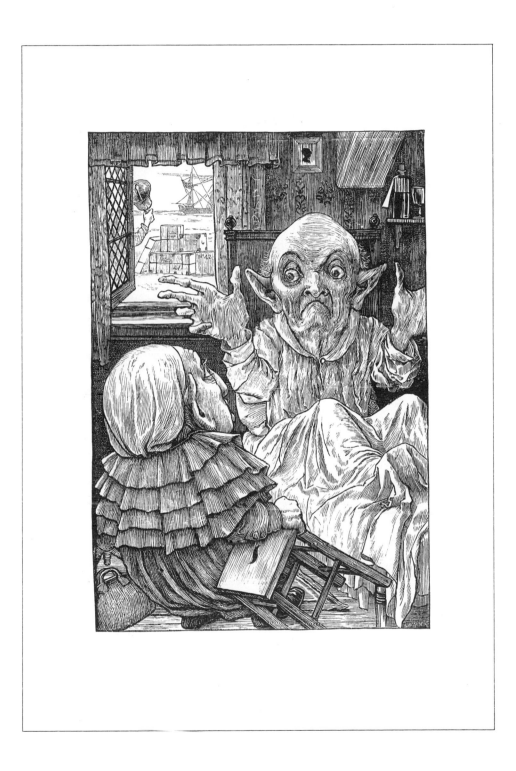

" It is this, it is this that oppresses my soul,

　　When I think of my uncle's last words :

And my heart is like nothing so much as a bowl

　　Brimming over with quivering curds !

" It is this, it is this——" " We have had that

　　before ! "

　　The Bellman indignantly said.

And the Baker replied " Let me say it once more.

　　It is this, it is this that I dread !

" I engage with the Snark—— every night after

　　dark——

　　In a dreamy delirious fight :

I serve it with greens in those shadowy scenes,

    And I use it for striking a light:

"But if ever I meet with a Boojum, that day,

    In a moment (of this I am sure),

I shall softly and suddenly vanish away—

    And the notion I cannot endure!"

FIT IV.—THE HUNTING.

F

Fit the Fourth.

THE HUNTING.

THE Bellman looked uffish, and wrinkled his brow.

   "If only you'd spoken before!

It's excessively awkward to mention it now,

   With the Snark, so to speak, at the door!

"We should all of us grieve, as you well may

   believe,

   If you never were met with again——

But surely, my man, when the voyage began,

   You might have suggested it then?

" It's excessively awkward to mention it now—

As I think I've already remarked."

And the man they called " Hi ! " replied, with a

sigh,

" I informed you the day we embarked.

" You may charge me with murder—or want of

sense—

(We are all of us weak at times) :

But the slightest approach to a false pretence

Was never among my crimes !

" I said it in Hebrew—I said it in Dutch—

I said it in German and Greek :

But I wholly forgot (and it vexes me much)

   That English is what you speak!"

" 'Tis a pitiful tale," said the Bellman, whose

   face

   Had grown longer at every word :

" But, now that you've stated the whole of your

   case,

   More debate would be simply absurd.

" The rest of my speech " (he explained to his men)

   " You shall hear when I've leisure to speak it.

But the Snark is at hand, let me tell you again !

   'Tis your glorious duty to seek it !

" To seek it with thimbles, to seek it with care ;

　　To pursue it with forks and hope ;

To threaten its life with a railway-share ;

　　To charm it with smiles and soap !

" For the Snark's a peculiar creature, that won't

　　Be caught in a commonplace way.

Do all that you know, and try all that you don't :

　　Not a chance must be wasted to-day !

" For England expects——-I forbear to proceed :

　　'Tis a maxim tremendous, but trite :

And you'd best be unpacking the things that

　　　　you need

　　To rig yourselves out for the fight."

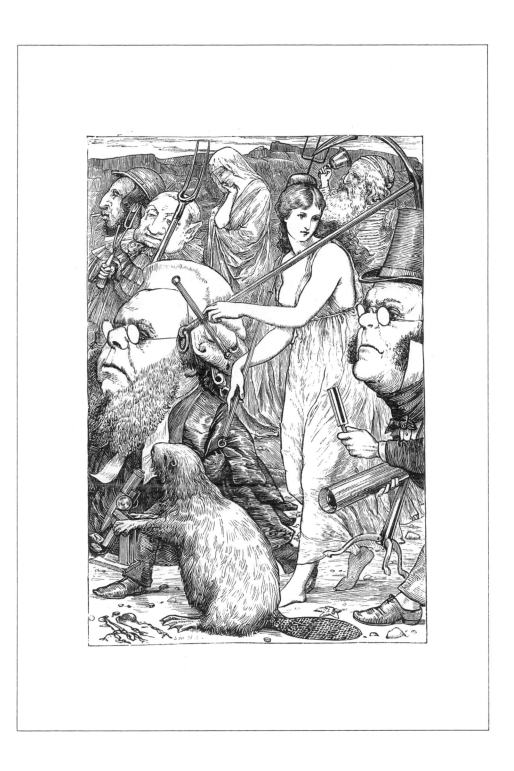

Then the Banker endorsed a blank cheque (which

    he crossed),

  And changed his loose silver for notes.

The Baker with care combed his whiskers and

    hair,

  And shook the dust out of his coats.

The Boots and the Broker were sharpening a

    spade—

  Each working the grindstone in turn :

But the Beaver went on making lace, and dis-

    played

  No interest in the concern :

Though the Barrister tried to appeal to its pride,

  And vainly proceeded to cite

A number of cases, in which making laces
    Had been proved an infringement of right.

The maker of Bonnets ferociously planned
    A novel arrangement of bows:
While the Billiard-marker with quivering hand
    Was chalking the tip of his nose.

But the Butcher turned nervous, and dressed
      himself fine,
    With yellow kid gloves and a ruff——
Said he felt it exactly like going to dine,
    Which the Bellman declared was all " stuff."

" Introduce me, now there's a good fellow," he said,
    " If we happen to meet it together !"

G

And the Bellman, sagaciously nodding his head,
   Said "That must depend on the weather."

The Beaver went simply galumphing about,
   At seeing the Butcher so shy :
And even the Baker, though stupid and stout,
   Made an effort to wink with one eye.

"Be a man!" said the Bellman in wrath, as he heard
   The Butcher beginning to sob.
"Should we meet with a Jubjub, that desperate
    bird,
   We shall need all our strength for the job!"

FIT V.—THE BEAVER'S LESSON.

G 2

Fit the Fifth.

THE BEAVER'S LESSON.

THEY sought it with thimbles, they sought it with
    care ;
   They pursued it with forks and hope ;
They threatened its life with a railway-share ;
   They charmed it with smiles and soap.

Then the Butcher contrived an ingenious plan
   For making a separate sally ;
And had fixed on a spot unfrequented by man,
   A dismal and desolate valley.

But the very same plan to the Beaver occurred :
 It had chosen the very same place :
Yet neither betrayed, by a sign or a word,
 The disgust that appeared in his face.

Each thought he was thinking of nothing but
  " Snark "
 And the glorious work of the day ;
And each tried to pretend that he did not remark
 That the other was going that way.

But the valley grew narrow and narrower still,
 And the evening got darker and colder,
Till (merely from nervousness, not from goodwill)
 They marched along shoulder to shoulder.

Then a scream, shrill and high, rent the shuddering
    sky,
    And they knew that some danger was near:
The Beaver turned pale to the tip of its tail,
    And even the Butcher felt queer.

He thought of his childhood, left far far behind—
    That blissful and innocent state—
The sound so exactly recalled to his mind
    A pencil that squeaks on a slate!

" 'Tis the voice of the Jubjub!" he suddenly cried.
    (This man, that they used to call " Dunce.")
" As the Bellman would tell you," he added with
    pride,
    " I have uttered that sentiment once.

" 'Tis the note of the Jubjub! Keep count, I
  entreat ;
 You will find I have told it you twice.
Tis the song of the Jubjub! The proof is
  complete,
 If only I've stated it thrice."

The Beaver had counted with scrupulous care,
 Attending to every word :
But it fairly lost heart, and outgrabe in despair,
 When the third repetition occurred.

It felt that, in spite of all possible pains,
 It had somehow contrived to lose count,

And the only thing now was to rack its poor
    brains
    By reckoning up the amount.

" Two added to one—if that could but be done,"
    It said, " with one's fingers and thumbs ! "
Recollecting with tears how, in earlier years,
    It had taken no pains with its sums.

" The thing can be done," said the Butcher, " I
    think.
    The thing must be done, I am sure.
The thing shall be done !   Bring me paper and ink,
    The best there is time to procure."

H

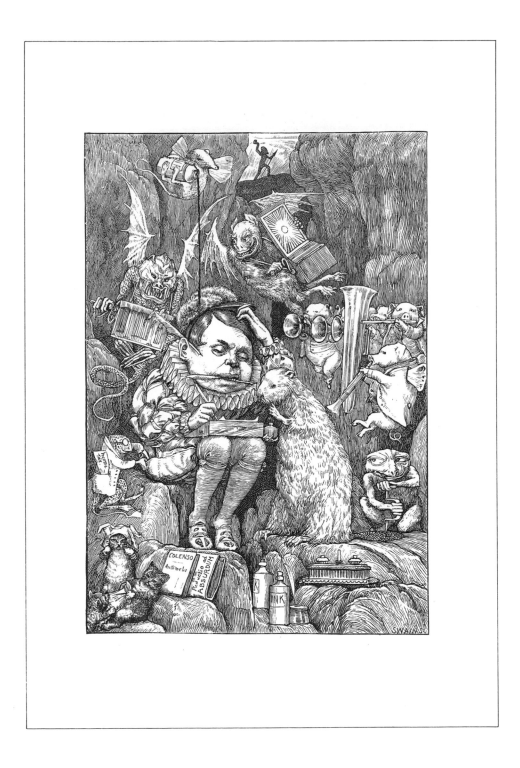

The Beaver brought paper, portfolio, pens,

    And ink in unfailing supplies:

While strange creepy creatures came out of their

       dens,

    And watched them with wondering eyes.

So engrossed was the Butcher, he heeded them not,

    As he wrote with a pen in each hand,

And explained all the while in a popular style

    Which the Beaver could well understand.

" Taking Three as the subject to reason about ——

    A convenient number to state——

We add Seven, and Ten, and then multiply out

    By One Thousand diminished by Eight.

" The result we proceed to divide, as you see,
　　By Nine Hundred and Ninety and Two :
Then subtract Seventeen, and the answer must be
　　Exactly and perfectly true.

" The method employed I would gladly explain,
　　While I have it so clear in my head,
If I had but the time and you had but the
　　　brain——
But much yet remains to be said.

" In one moment I've seen what has hitherto been
　　Enveloped in absolute mystery,
And without extra charge I will give you at large
　　A Lesson in Natural History."

In his genial way he proceeded to say

   (Forgetting all laws of propriety,

And that giving instruction, without introduction,

   Would have caused quite a thrill in Society),

" As to temper the Jubjub's a desperate bird,

   Since it lives in perpetual passion :

Its taste in costume is entirely absurd——

   It is ages ahead of the fashion :

" But it knows any friend it has met once before :

   It never will look at a bribe :

And in charity-meetings it stands at the door,

   And collects——though it does not subscribe.

" Its flavour when cooked is more exquisite far
    Than mutton, or oysters, or eggs :
(Some think it keeps best in an ivory jar,
    And some, in mahogany kegs :)

" You boil it in sawdust : you salt it in glue :
    You condense it with locusts and tape :
Still keeping one principal object in view——
    To preserve its symmetrical shape."

The Butcher would gladly have talked till next
        day,
    But he felt that the Lesson must end,
And he wept with delight in attempting to say
    He considered the Beaver his friend.

While the Beaver confessed, with affectionate looks
   More eloquent even than tears,
It had learned in ten minutes far more than all
      books
   Would have taught it in seventy years.

They returned hand-in-hand, and the Bellman,
      unmanned
   (For a moment) with noble emotion,
Said "This amply repays all the wearisome days
   We have spent on the billowy ocean!"

Such friends, as the Beaver and Butcher became,
   Have seldom if ever been known;

In winter or summer, 'twas always the same——
  You could never meet either alone.

And when quarrels arose——as one frequently finds
  Quarrels will, spite of every endeavour——
The song of the Jubjub recurred to their minds,
  And cemented their friendship for ever!

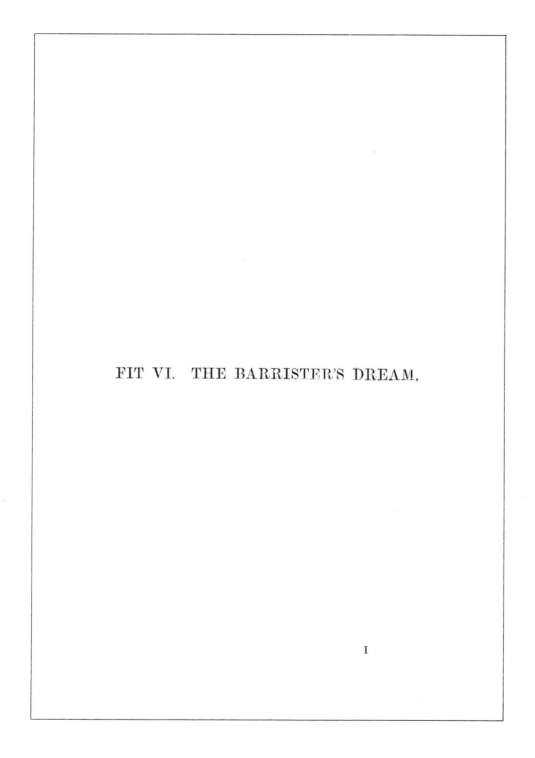

FIT VI.   THE BARRISTER'S DREAM.

I

Fit the Sixth.

THE BARRISTER'S DREAM.

THEY sought it with thimbles, they sought it
    with care ;
  They pursued it with forks and hope ;
They threatened its life with a railway-share ;
  They charmed it with smiles and soap.

But the Barrister, weary of proving in vain
  That the Beaver's lace-making was wrong,
Fell asleep, and in dreams saw the creature
    quite plain
  That his fancy had dwelt on so long.

I 2

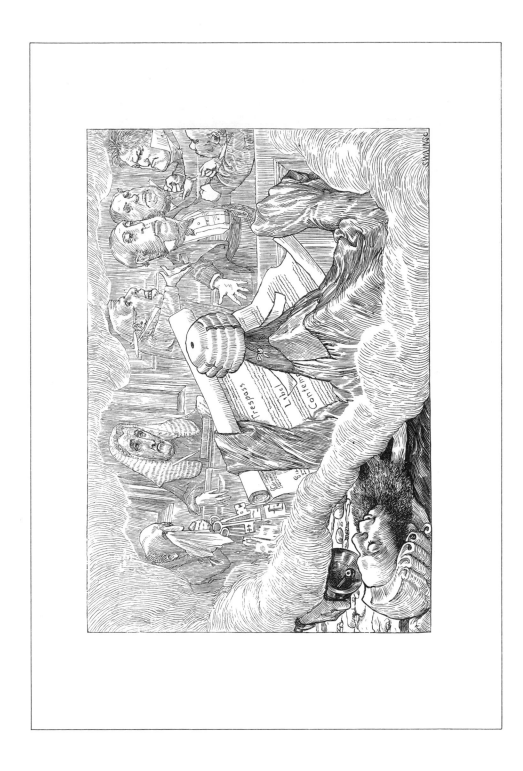

He dreamed that he stood in a shadowy Court,
  Where the Snark, with a glass in its eye,
Dressed in gown, bands, and wig, was defending
    a pig
  On the charge of deserting its sty.

The Witnesses proved, without error or flaw,
  That the sty was deserted when found:
And the Judge kept explaining the state of the
    law
  In a soft under-current of sound.

The indictment had never been clearly expressed,
  And it seemed that the Snark had begun,
And had spoken three hours, before any one
    guessed
  What the pig was supposed to have done.

The Jury had each formed a different view

   (Long before the indictment was read),

And they all spoke at once, so that none of

   them knew

   One word that the others had said.

"You must know ——" said the Judge: but the

   Snark exclaimed "Fudge!

   That statute is obsolete quite!

Let me tell you, my friends, the whole question

   depends

   On an ancient manorial right.

"In the matter of Treason the pig would appear

   To have aided, but scarcely abetted:

While the charge of Insolvency fails, it is clear,
   If you grant the plea 'never indebted.'

"The fact of Desertion I will not dispute:
   But its guilt, as I trust, is removed
(So far as relates to the costs of this suit)
   By the Alibi which has been proved.

"My poor client's fate now depends on your votes."
   Here the speaker sat down in his place,
And directed the Judge to refer to his notes
   And briefly to sum up the case.

But the Judge said he never had summed up
    before;
   So the Snark undertook it instead,

And summed it so well that it came to far more
    Than the Witnesses ever had said !

When the verdict was called for, the Jury declined,
    As the word was so puzzling to spell ;
But they ventured to hope that the Snark
        wouldn't mind
    Undertaking that duty as well.

So the Snark found the verdict, although, as it
        owned,
    It was spent with the toils of the day :
When it said the word " GUILTY !" the Jury
        all groaned,
    And some of them fainted away.

Then the Snark pronounced sentence, the Judge
    being quite
  Too nervous to utter a word:
When it rose to its feet, there was silence like night,
  And the fall of a pin might be heard.

" Transportation for life " was the sentence it gave,
  " And *then* to be fined forty pound."
The Jury all cheered, though the Judge said he
    feared
  That the phrase was not legally sound.

But their wild exultation was suddenly checked
  When the jailer informed them, with tears,
Such a sentence would have not the slightest effect,
  As the pig had been dead for some years.

K

The Judge left the Court, looking deeply
    disgusted :
  But the Snark, though a little aghast,
As the lawyer to whom the defence was
    intrusted,
  Went bellowing on to the last.

Thus the Barrister dreamed, while the bellow-
    ing seemed
  To grow every moment more clear :
Till he woke to the knell of a furious bell,
  Which the Bellman rang close at his ear.

FIT VII.—THE BANKER'S FATE.

Fit the Seventh.

THE BANKER'S FATE.

THEY sought it with thimbles, they sought it
    with care;
They pursued it with forks and hope;
They threatened its life with a railway-share;
    They charmed it with smiles and soap.

And the Banker, inspired with a courage so new
    It was matter for general remark,
Rushed madly ahead and was lost to their view
    In his zeal to discover the Snark.

But while he was seeking with thimbles and
  care,
  A Bandersnatch swiftly drew nigh
And grabbed at the Banker, who shrieked in
  despair,
  For he knew it was useless to fly.

He offered large discount—he offered a cheque
  (Drawn " to bearer ") for seven-pounds-ten :
But the Bandersnatch merely extended its neck
  And grabbed at the Banker again.

Without rest or pause—while those frumious jaws
  Went savagely snapping around—
He skipped and he hopped, and he floundered
  and flopped,
  Till fainting he fell to the ground.

The Bandersnatch fled as the others appeared
   Led on by that fear-stricken yell :
And the Bellman remarked "It is just as I
      feared !"
   And solemnly tolled on his bell.

He was black in the face, and they scarcely
      could trace
   The least likeness to what he had been :
While so great was his fright that his waistcoat
      turned white—
   A wonderful thing to be seen !

To the horror of all who were present that day.
   He uprose in full evening dress,
And with senseless grimaces endeavoured to say
   What his tongue could no longer express.

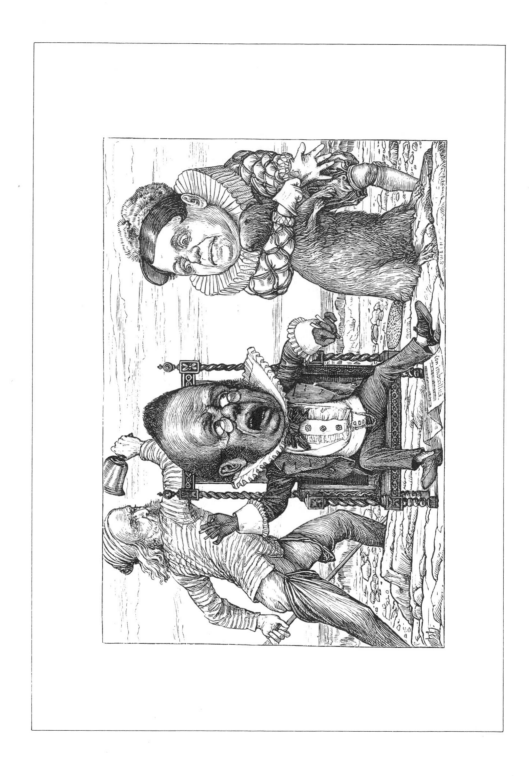

Down he sank in a chair—ran his hands through
    his hair—
   And chanted in mimsiest tones
Words whose utter inanity proved his insanity,
   While he rattled a couple of bones.

" Leave him here to his fate—it is getting so
    late ! "
   The Bellman exclaimed in a fright.
" We have lost half the day.   Any further delay,
   And we sha'n't catch a Snark before night ! "

L

FIT VIII.—THE VANISHING.

Fit the Eighth.

THE VANISHING.

They sought it with thimbles, they sought it with
　　care ;
　They pursued it with forks and hope ;
They threatened its life with a railway-share ;
　They charmed it with smiles and soap.

They shuddered to think that the chase might fail,
　And the Beaver, excited at last,
Went bounding along on the tip of its tail,
　For the daylight was nearly past.

"There is Thingumbob shouting!" the Bellman
    said.
  "He is shouting like mad, only hark!
He is waving his hands, he is wagging his head,
    He has certainly found a Snark!"

They gazed in delight, while the Butcher ex-
    claimed
  "He was always a desperate wag!"
They beheld him—their Baker—their hero un-
    named—
    On the top of a neighbouring crag,

Erect and sublime, for one moment of time
    In the next, that wild figure they saw

(As if stung by a spasm) plunge into a chasm,

 While they waited and listened in awe.

" It's a Snark !" was the sound that first came

  to their ears,

 And seemed almost too good to be true.

Then followed a torrent of laughter and cheers :

 Then the ominous words " It's a Boo—"

Then, silence. Some fancied they heard in the

  air

 A weary and wandering sigh

That sounded like "—jum!" but the others de-

  clare

 It was only a breeze that went by.

They hunted till darkness came on, but they
    found
    Not a button, or feather, or mark,
By which they could tell that they stood on the
    ground
    Where the Baker had met with the Snark.

In the midst of the word he was trying to say,
    In the midst of his laughter and glee,
He had softly and suddenly vanished away——
    For the Snark *was* a Boojum, you see.

THE END.

LONDON:
R. CLAY, SONS, AND TAYLOR, PRINTERS,
BREAD STREET HILL.

[TURN OVER.

WORKS BY LEWIS CARROLL.

Forty-ninth Thousand.

ALICE'S ADVENTURES IN WONDERLAND. With Forty-two Illustrations by TENNIEL. Crown 8vo. cloth, gilt edges, price 6s.

"An excellent piece of nonsense."—*Times.*

"That most delightful of children's stories."—*Saturday Review.*

"Elegant and delicious nonsense."—*Guardian.*

GERMAN, FRENCH, AND ITALIAN TRANSLA-TIONS of the same, with TENNIEL's Illustrations. Crown 8vo. cloth, gilt edges, price 6s. each.

The *Spectator* in speaking of the German and French translations says : "On the whole, the turn of the original has been followed with surprising fidelity, and it is curious to see what slight verbal alterations have often sufficed to preserve the humour of the English."

Thirty-eighth Thousand.

THROUGH THE LOOKING-GLASS, AND WHAT ALICE FOUND THERE. With Fifty Illustrations by TENNIEL. Crown 8vo. cloth, gilt edges, 6s.

"Will fairly rank with the tale of her previous experiences."—*Daily Telegraph.*

"Many of Mr. Tenniel's designs are masterpieces of wise absurdity." —*Athenæum.*

"Whether as regarding author or illustrator, this book is a jewel rarely to be found now a days."—*Echo.*

"Not a whit inferior to its predecessor in grand extravagance of imagi-nation, and delicious allegorical nonsense."—*British Quarterly Review.*

MACMILLAN & CO., LONDON.

Designed by Roderick Stinehour.
Composed in Monotype Baskerville and Monotype Bell by
The Stinehour Press, Lunenburg, Vermont.
Printed offset by
Braun-Brumfield, Inc., Ann Arbor, Michigan.
Cloth Trade Edition printed on
fifty-pound Warren's "1854" Regular
in an edition of 5,000 copies.